MIDWAY ISLANDS

HAWAIIAN ISLANDS

JOHNSTON ISLAND

POLYNESIA

PHOENIX ISLANDS

MALDEN ISLAND

...ANDS

MARQUESAS ISLANDS

TOKELAU ISLANDS

...ALLIS
...UNA

SAMOAN ISLANDS

TUAMOTU ARCHIPELAGO

TAHITI

COOK ISLANDS

SOCIETY ISLANDS

GAMBIER ISLAND

TONGA ISLANDS

AUSTRAL ISLANDS

PITCAIRN ISLAND

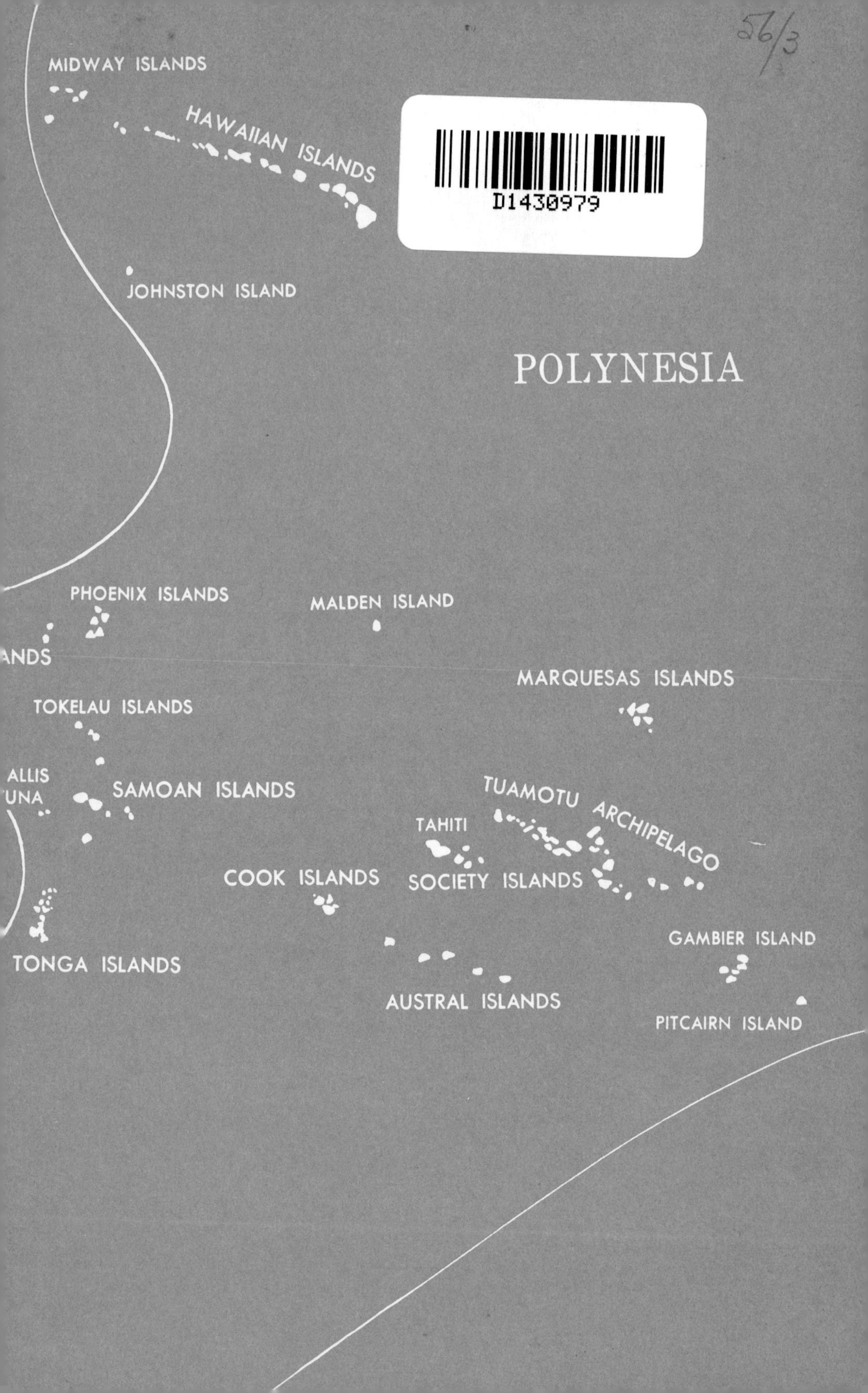

Bumayong Schools
Lutheran Mission
Box 80, Lae
Territory of New Guinea
Christmas, 1963

SOUTH SEA ISLANDS

To Dad with much
love and admiration,

Rolf

by the author of

OCEANIA

HE SAILED WITH CAPTAIN COOK

HAWAII: FIFTIETH STATE

South Sea Islands

By CHARLES A. BORDEN

MACRAE SMITH COMPANY, PHILADELPHIA

ACKNOWLEDGMENTS

The author wishes to thank the following for permission to reproduce photographs in this book: Australian National Travel Association, p. 13; Australian News and Information Bureau, p. 14 (V. Gadsby, photographer), pp. 18, 24, 28, 167, 172, 174, 177, 179, 181 (W. Brindle, photographer); Bishop Museum, pp. 31, 35; British Information Services, p. 141; Robin Kinkead, P.A.W.A., pp. 16, 21, 23, 185, 194, 199, 220; Matson Lines, pp. 83, 90, 105, 109, 187, 213, 243; Bill Murnan, p. 92; New Zealand Steamship Company, p. 200; Pacific Area Travel Association, pp. 128, 133, 135, 209, 219, 238; Pan American World Airways, pp. 86, 110; Science Museum, London, p. 32; United Nations, p. 75; U.S. Coast Guard, p. 148; U.S. Fish and Wildlife Service, p. 224 (H. J. Spencer, photographer), p. 225 (Philip A. DuMont, photographer); U.S. Navy, pp. 48, 58, 74; University of Hawaii, p. 241. End paper map by Guy Fry.

TO

JIM AND ELSIE of The Lighthouse
BILL AND CEICE of The Schooner Seven Seas
DENISE of Tahiti
BOB McKITTRICK of Hiva Oa
LAISHA AND ENESI of Tonga
EPINERY TITIMUA of New Guinea
and to
ALAIN GERBAULT who rests at Bora Bora

PREFACE AND ACKNOWLEDGMENT

Although each archipelago, often each island, has distinctive attributes and enough material for a book of its own, I've tried to show change, conflict and current problems through key island closeups and a broad, general picture of the South Sea people as they are today. In the scope of this book Hawaii has not been given individual treatment because it is in the North Pacific and because it requires a volume by itself (see *Hawaii: Fiftieth State*).

As used here the term native means simply born locally and is used in the sense that we all are natives whether our "island" happens to be San Francisco, Manhattan or Tahiti. It seems hardly necessary to say that beneath any color of skin, any pattern of language or culture the broad human values—the springs of hope, passion and fear—are much the same.

Polynesians who have always known that man needs love as much as food or shelter are looking beyond their own horizons and realizing that there is but one race in the Pacific—the human race. An increasing number of South Sea leaders who realize that faith in the old ways can no longer be a substitute for action also know that the time is short and we must co-operate with each other or perish.

It's good to remember obligations incurred in many ports and latitudes because it brings to mind friends and acquaintances scattered from Honolulu to Apia to Suva and from Tahiti to Port Moresby and beyond. Full acknowledgment would require another book—would have to include friends of a day or week, met in villages, port towns and occasionally along a lonely beach or lagoon road. Dropping formality, I doff my sea cap and thank wholeheartedly those who have helped in one way or another. I especially thank Eleanor Dixon, chief typist (and sometimes stern worrier), for careful attention to many things.

To Natalie Mayo—upon her longer voyage—I owe more than this or any acknowledgment can say.

Charles A. Borden, SPINDRIFT POINT, 1961

CONTENTS

CONTENTS

SOUTH SEA ISLANDS

BOSWELL:

I can give an entertaining narrative with many incidents, anecdotes, Jeux d'esprit, and remarks, so as to make very pleasant reading . . .

JOHNSON:

Why, Sir, the world is not now contented to be merely entertained by a traveller's narrative: they want to learn something.

New Guinea Highlander from Mount Hagen wears his finest for the yearly agriculture show at Goroka.

Traditional artistic native canoes on the Kikori River in the swampy Gulf of Papua.

Chapter One

THE SOUTH SEAS TODAY: THE PEOPLE

As the jet age shrinks the world, the two and a half million people of the South Seas, ranging from stone-age natives of New Guinea to modernized Polynesians, are becoming neighbors of ours who live only a few air hours away from Pacific Coast ports.

For over a century the South Sea Islands have stirred the imagination of the Western world, but for most people they were too far off. Today visiting the island of one's choice is a small matter, with super-jets cutting the tradewinds once sailed by clipper ships and tramp trading schooners. As this is being written, tiki carvers and thatch weavers of split bamboo are putting the finishing touches on Tahiti's new million-and-a-half-dollar hotel where barefoot Tahitian girls in pareus will serve breakfast to travelers who wing in from the Pacific Coast in seven and a half hours.

Reaching across the Pacific from the green mountains of Hawaii south to the glaciers of New Zealand, and from the island-continent of Australia to Easter Island, the South Seas cover one-eighth of the earth's surface and contain the most important group of islands in the world. Many are islands of deep mystery. Easter, Nan-Matal and Pitcairn pose questions that have not to this day ever been solved. There is still high adventure to be found in the South Seas, and more often than not white men are in the thick of it. "Shangri-La," the hidden valley of Lavani in the Southern Highlands district of Papua, remained undiscovered until just a few years ago.

The former head-hunters beyond the upper Sepik River are still as typical a part of the South Seas as descendants of the Bounty mutineers on Pitcairn, or the sophisticated Papuan who has discarded his lap-lap for shirt and shorts, or the modern teen-age

15

Polynesian men are friendly, romantic and often handsome by any standards. This Tahitian youth ponders the scenery his ancestors knew.

Samoans of Upolu who play cricket and soccer and wham out "Tiger Rag" or the "Beer Barrel Polka" in their high school bands.

Appealing and sometimes absurd fairy tales have been told and retold about the South Sea people for more than a century. To begin with, there is no such thing as a "typical South Sea Islander." Nor can the islanders be thought of simply as "two and a half million natives." Today they are a widely mixed people like the Americans. They comprise three large groups of human beings, vastly different individually, who live in Polynesia ("many islands"), Micronesia ("little islands"), and Melanesia ("dark islands").

It should be remembered that any single islander is as much a person in his own right as any reader of this book, though his ways may be vastly different. Many young islanders have a deep desire "to do things modern people do" and to establish new standards of living in their own communities. In Apia, Suva, Rarotonga,

16

Noumea and other port centers one sees young, racially-mixed people of outstanding qualities. Sometimes it would seem that the most attractive island people are those whose inherent native attractiveness has been enriched by mixtures of European, Oriental or American ancestry.

The brown Polynesians, closest relative to the Caucasians of the three main groups of South Sea people, live within a huge triangle in the central Pacific with its corners in Hawaii, New Zealand and Easter Island. The one hundred and fifty thousand people of Micronesia live for the most part north of the equator on more than two thousand islands scattered over an area larger than the United States. The Melanesians, who inhabit the islands south of the equator from the Fijis to New Guinea, are basically of negroid stock. The greatest differences among these three geographical groups are their physical appearances and folkways.

Generally, Melanesians have fuzzy hair and thick lips and vary in color from a dark brown in Fiji, New Caledonia and the New Hebrides to a deep black in the Solomons. As in Polynesia and Micronesia, there are wide differences within each archipelago due to contact with other peoples. From the dense tropical jungles of New Guinea to the wind-swept, almost soilless coral atolls of Micronesia living conditions are vastly different. In some areas most of a person's waking hours are spent in some ceremonial or other, while in other areas getting a bare existence requires all of an islander's effort.

In Melanesia there are stone-age gardeners and fisherfolk living in the same way they did thousands of years ago. In the high interiors of New Guinea and New Britain large areas of people are not yet under any form of civilized control. After a hundred years there, missionaries have been able only to establish rudimentary health and education services in the coastal areas. Occasional cannibals and blow-gun and poison dart people still lurk beyond the shadows of the upper Sepik.

Single continental islands that can now be flown across in a few minutes contain hundreds of communities speaking different languages and living different ways of life. In some parts of New Guinea, yesterday's head-hunters are now hunting crocodiles or raising peanuts for a meagre living. Side by side with an agricultural people, another people may be living entirely on wild things. Next to a seafaring community, perhaps only a few miles inland, may live

17

New Guinea Southern Highlands leader reports a death among his people by bringing the finger of a man killed in a fight to a remote patrol station.

a root-and-grub-eating peasantry who have never even seen salt water. On some islands every valley and mountain area has its own different customs. The dried-human-head trade and the practice of human sacrifice has been abolished, but on many islands the people still live in deathly fear of voodoo.

Much of Melanesia is still an area of yaws, tuberculosis, malaria, dysentery, dengue fever and other plagues. The line between black and brown peoples in the South Seas follows, even today, what is called the malaria line. Brown Polynesians are an easy prey to the disease and are generally found only in areas that are free of it.

The modernized Polynesians, Micronesians and Melanesians who live in Papeete, Pago Pago, Guam, Suva and other port towns are a vastly different people from the Kukukuku pygmies and other

18

nomadic groups who live on insects and grubs in the remote forests and mountains of New Guinea. In many urban centers peroxide, rouge, pomade and cheap perfumes from Japan have taken the place of the old beauty preparations, lime, ocher, coconut oil and the scent of the hibiscus.

On some islands the blending of races and ways of life has erased many of the distinct differences between peoples. On most of the main islands of the Pacific white men and white men's ways predominate, but in the kingdom of Tonga, at the extreme western end of Polynesia, Polynesian customs still hold sway. The proud and independent Tongans have retained their racial identity and natural ways of life more carefully than any other Polynesians. Here white settlers and tourists are not encouraged, because Tongans realize that in port centers where tourists congregate true native culture degenerates in a sort of carnival atmosphere.

The black, fuzzy-haired Fijians, at the extreme eastern end of Melanesia, are among the most intelligent and likeable of islanders; in the nineteenth century they were the fiercest cannibals in the Pacific. Today, most Fijians want "new things" that money can buy but are reluctant to give up the dignity and satisfactions of their old customs for efficient money-making ways. The educated Fijians are as advanced in most ways as the native Hawaiians.

Samoa has a quieter, softer beauty than Tahiti. Robert Louis Stevenson, who lies buried in Western Samoa on the island of Upolu, thought its native inhabitants "the sweetest people God ever made." Pago Pago, America's outpost harbor, is one of the most beautiful harbors in the South Pacific. It is also probably the cleanest of the capital islands. Modern Samoans are a proud, dignified, handsome and fun-loving people. Like ourselves, they face big problems in trying to adjust to the world of today. In Western Samoa the biggest problem is the rapidly increasing population which is expected to double in the next twenty years.

Many Polynesians are as far from the old ways as most Americans are from the ways of the pilgrim fathers. If Herman Melville, who wrote his classic *Omoo* after imprisonment as a mutineer in Papeete, could revisit Tahiti in 1962, he would find that the life of an omoo, or beachcomber, is now not only illegal but impossible. Yesterday's "white shadows" have had to get out or seek a place in the sun. Today the French government requires that visitors wishing to stop over in Tahiti must have a return ticket and enough money to cover

19

the expenses of their stay. Normal expenses are calculated at two hundred to five hundred dollars per month.

Melville would find that, in the one hundred and seventeen years since the Nantucket whaler *Charles & Henry* sailed out through the pass, nearly every Tahitian has acquired some degree of white or Oriental blood, although the dominant strain is still Polynesian. At night, under the flamboyant trees along the Quai Bir Hackeim, he would hear the young cosmopolitan people of Papeete speaking French, English and Tahitian. He would hear brassy island bands rendering a medley of French songs, Tahitian tunes and American jazz.

None of the South Seas people have a written language but they possess traditions and an oral literature comparable to that of the ancient Greeks. Today hundreds of different languages are spoken in the islands. Polynesia has about a dozen dialects, Micronesia has about fifteen, and Melanesia is a babel of different tongues changing almost from village to village. Added to the native languages are Chinese, Hindi, English, French and Beach-la-Mar (pidgin English).

It would be difficult for a trader, planter or merchant to do business in many parts of Melanesia without knowing Beach-la-Mar. In this strange tongue "schooner-belong-bush" means an auto. "Pull-'im he come, push-'im he go" means a saw. "Sore leg" means pain, so a headache is indicated by saying, "sore-leg-belong-head." When confused by English questions or phrases the Melanesian says simply, "Talk belong me, he straight; all other kind talk, he cranky."

Government officials frown on Beach-la-Mar but it remains in wide general use today and probably always will. Books have been written, dictionaries compiled and newspapers are printed in the local versions. Lessons in pidgin are broadcast regularly from the A.B.C. station at Port Moresby. Airline hostesses that fly Melanesian routes are given a special course in Beach-la-Mar.

Once an island was noted for its guano, pearl shell or copra; today its place on the map determines its importance in Western eyes. Since the first experimental trans-Pacific flights of 1937, island after island has become important overnight. First it was Midway, Wake and Guam, then Pago Pago and a host of others, including Howland, Baker and Canton. Bora Bora and Tahiti have become the latest important stops on Pacific travel routes.

On Moorea beside a road scented with vanilla and frangipani Tahitian girls gather
fronds for an evening feast and dance. Jagged peaks of Paopao (Cook's) Bay
in background.

Papeete, long known as the "little Paris of the South Seas," and the French islands of Moorea and Bora Bora, probably represent, more than other islands, what the average traveler hopes to find in Polynesia. The price tag is another matter. Although tipping is taboo and fruit, vegetables and fish are cheap, Tahiti is now the most expensive island in the South Seas. The cost of living in Papeete and other port towns is higher than in towns of comparable size in the United States partly because most of the things an American requires have to be imported from Australia, New Zealand or the Pacific Coast.

"*Mon dieu!* One cannot live on coconuts [copra] any more," shrugged a French official a few months ago in Tahiti. "At night there are more girls, more singing and dancing than ever before. Soon, perhaps we can live on the tourists."

Ambitious plans are now under way at Tahiti, Suva, Fiji and Noumea, New Caledonia, to attract tourist dollars. All three hope to become tropical centers for the booming travel trade. Even lesser islands that have small returns from copra, pearl shell or other natural resources are looking to their dancing girls, swaying coco palms and blue lagoons to attract the overflow of travel dollars.

Matches, soap, kerosene, canned meats, sewing machines and bicycles are now considered necessities—even on the outer islands, and these things cannot be bought with the proceeds from a few sacks of copra. Land and sea products that tourists want and native craft work are becoming "big business." Despite the dangers from man-eating sharks, giant eels and rays, diving for mother-of-pearl shell supplies dollars for many islands, especially in the Tuamotus and in the Torres Straits.

When the first big jets whined down over the blue lagoons of Tahiti the travelers aboard found that the best dressed Polynesian girls wear Parisian-style skirts and dresses and prefer cosmetics and perfumes that are imported from New York or Paris; that thatch-top cottages rent for one hundred and fifty to three hundred and fifty U. S. dollars per month; that the island "sleeps" from 11:00 A.M. to 2:00 P.M., not because it's too hot but simply because the Tahitians think it's a good idea.

Visitors will find that Tahiti is still an evergreen island fragrant with the scent of creamy white to golden amber frangipani blossoms. All the girls of Papeete can sing, play the guitar and dance the *tumare* (local hula). The big difference in the Hawaiian and Tahitian versions is that in Tahiti the hips instead of the hands tell the story.

At a *tamaaraa* (Tahitian feast) there is suckling pig, breadfruit, *eia ota* (raw fish), *pota* (spinach), *fei* (wild bananas). There may also be tiny fresh-water shrimp and hearts of palm served in a split coconut shell. Raw fish dipped in coconut milk and eaten with the fingers is much more tasty than it sounds. People of Tahiti love to eat, dance and sing. They also know that there are many things the *popaa* (white man) needs that they can get along happily without. A few educated native leaders are concerned lest their young people be "quarantined" to a tourist version of the simple life and the "old ways" solely to provide a tropical sanatorium or spiritual retreat for weary Americans.

The charm and beauty that inspired Stevenson, Melville and Gauguin are still there but are not always to be found in port towns. In the remote areas life is just about the same as ever. The acrid

Tahitian dancers on Moorea warm up for a festive tamaaraa. (The flower over the girl's right ear indicates she has no boy friend.)

Tapini airstrip, a "Shangri-La"-type village in the Owen Stanley Mountains of Papua that only a few planes can penetrate because of air pockets and narrow maneuverability.

odors of native cooking and the pungent scent of copra drying in the sun mingle strangely with the smell of the salt sea and the trade-winds; picturesque native villages still border the lagoons; flaming torches of dried coconut still split the darkness on festival nights. One can find Melanesians and Polynesians, scattered in small groups on remote islands, living almost as simply as they did a half century ago, but few travelers stop over and still fewer get beyond the main ports. Dozens of islands that are only a hundred miles or less from such centers as Pago Pago, Rarotonga, Rabaul, Port Moresby, Apia and Nukualofa are rarely visited by outsiders other than a few officials and missionaries.

24

Americans sometimes unfairly label outer islanders as lazy because they work in a vastly different way. Even their biggest tasks are frequently accompanied by singing, dancing, feasting and ceremonies.

South Sea Island real estate ranges from thirty cents an acre in parts of Melanesia to three dollars a square foot in more than one major port town. On New Guinea, a snow-capped island more than twice the size of Japan (fifteen hundred miles long), and on other continental islands including New Caledonia, Guadalcanal, Bougainville, New Britain and New Ireland, land still can be had for a few cents up to a few dollars an acre. These islands, which are the exposed peaks and ridges of vast mountain ranges that traverse the floor of the Pacific, are kept green and luxuriant by the moisture-laden tradewinds.

Ocean currents, rainfall and winds greatly affect human existence in the South Seas. Some islands have an ideal year-round climate; others are breeding grounds for terrible typhoons. To a large extent the weather is controlled by the Southeast and Northeast tradewinds, by the prevailing Westerlies and sometimes by the "Roaring Forties" and "Furious Fifties" that blow between forty and fifty degrees South.

Land values are high near port centers on high islands like Samoa and French Polynesia, where the weather is moderate and where every type of growing thing needed by islanders can be found.

On some of the low islands there is no soil at all and the people have to bring it in sailing vessels from the nearest high islands. The lowest islands, called atolls, are like great irregular-shaped doughnuts with openings through which the tides flow to the inner lagoons. Some, like Canton and Howland, are treeless; others, like the Gilberts, have been raised by coral growth to several hundred feet and support luxuriant vegetation. Most of them, however, are low-lying, rising less than ten feet above the sea and some are almost completely awash at high tide.

It takes great courage to live on an atoll. During storms one feels the whole island tremble before the impact of heavy, pounding seas. Sometimes in great storms vast seas sweep completely over an island and carry everything to destruction, including men, women, children, houses and trees.

Some islands, such as New Guinea, have as few as four people to the square mile, while parts of Suva, Apia and Honolulu are among the most densely populated areas in the world. Young people crowd into the port towns, some attracted by bright lights and new experiences, others seeking higher educational standards and a better way of life. In the towns they see the stimulating reality of modern things from the outside world. Unfortunately, they also see and perhaps live in shacks in crowded slum areas. Only a small number of them can obtain white collar jobs. A small percentage adjust to and benefit from modern ways, but many lose more than they gain and become a confused people living on the fringes of a dollars and cents world that they cannot either escape or join.

The white man has always acted on the assumption that he had a God-given right to exploit the South Seas peoples and their islands for his profit and for "their own good." Many have also felt impelled to deliver reams of lofty advice. In large areas, especially in Melanesia, natives are still considered useful principally for laboring on white plantations or other enterprises, attracting tourists or performing household duties. Although most island peoples are on the increase, many of the pure native races continue to decline and a new population emerges in control: Chinese, Indians, whites and mixed races.

Commercially, Fiji, New Caledonia and the temperate uplands of New Guinea have provided large returns for white investors. Gold is still drawing white prospectors to New Guinea, Fiji and the Solomons and oil is being sought in New Guinea. All of the big money and politics is in the hands of white people although much business enterprise is controlled by Chinese, part-Chinese and Indians. Local white residents are mostly merchants, missionaries, government employees, planters, miners and employees of large trading firms.

Although the white population of the South Seas generally constitutes less than one percent of the total inhabitants, the main groups and all of the outlying islands have come under the control of Great Britain, the United States, France, Australia and New Zealand. In recent times these nations have worked toward a common cause both in defense and in peace. One of the earliest co-operative measures was the establishment of the Central Medical School for native practitioners at Fiji, which was followed by a similar school at Guam. The South Pacific Commission, established to study and recommend measures for the welfare and advancement of South Sea Islanders, is a further step in the right direction.

Despite the good work that is being done in the South Seas the danger exists that the ruling powers may bring disaster to the islanders by their increasing military rivalries. Since the United States and Great Britain have tested atomic bombs and Russia has dropped intercontinental missiles in the South Pacific the fear of danger from the sky has replaced the fear of black magic in the hearts of many islanders, especially in Micronesia.

In the U. S. Trust Territory the inhabitants of Bikini were uprooted from their homes so that Westerners could experiment with the atomic bomb. And in 1954, when meteorologists of the U. S. Atomic Energy Commission miscalculated, two islands outside of the experimental area were hit by atomic fallout, requiring the evacuation of the entire population for safety and medical treatment.

The Samoans and the Marshall Islanders protested to the United Nations against the endangering of their lives and homes and pleaded that no further nuclear tests be made in the South Seas. The Micronesians were told that only thermonuclear bombs would be tested in the future. These bombs were "clean" and "safe," they were assured. "If the new bombs are safe," replied the Micronesians, "then why don't the ruling powers test them on their own homeland and leave us in peace?"

Educated modern islanders now realize that their islands are an important part of the world. Some, as in French Polynesia, Fiji, Samoa, the Ellice Islands and other groups, have asked for more rights of self-determination and a larger share of profits from their land, sea and forests. On all major archipelagos the white man is being called upon to return some of the lands he has taken from the brown and black people of the South Seas.

"You have been here fifty years and that is too long. When are you going to give us our independence?" Epinery Titimua, spokesman for the most advanced tribal group in New Guinea (the Tolai people), asked the Australian administrator at an official meeting in Rabaul.

Nationalist feelings are strong in many groups. Some of the jobs held by white people are being taken over by college-educated native islanders. Some have become professional and business leaders and hold responsible positions. The energetic and prideful Samoans have long asked themselves, "Why should we, who were here for centuries before the white men ever heard of the South Seas, be under their dominance?" After half a century of working toward

27

" 'Bik pella government' (Australian administration headquarters) is here," says Kibunki, wealthy Wabag coffee grower and leader, as he points out Port Moresby to several of his 110,000 constituents.

complete independence from New Zealand, Western Samoa will become an independent state early in 1962.

The Marshall Islanders, under American Trusteeship, pointed out to the United Nations Trusteeship Council that they would like to be returned to their former freedom, as they felt they could govern themselves just as well as the peoples of Africa and Asia who are now gaining their independence.

There is rising hope among many island leaders that their people will eventually become self-governing within the framework of some sort of International Trusteeship Council. On the whole, the natives of Melanesia, Polynesia and Micronesia have proven intensely loyal to the white powers that ruled them, although until recently little was done to deserve such loyalty.

Americans are now answerable directly for the well-being of more than one hundred and thirty thousand islanders in Micronesia and Polynesia, and indirectly for the best interests of more than two million people in the South Seas. This vast island world is part of a tra-

28

dition that goes back to the pioneering of Yankee whalers and guano seekers and to the high adventures of Herman Melville, Commodore Wilkes and Captain Porter of the frigate *Essex*.

It took the greatest defeat in American history, Pearl Harbor, to make most Americans realize how important such tiny distant islands as Wake, Midway, Guam, Saipan and dozens of others are to insure the safety of mainland United States. During World War II huge American bases in New Caledonia, Fiji, the New Hebrides, the Solomons and in French Oceania became known around the world and today those islands, as well as New Guinea, New Britain, the Carolines, Marshalls, Gilberts and many others are a heroic part of modern history.

Most islanders, regardless of whether their island flies the Stars and Stripes, the Tricolor, the Southern Cross, or the Union Jack, look to the United States in one way or another. Their strategic location and the arrival of the jet era has linked their destinies with our own.

Chapter Two

MICRONESIA

Long before the dawn of written history Micronesia provided a sea-path for the great Polynesian migrations. Centuries before Columbus groped his way to America, while Europe was still in the dark ages and navigators lived in constant fear of the Atlantic, bold Polynesian explorers labored with the crudest of stone tools on the shores of southeastern Asia to build great fleets of long double-canoes, and sailed forth into the lonely reaches of the South Pacific bearing full cargoes of women, children, plants and pigs.

Without compasses, with no charts or mathematical knowledge, the occupants of many canoes were lost, perishing miserably in the great void of long, rolling seas. But others reached the westernmost islands of the vast Micronesian world that was to become their new home. And still others, in vessels built with shell chisels and adzes, and bound together with coconut fibre, sailed farther eastward to Polynesia.

The first of these fearless voyagers presumably dropped their stone anchors in the small scattered lagoons of the Palau Archipelago, sailing thence to the Carolines, and later to the Marshalls, Gilberts, and the Ellice Group.

These first settlers in Micronesia were Caucasian-featured Poly-nesians. They found the islands so poor in natural resources that they had to give up many of their original arts and crafts. Later, great numbers questing for better homes sailed eastward toward the verdant, bountiful lands of Tahiti and Samoa. Those who remained acquired various Mongoloid characteristics in the flux of inter-marriage with other peoples who pressed into Micronesia from Asia and Melanesia.

Marshall Islanders, the ancients of Yap and other Micronesian people had names for all of the stars and were skilled observers of sea and sky phenomena and of the migratory flights of sea birds. For many hundreds of years they made long sea journeys over the vast length of their widely separated island groups and to distant archipelagos in their *popos,* or flying canoes. Long after the Spaniards arrived, the men of Uleai, Lamotrek and other groups sailed in flotillas of twenty to thirty canoes on regular yearly trading expeditions five hundred miles north to Guam, in the Marianas. Fishermen blown far out to sea in their outrigger canoes have been known to sail as far as New Guinea and the Solomons. Early legends tell of ancient Ponapean navigators venturing east as far as Hawaii; of trading vessels from Timor and Sumatra, and pirate proas from Borneo and the Sulu Sea.

Primitive stick-charts based upon the accumulated experience and knowledge of interisland navigators were widely used. These were usually made of the thin inner ribs of coconut fronds, tied together, forming a frame upon which tiny cowry shells were securely placed to designate the positions of various atolls. Curved

Early Polynesian double canoe with lateen sail, used on long voyages to distant archipelagos.

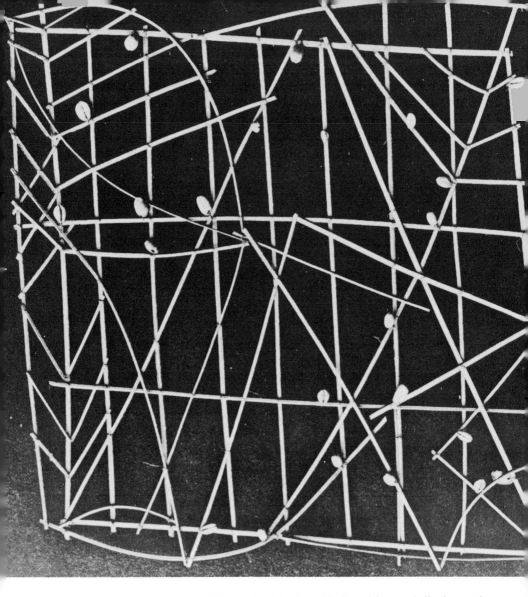

Early sea chart used in Micronesia. Islands are indicated by sea shells, long strips indicate certain reefs and curved strips show the direction of ocean waves.

leaf strips indicated the direction of the ocean swells, and the places where cross-directional waves met, causing a confused sea, were marked by intersecting leaf ribs. Long strips told of the location of certain reefs and short strips were used to indicate the seasonal direction of ocean currents.

The most accomplished navigators often acted as instructors and conducted small classes where young villagers were coached in the lore of the sea and the sky. When one of the first white traders attempted to explain and sell a small pocket compass to a gathering of island leaders they showed but slight interest and when the trader persisted in his efforts the chiefs pointed to each other and said in the native language, "Heads all the same compasses."

More than in any other medium the people of the Carolines excelled in the art of canoe-making. Their skill and fine craftmanship was especially apparent in the seagoing trading canoes. On the largest of these, thatched cargo huts for provisions, trade goods and booty were erected on rectangular platforms projecting out over the weather and lee sides of the hull. A third platform and hut was sometimes erected over the center of the canoe for passenger accommodations. Rigging was of sennet and the large triangular sails were of woven pandanus matting. With shell-blade adzes, shark's-tooth awls, rayskin files, shell drills, bone needles and mother-of-pearl knives, craftsmen working in wood, fibre, bone and shell produced a wide variety of canoes and other beautiful things.

Just as the prepared foods and the cultural pursuits of the various groups were controlled by the raw products available, so, too, was the manner of canoe construction. On islands where there were large trees, as in Yap, almost the entire canoe was hewn from a single tree trunk. On other islands where no large trees were available, the canoe hulls were skillfully fitted and sewn together from a large number of individual pieces of wood. After the seams were caulked with a mastic made of burnt lime, the completed hulls were finished to a fine smoothness and painted various designs in black and white.

Most canoes, especially those belonging to the chiefs, were artistically decorated with featherwork ornaments at both ends and with frigatebirds' feathers attached to the masthead and often to the leech (the outer and after edge) of the sail. Symbolic bow figures were used, including one that was quite similar to the lotus figure-heads of ancient Egypt.

Great faith was placed in the black arts of the soothsayers and most appeals to heavenly gods and to earthly spirits were made through them. No large project was ever undertaken without first determining from the bei leaves of a dealer-in-charms how it would turn out. When one of the big outrigger canoes was caught in a storm the native sorcerer, who was always carried on important voyages, stood erect at the bow and in defiance of the gale would violently wave a barbed spine from the tail of a sting-ray at the God

33

of Storms, imploring him in the name of the good islanders to cease his wrath and compose the sea until they could reach their destination.

Occasionally terrible disasters occurred. A fleet of thirty-five to a hundred canoes would sometimes be overtaken by typhoons and the entire flotilla with all of its occupants lost at sea. On one of Louis Becke's voyages to the Carolines as supercargo of a trading schooner, he came upon a huge Marshall Island sailing canoe that had been unexpectedly blown offshore and, unprepared for sea, had drifted six hundred miles to the west. Of the seventy natives aboard the battered craft, thirty were dead; the others, although in a very weak state, refused to leave their canoe. Accepting provisions and water, the natives proceeded on their way and finally arrived at Kusaie with thirty-six alive and thirty-four dead.

Ferdinand Magellan, Captain General of His Majesty's Armada bound for the Spice Islands, was the first white explorer to enter the Pacific. After overcoming mass mutiny, shipwreck and starvation in the straits which bear his name, the iron-willed commander, with his two carracks *Conception* and *Vittorio* and the seventy-eight foot flagship *Trinidada*, blazed a long and tortuous trail across the South Seas, a voyage described by some historians as "the greatest achievement in the history of the human race."

"We sailed about four thousand *leguas* during those three months and twenty days through an open stretch in that Pacific Sea," wrote ship's chronicler Antonio Pigafetta. "We ate biscuit, which was no longer biscuit, but powder of biscuits swarming with worms, for they had eaten the good. It stank strongly of the urine of rats. We drank yellow water that had been putrid for many days. We also ate some ox hides that covered the top of the mainyard and which had become exceedingly hard because of the sun, rain and wind. We left them in the sea for four or five days, and then placed them for a few moments on top of the embers, and so ate them; often we ate sawdust from boards. Rats were a delicacy selling for one-half ducat apiece, and even then we could not get them. The gums of both the lower and upper teeth of some of our men swelled, so that they could not eat under any circumstances—nineteen men died from that sickness. Thirty men fell sick in the arms, legs, or in another place, so that but few remained well."

On the morning of Wednesday, March 6, 1521, the three small vessels were slow and sluggish, foul with barnacles and long trailing weeds. Men with long matted beards and swollen joints lay about the decks half-dead. Those at the pumps groaned in despair. The helmsmen, weak, dizzy and in pain, were barely able to steer. Only a handful were able to stand. Still fewer could climb aloft.

As the gromet of the dawn watch recited the daybreak Pater Noster and Ave Maria the lookout at the masthead of the flagship *Trinidada* could barely raise his head into the sun's glare to scan the

Because timber was scarce, islanders made this ingenious seagoing vessel of whatever planks they had—carefully shaped to match and sewn together with coconut fibre twine.

horizon. His burning eyes pained more than his swollen lips. He reeled occasionally and clutched the railing in terror of falling. As the last *ampolleta* (sandglass) of the dawn watch was turned he straightened up weakly, and looking ahead, stiffened and quickly made the sign of the Cross. Bending over the railing of the top he cried out in a voice that trembled and was barely heard on deck, "*Vigia! Vigia, vigia!*" "Land! Land, land!" The cry ran through the ship.

When the high peaks of Rota and Guam came into view the *Trinidada* hoisted her Royal Standard. Old Master Andrew, the gunner, fired a bombard and those of the crew who were strong enough to rejoice shouted and screamed as though possessed. Others prayed aloud, and still others who were unable to open their swollen mouths mumbled prayers and crawling to the bulwarks gazed out into the looming blue as the vivid green slopes of Guam took shape. A few who were unable to reach the bulwarks screamed in pain and, falling back, coughed up blood.

Under patched and ragged canvas filled with a bare cat's-paw of wind, the gray, weather-streaked vessels of the tiny armada stood slowly into the south of the island. A few shaking, skinny men groaned as they crawled to the braces and halyards. Some who tried to help found that the fluid had left the joints of their limbs and that they could not move. Nothing was done shipshape. It was incredible that anything at all was done. Halyards were let fly on the run and the sails came down in great clumsy folds as the *Trinidada* followed by the *Conception* and the *Vittorio* rounded to and splashed their long shanked anchors into the placid waters of Apra Bay. After the setting of anchor watches, the church signal was made and an hour of fervent High Mass was said on each vessel.

No ship had ever anchored off these islands—no white men had seen them before. Had the vessels remained at sea another two weeks all would have perished and the Marianas might have remained undiscovered for another century.

To the long-suffering Magellan, the Marianas meant water, food, new strength for his crews and new hope for the westward voyage to the Isles of Spice and the long homeward journey around the Cape of Good Hope. Unaware that he was in the southernmost of a five hundred and fifty mile north-to-south-reaching chain of fifteen islands, Magellan little knew that he had discovered the largest island and the best natural harbor between Hawaii and the Philippines, an island destined to become a vital link in the path of man's questing toward the Far East.

It was an exciting day and a great event in the lives of the islanders when the first great ships without outriggers anchored in their blue lagoon. They prostrated themselves in wonder and awe before the heavy-bearded captain-general and his gaunt, sea-weary crew. Viewing in amazement and childish delight the strange iron objects and wearing apparel of which the new gods appeared to have more than enough, the benign islanders ran off with buckets, knives, ropes, clothing and everything in sight that was not fastened to the ship. One group, eager to ride in one of the strange, outriggerless boats, took off in the precious ship's boat that had just been lowered over the side of the *Trinidada*.

This act so enraged the weary Magellan that he hurried ashore with forty men armed with crossbows, shafts and arquebuses. Burning scores of houses and boats, the Spaniards killed seven and wounded a large number of astounded natives. The utter simplicity of the islanders and the tragedy of their first contact with white men is graphically described by one of the avengers, Antonio Pigafetta: "When we wounded any of those people with our crossbow-shafts, which passed completely through their loins from one side to the other, they looked at it, and then pulling on the shaft withdrew and gazed at it with great astonishment as they bled to death."

The Spaniards, after recovering their boat, helped themselves to large quantities of native coconuts, yams, and other food supplies, and took everything of value in the village. In pious indignation they renamed the group Isles of Thieves, and following devout prayers, made sail to the westward. Only a few months later Magellan was killed by a native in the Philippines.

During the Age of Discovery, when great continents and oceans were still to be found, the discovery of the Mariana Islands by Ferdinand Magellan was a matter of small concern to his employers, King Charles I and the rich knights and merchants of old Seville. Court circles were humming with bigger things. Already, at the Royal Quays, cargoes of treasure were arriving from the lands of Columbus, in the west.

The islands of Micronesia were merest pinpricks in the vast watery wastes of Mar Pacifico. There was little likelihood that they would ever add to the gold and silver in Andalusia's Tower of Gold. There were few who realized how profoundly it would have affected the Spanish Empire if Magellan and his men had missed the Marianas and perished at sea.

Long after Magellan had blazed the trail for the Golden Era of Discovery in the Pacific, Spain and Portugal, the great Catholic sea powers of the day, were still bickering over the Papal Bull of 1493, and the Treaty of Tordesillas, which established a line of demarcation dividing the entire world between them.

While the most advanced scholars of geodesy and "sacred theology" expounded at great length in behalf of each, Spain declared her determination to take possession of all the South Sea Islands and Portugal reaffirmed that she would "hang by the neck" any Spaniards trespassing on her side of the line, especially if caught near the Moluccas.

The Portuguese Crown having but recently acquired the Spice Islands, and Spain the promising Philippines, both were eager to add to their mighty colonial empires. While grandees and knights bustled to and fro between Lisbon, Rome, and Madrid, Spanish and Portuguese buccaneers were out scouring the Pacific for new discoveries.

The story of the vast, sprawling Caroline Archipelago begins with a small group of early sea rovers and armored knights from the Spanish Main whose love for gold and riches overcame their fear of the great South Sea and sent them roving through Micronesia during the early sixteenth century. It was during this period that the Pacific Ocean became widely known as a "Spanish Lake."

When word finally reached Vera Cruz of Magellan's great voyage of discovery to the Western Islands, Hernán Cortes, conquerer of the Aztec Empire, and his cousin Alvaro de Saavedra were busily involved considering ways and means of cutting a canal through the Isthmus of Panama. Ordered by royal decree to send vessels in search of Magellan's lost flagship, the *Trinidada*, and for news of Loaisa's and Cabot's expeditions, Cortes, having well ravished Mexico, was not the one to overlook new possibilities. Like many another don of Aragon and Castile, he was stirred to fabulous dreams of the gold and silver that might be found somewhere out in this new region. Perhaps there were natives even richer than the ancient Aztec and Inca people, or possibly fragrant isles of spice and pearls, like the Moluccas.

Deciding to send Saavedra in charge of the expedition, Cortes ordered three vessels built of the best materials to be found on the west coast of New Spain. Both men had a great respect for Mar Pacifico and Saavedra, having heard in detail of the terrifying hardships suffered by Magellan, was determined to prepare well before putting to sea.

The ships were well caulked and tarred, staunch rigging was set up, heavy sails were bent and ample spares were stowed. The rate of the newly arrived sandglasses and the astrolabes were checked. The latest *portolanos*—parchment navigating charts—were procured, with the puffed cheeks of Boreas blowing from the north and imaginary sea monsters lurking where the islands of Micronesia are today. Artillery, articles of barter and other supplies sent from Seville by the Indian House of Trade were stowed against shifting in the heavy Pacific swells. Finally the crews were sent to a last confession and special masses were said in the mission churches of Vera Cruz.

In October 1527, Saavedra's tiny armada stood out past the forts of Zaguatenejo. With the brilliant Royal Standard and the pennant of Cortes flashing at her truck the flagship bore away westward to gain a place for Spain in the South Seas—a voyage on which "the king's rights, especially of gold, silver, precious stones and pearls shall be one-half of all treasure found in graves or places of worship or buried."

During the time that Saavedra was fitting out and preparing his expedition, a Portuguese navigator, Diego da Rocha, sailing under the flag of "Pious" John the Fortunate, ventured into Micronesian waters and discovered the Yap and Ulithi Islands early in 1527, becoming the first white man to visit the Caroline Archipelago. Naming his discovery the Sequeira Islands, da Rocha returned to the Moluccas without knowing that he had reached only the westernmost of a long chain of islands and low-lying atolls reaching from Yap nearly two thousand miles to the easternmost Kusaie Group. Had da Rocha sailed to the east he probably would have made further discoveries among the many hundreds of islands that comprise this far-reaching archipelago and quite possibly would have met Alvaro de Saavedra, the discoverer of the central and the eastern Carolines.

Driven westward in the tradewinds, navigating by latitude and dead reckoning, Saavedra's fleet was beset with gales, mutiny and disaster. On New Year's Day, 1528, Saavedra brought his one remaining vessel, a broad, lateen-rigged caraval, to a safe anchorage in the Ulithi Group. It was the first ship from the Americas to enter the Carolines. After taking possession of the group in the name of the crown, Saavedra sailed on to the great lagoon of Truk. While amazed at the sight of the forty-mile-long lagoon and its great number of verdant mountainous islands, the captain-general could not have known that he had anchored his flagship in the largest atoll in the world.

He described the native women as "tall and handsome but without shame," and reported "they were so overjoyed upon seeing goats for the first time that they did not resent in the least when the goats ate their grass skirts clean to the girdle."

Once convinced that there were no quantities of cinnamon, gold or pearls to be found in the lovely central and eastern Caroline Groups, and failing in his attempts to sail east, Saavedra returned to the Moluccas.

So it was that the Spanish Crown obtained its claim to the Carolines. And since discovery—or first sight—somehow is always associated with ownership, this vast area roughly three thousand miles west-southwest of Honolulu came to be considered as belonging to Spain.

Far from bringing a bright new era to Micronesia, the arrival of the first white explorers heralded a cloud of evils that soon cast shadows over every island, atoll, and motu, until entire archipelagos became so ravaged with bloodshed and disease that they lost as high as ninety percent of their populations.

Many other islands in Micronesia became known to the Spanish and Portuguese during the sixteenth century. But, since the explorers were bitterly disappointed in not finding treasures of gold, silver, or precious stones and their countries were not interested in islands with less possibilities for exploitation than the Philippines and the Moluccas, Spanish rule remained for long loose and inactive. Except for the introduction of cattle, pigs and fowl, and the cultivation, on a small scale, of maize, sugar cane, coffee and tobacco in the Marianas, little was done.

When offered meat for the first time the people of the Marianas, called Chamorros, shuddered at the thought of eating it. They were amazed at the sight of the first Spanish horse landed in the islands. Because it had a bit in its mouth they thought that iron was part of its regular diet and endeavored in every way to gain the friendship of such a superior creature.

Spanish administrators, prompted by Jesuit missionaries in the

40

latter part of the seventeenth century, introduced Christianity to the natives. Almost overnight there began a vigorous reign of terror and cruelty. No patience or mercy was shown those unfortunates who failed quickly to see the new light. The Spaniards were determined to destroy swiftly the ancient customs and deep-rooted ways of life by which the natives had lived happily for centuries.

Baptism and conversion were forced at the point of steel. Disobedience meant death.

Valiant islanders armed with bone spears, slings and stones fought relentlessly for nearly thirty years against the gunfire of Spanish troops. Thousands were slaughtered and the once proud, freedom-loving Chamorros were finally reduced to a broken-hearted remnant. High over the sea and cliffs, on the steep terraced mountainsides of Agrihan, this great race made their last stand against the superior arms of the Spanish soldiers.

Of the fifty thousand Chamorros first estimated by Padre Sanvitores, there were less than one thousand remaining at the start of the eighteenth century. All were living in concentration near the churches that had been built with forced labor on the island of Guam. Twenty years later there was only one pure-blooded Chamorro family surviving from the original race. Apace with the tragic decline in population, island culture crumbled; with the total disruption of native faith in simple things, the vast archipelago became a land of confusion, sickness, and despair.

After 1606, following the last of the great Spanish voyages of discovery, that of de Quiros in the *Almirantes* and *Capitana,* there was hardly a sail to be seen in the lonely reaches of Micronesia for more than one hundred and fifty years.

Native history in the Gilberts tells of a huge white man with a red beard and red hair who came ashore, presumably about 1600, more dead than alive, "in a strange box." After a remarkable recovery, he married all eight of the chief's sisters and had twenty-three children by them, some of whose descendants are still scattered throughout the Gilberts.

Commodore "Foul-weather Jack" Byron, cruising the Gilberts in 1764 in his Majesty's three-hundred-ton frigate *Dolphin,* was first of the many British sea rovers in their little brigantines, barques, corvettes, frigates, and sloops-of-war who were to discover several islands of this vast South Sea area, and reveal many more to the doubting geographers of Europe.

41

In the early nineteenth century Russia looked toward the South Sea Islands with a great deal of interest. At the height of this awakening, the one hundred and eighty ton *Rurik,* commanded by twenty-eight year old Lieutenant Otto von Kotzebue, was dispatched on a voyage of exploration around the world.

The *Rurik* arrived in the Marshalls on January 1, 1817 from "Hana-ruru," Hawaii. Her crew bartered hoop iron, hatchets, hammers and nails in exchange for native mats, carving and shell work. The native chiefs, astute and dignified in their trade relations, quickly presented an item as a gift if the visitors haggled over the barter or considered the exchange too high.

Kotzebue has been compared to Captain James Cook because of his broad understanding and respect for the rights of the natives and because of his excellent hydrographic reports and authentic, colorful accounts of the flora and fauna and the ways of the people. He gave the natives goats, chickens, pigs and many new plants including yams, pineapples and melons. More than any other voyagers of the nineteenth century young Kotzebue, aided by Chamisso, a German naturalist, and Choris, a Russian artist, made the Marshall Islands known to a world-wide audience. Their fascinating works were often reprinted and translated into many different languages.

The Stars and Stripes first reached Micronesia in 1791. Yankee seafarers discovered a number of islands in the Ellices, Gilberts, Marshalls and Carolines, and were the first to chart and thoroughly explore these archipelagos, calling them the Kingsmill Group. Because of these and a score of other American "firsts," previous to 1860, several European cartographers consistently labeled the whole central Pacific area "American Polynesia."

American whalers from New England ports became such frequent visitors in the Marshalls and Carolines that at one time the whaling bases of Kiti in Ponape, and Port Lele in Kusaie, were known as the little Bangor and New Bedford of the South Seas. Ebon in the Marshalls became known as Boston Atoll. Although light skins have darkened with each generation, today there are still many traces of New England blended variously throughout Micronesia. It was due in no small part to ships' logs and whalers' accounts that these islands became known to the outside world. And it was through the whalers that islanders were introduced to hard liquors, guns and venereal diseases.

42

Often there would be as many as twenty to thirty ships at anchor and when their hundreds of crew members were given shore liberty, they proceeded to run rampant through the villages, raping native girls and remaining drunk for weeks on palm wine. During these periods the lives of a few natives, more or less, was of small concern, and often in the morning from one to five dead bodies would be found on the beach. In addition, there was a good deal of what one chronicler described as "unabashed piracy." Catch-catch vessels from Australia, seeking slaves for plantations in Melanesia, frequently raided remote islands.

The Marshall Islanders, seeing their women and children mistreated by Americans, with their villages sacked and large numbers of their bravest warriors slaughtered for protesting, decided to reverse the treachery by singling out and attacking foreign ships when least expected. Thus they became known as "blood-thirsty reef pirates." It finally became unsafe for ships to anchor in the Marshalls, especially those flying the Stars and Stripes. A number of Yankee vessels were destroyed and the heads of more than a few New Englanders came to decorate the houses of native chiefs.

As in other Pacific archipelagos, tuberculosis, influenza, measles and other diseases brought in by the early whites soon decimated once-populous islands. Gonorrhea, called by Marshall Islanders "Amereke"—the American disease—spread widely during early contacts with Yankee whalers. In 1853, Captain Wicks of the American sailing ship *Delta* brought several cases of smallpox to Ponape, causing a severe epidemic that took the lives of nearly three thousand natives. Other such cases were numerous.

The population of Truk dropped from thirty-five thousand to eleven thousand in less than a hundred years. Ponape was reduced from fifteen thousand in 1800 to less than three thousand a half century later. Houses, canoes and sometimes whole villages were abandoned. In Yap, the high death rate, which began during the Spanish regime, increased to more than double the birth rate in the first part of the twentieth century.

During the middle of the nineteenth century New England missionaries were deeply aroused by thoughts of the dangers of damnation threatening the idolatrous islanders and the first of the Boston puritans hastily departed to "snatch the souls of South Sea heathens from the claws of Satan."

Following the presentation of a large number of red shirts,

turkey-red quill and scissors to "Good King George" of Kusaie, so called because he forbid the manufacture of coconut toddy, good feelings were established and the king agreed to help the missionaries. In 1852 the first American mission was established at Kusaie. Conversions came slowly and more often from gratitude for having received medical treatment than from any sincere convictions as to the benefits of Christianity.

After their first enthusiasm over the new teachings many native people came to believe that the price of salvation came too high. The more sensitive and intelligent chiefs resented "foreigners" who spoke of truthfulness, honesty and brotherly love as if these virtues were a monopoly that came first from across the sea. They were puzzled by the fact that when the missionaries wanted land, houses, food, labor, furniture or boats, whatever they wished or admired was given to them. But when islanders coveted small items belonging to the missionaries they were told at length of the virtues of hard work as a step toward obtaining such items in the glorious future. On occasions when they, as children might, took such items, they were labeled "thieving heathens" and shamed before the eyes of the whole village.

Nevertheless, many missionaries in Micronesia have accomplished great good. Among them there have been a few broadminded, progressive individuals with as great a concern for the natives' welfare as for saving their souls. On the whole, missionary activity has been instrumental in abolishing tribal warfare, giving medical care and improving hygienic conditions. It took great courage, self-sacrifice and devotion to accomplish good in a world almost wholly concerned with exploiting the natives. Also, the voice of the missionary was almost the only voice ever raised in protests to home governments against the ruthless exploits of ship captains and others who, on occasion, ravished and slaughtered natives at will.

Such men as Padre Jose Palomo and Father Calvo, Catholic Chamorro priests of Guam; Reverend Carl Heine and Miss Hoppin of the Marshalls; the Swiss missionaries in Truk and the Carolines; and a number of others, have done outstanding work in Micronesia, and their large success has been well merited.

American missionary efforts in the Marshalls were pre-eminent. The Boston puritans sailed boldly into atoll lagoons and took up residence among natives who had long been aroused to a murderous hatred of all outsiders, especially Americans. Persistent and uncompromising, they remained for years on end, lived on native foods, translated the Bible, preached the gospel in the native language and brooked no interference, brown or white, in their determination to change "the naked witchcraft-ridden savages into a well-clothed God-fearing people." Much credit is due to mission schools for teaching the native language rather than the language of the missionaries or that of the ruling power.

Official American interest in Micronesia dates from the end of the nineteenth century, when Guam, southernmost of the Marianas, was acquired as a strange and unexpected development of the Spanish-American War—a war ostensibly fought to free the Cubans, on the other side of the earth, from the yoke of Spain.

After Dewey's victory, official Washington was undecided about what to do with the Philippines and Guam. President McKinley, strongly influenced by pious considerations, was most uncertain of all.

"I thought first that we would take only Manila; then Luzon; then the other islands, perhaps also. I walked the floor of the White House night after night until midnight; and I am not ashamed to tell you, gentlemen, that I went down on my knees and prayed Almighty God for light and guidance more than one night. And one night late it came to me this way—I don't know how, but it came—that there was nothing left for us to do but to take them all and to educate and uplift and civilize and Christianize them, and by God's grace do the very best we could for them as our fellow men for whom Christ also died. And then I went to bed and went to sleep and slept soundly. . . ."

Less moved by pious considerations, Mark Hanna, the man most responsible for McKinley's election as President and one of his closest advisors, said, "If it is commercialism to want possession of a strategic point giving the American people an opportunity to maintain a foothold in the markets of the East—for God's sake let us have commercialism."

Wisely realizing that her days as a colonial power in the Pacific were over, Spain sold the Mariana and Caroline Archipelagos to Germany. Thus, Germany entered the twentieth century in possession of the Palaus, Marshalls, Marianas, and Carolines, comprising all of Micronesia except for the British-held Ellices and Gilberts, and American Guam.

45

The Germans, in order to exploit natural resources more profitably, leaned heavily toward the Dutch policy of leaving the natives to their own beliefs. Their administrators concentrated on trade and copra production and cared little whether natives worshipped a stone god or Jesus Christ. Besides tobacco and iron, "pain killers" and "guaranteed" cure-all pills became popular trade items.

German activities prospered. At the outbreak of World War I, hardly a shot had been fired before the warships of Australia and Japan were racing toward Micronesia to gain that long-coveted prize. The Australians, arriving belatedly and finding the Japanese in possession of all the islands north of the equator, had to soothe their disappointment by taking the German possessions south of the line.

Thus, within three months of the outbreak of World War I, the spoils in the Pacific were informally divided; and as far as the new possessors, Australia, New Zealand and Japan, were concerned, they were going to remain that way. As early as 1915, Japan's Viscount Ishii and Great Britain's Sir Edward Grey had informally arrived at their now well-known but at that time closely guarded agreement as to such disposition. Great Britain had secretly agreed to recognize and support Japanese claims to all the islands of Micronesia west of the Gilberts in exchange for Japanese support of British claims to the German islands south of the equator.

Although, by the Treaty of Versailles, Germany renounced "all rights and titles over her overseas possessions" to the five principal Allied Powers, of which the United States was one, America did not receive so much as a single coconut tree in return for her one-fifth ownership in Micronesia.

In German hands the Caroline Islands were strategically unimportant because of the long distance from the Fatherland and other factors. But under Japanese administration they soon were considered of major importance by all nations bordering the Pacific, especially by the United States, Australia and New Zealand.

Profiting from Germany's mistakes, Japan discounted native labor as undependable. With an eye to the American policy in Hawaii, and that of the British in Fiji and the French in New Caledonia, the Japanese imported great numbers of Japanese sugar workers from the Loochoo Islands. Eighty percent of these were employed in the sugar industry on the Marianas. Almost overnight many tranquil green islands became busy agricultural centers humming with activity.

46

Upon taking over the development of copra production in the Marshalls and Carolines, the new managers found that one of their biggest problems was the eradication of great numbers of fat, coconut-eating rats that were annually ruining much of the coconut yield. Huge monitor lizards imported from the Marianas, some measuring up to six feet in length, promptly proceeded to kill off the rats. When the rats became thin and wary and remained out of reach of the lizards, the wily reptiles tired of the arduous labor and developed a decided preference for native chickens. Eventually a breed of husky cats took over the job abandoned by the lizards and it became a much-encouraged pastime among young islanders to stimulate the cats to rat-chasing among the coconut trees, where the rodents could always be found nesting, sampling, or gorging themselves high amid the coco fronds.

By developing the mandate, and at the same time refraining from forced native labor, Japanese Micronesia became the proving ground for the most outstanding economic development of any Pacific mandate. In less than twenty years, trade was increased more than twentyfold, more than during the entire four centuries under Spanish and German rule.

Early in 1941 Congress became aware of the possibility of an attack against American islands in the South Seas and passed an appropriation for harbor improvements and the construction of bomb shelters on Guam. During the following months the Navy ordered all American women and children on Guam to return to the United States.

Congressional fears were well-founded, for Japan—having finally realized that the United States could not and would not accept Japanese plans for domination of the Western Pacific—became suddenly alarmed at the speed of America's accelerated armament program and executed a surprise attack on Pearl Harbor on December 7, 1941.

Although Guam was under United States Naval rule for nearly half a century, ostensibly for reasons of national defense, at the outbreak of war there were no American planes, not a single combat vessel in the harbor, and no heavy arms—not even a field piece —on the island. Guam became the first American territory to be captured by an Asiatic power.

During the subsequent period of Japanese military rule over all of the Marianas, the United Nations Forces suffered several of their worse defeats: that of Bataan in the Philippines, the loss of

47

A collage of U.S. bases in Micronesia, showing forces and equipment required to retake these islands during World War II.

the Dutch East Indies, the fall of Singapore, the Battle of the Java Sea, and the loss of Burma.

The turning point of World War II came late in 1942, presaged by Allied victories at the Battle of the Coral Sea and the great Battle of Midway. In July 1944 the Stars and Stripes was raised once again over the capital of Guam.

After four hundred years of civilized disruption the tragedy of World War II was nothing new to long-suffering islanders, except that it had brought a greater degree of misery and destruction than ever before; except that great bulldozers scraped and scarred whole sides of islands raw and entire populations were moved where they didn't want to go.

Contrary to what many believe, the bewildered Micronesians did not consider Americans as heavenly saviors, or as saviors at all. But Americans soon won their way deeply into the hearts of the islanders by numerous acts of kindness and a real concern for the betterment of native welfare. It was not long before many islanders decided that they liked working with Americans "because they have so many machines to do all the hard work."

Chapter Three

UNITED STATES TRUST TERRITORY
OF THE PACIFIC

After winning the islands of Micronesia from Japan the United States assumed responsibility for all of them, excepting the British Ellices and Gilberts, under a United Nations Trusteeship that made her the major island power in the South Seas. She now has, in addition to Guam, Eastern Samoa and the Line Islands, the full responsibility for governing an island area far larger than her own mainland. These 2,124 islands that comprise the United States Trust Territory of the Pacific are an important part of the South Seas that most Americans know little about.

As late as 1961 Americans were still writing to the administration wanting to buy islands or homesteads or start businesses in Micronesia. Some planned to sail down in their own schooners and ketches. All were dismayed to find that the Trust Islands, called by some journalists "the last paradise," are now closed to all tourists and nonofficial visitors. The Trust Territory Code also prohibits any alien (nonlocal native) from owning land. There would be fewer seekers after lotus islands if young Americans realized that Micronesia's coral atolls are something far less than a paradise—even for those who like coconuts, fish and pandanus as a steady diet.

Micronesians today are a young people. Over half of the population are teen-agers and younger. Their average intelligence is high and there are a few who understand Spanish, German, Japanese, English and several Micronesian languages. Advanced boys and girls, some of whose parents wore grass skirts and lava-lavas, now study economics, English and world affairs and read the *New*

York Times in their new, typhoon-proof Pacific Islands Central School Library. Outstanding students are taking advanced training in medicine, business administration and general education at Suva, Guam and Honolulu. They are being trained to replace Americans and to become the leaders of tomorrow in Micronesia.

Grouped within six main archipelagos, the islands of Micronesia scatter from the Marianas and westerly Palaus eastward through the Carolines to the Marshalls and southeast through the low, ribbonlike Gilberts to the Ellice Group, a thirty-five hundred mile crescent of islands two thousand miles wide.

In extreme contrast to the lofty green islands of Yap, Ponape, Kusaie, Guam and the Palaus, the many hundreds of low, windswept atolls that comprise the largest part of Micronesia barely thrust their white, coralline beaches above the thundering surf. They are islands without a middle—coral rings, built up layer upon layer in past centuries by numberless white, turquoise, shell-pink and pale-yellow polyps. Surrounding barrier reefs take the pounding seas and in normal weather protect the blue lagoons that encircle these atolls like huge ribbons.

Because of the vast, lonely stretches of sea and sky that separate the principal archipelagos, they are almost like separate countries, so distinctly different are their social, cultural and physical characteristics. In the westernmost islands the darker-skinned natives predominate; in the Marshalls, Gilberts and the smaller eastern islands the lighter Polynesian characteristics prevail. Not one island is inhabited by people of a distinct or uniform physical type. Within the confines of each is often found a wide range and variety, from short, slender natives to tall, powerfully-built islanders with color ranging through all the shades from yellow-tan to deep mahogany-brown.

Guam, an island with four-lane paved highways, used car lots and air-conditioned stores and movies, represents the center of civilization to most Micronesians, many of whom live more than a thousand miles away. In contrast to the pole and thatch standards found in outlying districts and islands, radios, refrigerators, store clothes and many modern conveniences are now commonplace in port towns. Islanders who live in "shanty town" settlements that have sprung up around main district centers often own a vehicle of sorts, usually an aged jeep that was bought as surplus property for one dollar. Many have learned to operate jack-hammers, dump trucks, cranes, bulldozers, tractors and agricultural machinery. Island mechanics have developed considerable skill at keeping ancient jeeps and trucks in running condition.

Old naval material still lies rusting on all of the main islands. Fifteen years after World War II, the salvaging of scrap metal from abandoned equipment was still going on. Much salvaged Japanese and American machinery became a permanent part of the new way of life. Ingenious local blacksmiths have made a variety of useful things, including fish spears, small tools and coconut huskers, from war metals that once were shells, planes and bombs.

Copra and handcrafts are exported and rice, sugar, clothing and tinned foods are the main imports. Tinned horsemeat sells well in the trade stores because Micronesians see little difference between eating horsemeat or tinned beef. Japanese cosmetics are popular because "they are cheaper and smell louder." In Truk's main trade store devil masks are stocked and a bachelor can buy a love stick for ninety-five cents that reputedly will help him to win the girl of his choice.

What is enjoyed because it is modern on Saipan, Koror or Ponape is vastly different from what is popular on the islands of Yap. Conservative and independent, the people of Yap have yielded little to modern trends. They are proud of the old ways and see no reason to adopt trousers, shirts and dresses when their traditional grass skirts, thirty pounds of grass and fronds, and *thu*, or loin cloths, for men are well suited to local conditions. Even in schools men teachers and boy students invariably wear only the thu. Yapese men, women and teen-age boys and girls enjoy chewing betel nuts that darken the teeth, and add herbs to complete the blackening to an ebony hue. "Any dog or shark can have white teeth," they say, "but it takes much care to have fine, black teeth."

On hundreds of scattered atolls in Micronesia outsiders are seen only a few times a year when the administrator calls or when a vessel comes to load copra. Life on an atoll is hard, and because of that, generally healthier than on the high islands. An "advanced" outer atoll dweller is one who owns perhaps a kerosene reefer (refrigerator), a kerosene stove, a tank for fresh water and a *benjo* (outhouse toilet). There is a solemn side to most remote islanders, no matter how joyous they may be at times. It is a solemnity bred of being surrounded on all sides by the loneliness of sea and sky.

Although the winds blow steadily over Micronesia, the low islands receive comparatively little rain. Lying close to the sea, they are tempered by ocean currents with frequent sea-breezes and squalls to moderate and freshen the atmosphere. There is generally a cloud or two hanging over and a little to leeward of low atolls because the reflected heat of the coralline sands is greater than that of the surrounding sea. Often, on an otherwise clear day, sailors can see the lovely turquoise of the lagoon reflected in such clouds many miles before the atoll itself appears above the horizon.

To coral islanders, whose material possessions are few, their tiny atolls are precious beyond all values. Schooner skippers have had to tie the hands of seamen while passing home-islands during the night or early morning—when the sweet odor of coconuts drying into copra can be detected as far as forty miles to leeward—so strong would be their desire to jump overboard and return to their soilless, coralline homes.

Living as they do, by and from the sea, it is as hard for remote islanders who have never been away from their islands to visualize the outside world as it is for an outsider to contemplate living a whole lifetime on a tiny bit of coral surrounded by the blue Pacific. Once, when a native Californian showed several Gilbert Islanders a picture of San Francisco and pointed out the great bridges and the Golden Gate, they impatiently exclaimed, "But where is the lagoon and where is the reef? Show us your reef!"

Fish, coconuts and pandanus fruit form the monotonous staple diet on most atolls because breadfruit, bananas, and other products requiring soil do not grow there. In late years, where enough soil exists for it to grow, arrowroot has been cultivated. Grated, squeezed, and cooked with coconut oil on hot stones, it is a sweet delicacy much enjoyed by islanders.

With squid, crabs and shellfish from the reefs, bonito and big fish from the sea, and small fish from the lagoons, sea food is the main item in the diet of low-islanders. Their only animals are fish-and-coconut-eating rats, cats, dogs and pigs. During severe storms, when fish scraps are scarce, coconut is their only food.

In one way or another Micronesians live off the coconut tree. On many islands the coco palm supplies food, drink, building material, fuel, cooking utensils and clothing. Ripe nuts are always available for eating or drinking, as the trees bear throughout the year. Copra, the dried meat of the coconut used in soap and other products, is the most important, and almost the only cash crop.

53

On the high islands, deer, water buffalo, cattle, horses, mules, goats and dogs thrive. Wild hogs inhabit the forests, living on scrub-breadfruit and roots; and "flying foxes," a species of bat, fly about in the daytime, feeding on choice guavas, custard apples, and breadfruit. The cattle and chickens feast off tender young banana and plantain leaves.

On these islands seafoods are supplementary rather than staple. The main foods consists of whatever vegetables or fruit grows most easily and in greatest abundance. On islands where large purple yams grow well in the cool valleys and on the verdant mountains, the chief food of the natives is yams; on other high islands where breadfruit is plentiful, it has become the principal food. In the Palaus where there are few yams or breadfruit, taro, a tuber resembling a yam, is the main diet. Taro, above all, is the Micronesian staff of life.

High islands can be recognized, long before any land is visible, by the woolly clouds that gather and remain above their peaks. In the volcanic Palau and Mariana Archipelagos, and on the high islands of the Carolines, the heavy rainfall nurtures a perpetually green background. Brilliant against it is a profusion of exotic-hued flowers that flourish along the coasts and in the villages and fertile valleys. Numerous seed-bearing plants and trees have been widely distributed over these high islands by fruit pigeons.

The forests are largely wild breadfruit, giant banyan, betel palms, Indian almond, and several tough-grained, indigenous trees. The bamboos that grow on the higher islands and the great leaves of the nipa palm are used extensively for house building. Near many villages, yellow-blossoming mango trees line the lagoon roads. In small family plantations, oranges, lemons, limes, taro, bananas, plantains, coffee and sugar apples are grown. On some of the islands there are tamarinds, cashew nuts and pomegranates.

To Micronesians the pandanus, with its long, slender leaves, is next in value to the coconut tree, and similar to it in that it furnishes wood thatch and fibre for dwellings, mats for beds, clothing, food and medicine. Like a pineapple in appearance, its fragrant orange and yellow fruit may be baked or roasted and the tender white tips at the base of the young leaves can be eaten raw or cooked. A pandanus house is far stronger and lasts much longer than one of coconut or other thatch.

Third in importance is the breadfruit tree. It bears three times a year, and its round, yellow-green, prickly-rinded fruit is sometimes as large as a man's head. Baked and eaten like a potato or pounded into poi, this is a valuable food item. The choicest white native cloth can be made from the supple underbark of the tree's young branches and its durable red wood is fine for canoe construction and figure carving. The adhesive fiber from the tree trunk is excellent for caulking the seams of boats.

Much of the leisure enjoyed by Micronesians is used in creative cultural pursuits. The plaiting and weaving of indigenous leaves and fibers into mats, baskets and hats; net and sailmaking; thatching, wood carving and other native arts and crafts have long been an essential part of their daily life.

Athletic contests between villages are a favorite pastime. In canoe racing, native craft thirty feet long and only thirty inches wide can attain the speed of twenty miles per hour. Crab racing is popular with children. They dig a trough in the sand and prod the crabs along. Toys are made from whatever materials are at hand—miniature boats out of coconut shells with frond sails, drums from sharkskin, and bamboo popguns with tiny coconut kernels for bullets. Flying homemade kites that are often bigger than twenty-five feet is a favorite sport.

Micronesians are just as sensitive of their culture and way of life as we are of ours. Rather than be known as Micronesians they prefer to be identified with their own particular island. On Guam the islanders want to be called Guamanians and on Saipan they are called Saipanese. Yap people are called Yapese and Marshall Islanders are Marshallese. Many feel that certain of the ways of their own particular island are superior to the ways of other islands as well as the introduced ways of the West. Islanders can teach the people of the great continents much in matters of co-operation and the creative use of leisure.

All of the Trust Islands of Micronesia are now officially known as The United States Trust Territory of the Pacific. Although administered by the U. S. Navy and the Department of the Interior, they are actually foreign soil and the people are subject to separate citizenship, taxes and immigration.

Having been highly critical of Japanese rule in this area the United States now faces the task of preparing the people of the Trust Islands for eventual self-government as an independent nation of Micronesia. The administration has worked quietly toward overcoming the old system of land control by island chiefs. With the introduction of democratic principles and the election of local officials by popular vote more than one native chief has been voted out of office. Special training programs are under way to enable Micronesians to take over a larger percentage of administration posts held by Americans.

Wage rates are low throughout the Trust Islands and many who work in urban centers must also do subsistence farming in order to support their families. In much of the Territory the wage scale set by the administration averages from twenty to sixty cents per hour. Elementary school teachers are paid approximately twenty-eight dollars per month and higher grade instructors receive up to seventy-five dollars monthly.

Only a few years ago English was taught in some outer island elementary schools by having the children sing "God Bless America" over and over, each day.

Today education has assumed an increasingly important role in order to equip the islanders for coping with changing conditions. The problems are complicated because of the big differences between primitive and advanced natives. From the Marshalls two thousand miles westward to the Palaus school textbooks are distributed in nine different languages besides English. A school that might be a model in energetic Honolulu or Guam could not answer the needs of the young people of Yap. The course of activities is geared by the administration to travel apace with the life and conditions of each island group.

At Ponape, the new educational center of the Territory, students from all the islands now attend the modern Pacific Islands Central School where advanced courses in general education, vocational arts and agriculture are stressed. Some go on to the Guam Territorial College for degrees, others to the University of Hawaii and to other American campuses. Some islanders are studying abroad under United Nations grants. Qualified Micronesians are expected to take over all of the staff posts at the school within the next few years.

Trust Islanders have taken full advantages of the opportunities offered under the American administration and today large trading companies are owned entirely by island stockholders and have their own Micronesian boards of directors. The Truk Trading Company, for example, which does more than a million dollar yearly business, is owned by nearly eight hundred Trukese shareholders who live on thirty-nine different islands.

When given the incentive and encouragement, Micronesians are capable of the highest achievements. They now serve in key positions in all levels of district government. Several hold some of the highest positions in the administration and have Americans working under them. Dwight Heine, a young Marshallese, is Director of Education and Dr. Arabati Hicking, a Gilbertese, is Medical Director for the Marshall Islands. A Ponapean, Dr. Ciro Barbosa, is Director of the Ponape Hospital.

All dental work is now performed by island dentists and an islander is director of dental services for the Territory. A number of Micronesians are good physicians and skilled surgeons capable of performing complex operations. It is expected that the Trust Territory Medical Department will soon be completely staffed by Trust Islanders and it is possible that the population of the islands may double in the next twenty years.

While avoiding the introduction of living standards that cannot be supported by the island people, the United States is quietly but steadily extending to the Micronesians new opportunities and a better way of life.

Guam and the Mariana Islands

The Mariana Islands, unlike the Carolines and the Marshalls, are a high volcanic group. As the northernmost of the Micronesias, on the direct route from Honolulu to the Orient, they are the crossroads of the western Pacific. Located in an area where severe storms are frequent, they play important roles, as a weather-tracking nerve center and as a vital transportation link for the air age. As an advanced fleet and air base they are as important to the United States Navy as Pearl Harbor and Hawaii, the fiftieth state.

Guam, the largest and most southerly of the Marianas, has been a Territory of the United States for sixty-three years and is now the principal western Pacific base of the Strategic Air Command. Apra, the best natural harbor between Honolulu and the Orient, has made the island a full-fledged naval defense base. Although military activity is now confined to Guam and Saipan all of the Marianas, except northerly Rota, are under United States Naval rule because of their strategic position in relation to the Orient.

North of Guam lie Rota, Saipan and Tinian. Three thousand Americans were killed and thirteen thousand wounded in the con-

Guam, principal U.S. wartime base in Micronesia.

quest of Saipan, a bright green island only thirteen miles long that became known to GIs as "Hell's Pocket." Because of its harbor, airfields and land area Saipan is now considered one of the Navy's most important forward bases. Over three-quarters of the population are supported by the Navy and live in Chalan Kanoa, the new capital town. Most Saipanese would like to see their island made a Territory of the United States. In petitioning for American citizenship they make it plain, however, that they want to preserve their own distinct ways and definitely don't want to be lumped in with Guam.

Most of the residents of Tinian and Rota are engaged in farming and small scale fishing enterprises. Only three miles of sea separate Tinian from Saipan. Because of its natural beauty five-by-ten-mile Tinian is considered by many to be the loveliest island north of the equator. Its low plateaus are well suited to agriculture and modern farm enterprises have been established under American agriculture specialists.

Rota, a small island sixty-five miles south of Saipan, reaches to a height of 1,614 feet above the sea. On a clear day, looking south from one of Rota's rugged southerly cliffs, the dim, purplish outline of

Guam can be seen forty miles away. Once the most primitive island in the Marianas, Rota is now a busy agricultural area.

The Guamanians, Saipanese, Tinians, Rotanese and other people of the Marianas are of mixed blood. Spanish names predominate and most people are Roman Catholics. Basically of Indonesian stock and descended from early native chiefs known as Chamorri, they intermarried with Spanish, Filipino and other stock and have adopted a modern way of living in advance of other islanders. They possess a deep pride of race and personal dignity and today have a higher standard of development than any other group in Micronesia.

Guamanians, distinct from the Trust Islanders, are American citizens and are ruled by a civilian governor. They have been given a degree of self-government and now elect their own twenty-one member legislature. Island courts are presided over by Guamanian judges and many local islanders have become government officials, teachers, engineers, lawyers and business men. The diffusion of "Stateside" ideals and standards has resulted in a mixed Guamanian-American way of life.

Before the postwar construction of huge U. S. Naval and air bases Guam was dependent upon an agricultural economy. It is a mountainous island, thirty miles long, shaped like the sole of a shoe, and its large southern valleys were almost wholly given over to farming. Five rivers flowing to the east provide an abundant water supply and the soil is rich and fertile, containing both coral and limestone formations. While one can almost never go more than a foot deep without striking hard coral, excellent crops are easily produced in the shallow top soil. The island climate, averaging eighty-one degrees, is healthy and well suited to farming.

Earthquakes are numerous. During the rainy season, from June to December, occasional typhoons come screaming in from the Carolines, accompanied by torrential downpours, and do considerable damage to crops and property. Because of the warm, damp humidity during this season those that have electric lights often keep them burning day and night to prevent books, shoes, clothing and many household items from developing mildew beards overnight.

Today the most important food of the Guamanian people is dry, boiled rice. Two to six pounds are consumed daily by an average family. Most often the grain is cooked in coconut milk, flavored and colored to an orange tint by a local berry. It is eaten with corn, the number two island staple, and both are liberally dipped in a red-hot sauce made of vinegar, peppers and onions, called *finadeni.* In some homes the old. Indian method of grinding corn with a stone mortar and pestle still persists. Ground corn tortillas are a favorite for lunch. *Faniji,* strange-looking bats, are considered a table delicacy by some islanders. They are roasted or boiled intact, with wings, claws, fur and all, and when served have a rather gamey flavor somewhat like young wild rabbit.

The mothers of Guam, in addition to supervising the household, often control the purses and the marriages, and manage all of the family's business affairs. Until fairly recent times, descent was through the female side of the family with children carrying on the mother's, rather than the father's, name. The bond between mother and son is especially strong and when island boys join the Navy it usually is their mother's picture that is pinned beside their bunk, rather than the American pin-up girl.

Guamanian girls have self-assurance, quiet dignity and a fine sense of humor. Spanish and Filipino traditions are still strong there. A conservative young lady, if unmarried, drapes her dress to the left; and if married, to the right. Many prefer to dress in the old Manila fashion with starched gauze blouses, fancy, embroidered butterfly sleeves and pinned-up trains. Sophisticated young moderns of Guam, especially those employed by the Navy and those who have been to school in mainland United States, peruse New York fashion magazines and dress in the latest American styles.

The Catholic religion, accepted lightly at first, in time took on a real and a deeper meaning and now holds the most important place in island life. Colorful church pageants, fiestas and fandangos are looked forward to and considered by the islanders the most important events of each year. The music, pomp and pageantry offer an emotional outlet from the monotonous routine of a military-dominated way of life.

Folk songs of the Chamorro fishermen and folk tales of ancient island heroes are still heard occasionally. Also heard are the low, soft chant of private novenas. The "Chamorita," a simple melody of old Guam, is widely sung around the island. Although the refrain remains, often new words are added or improvised for a special occasion. Sometimes the singing is accompanied by a peculiar wailing instrument called the *bilembau-tuyan.*

Island life is a strange mixture of old Chamorro and modern American ways. Some Guamanians who represent the aristocracy of Micronesia have an elite and exclusive social set. Many are rich according to island standards and live in spacious, modern homes. An average Guamanian middle or working class home consists of two or three rooms set several feet above the ground on heavy posts roofed over with galvanized iron in place of the former nipa thatch. Floors are usually built of ifil—"Guam mahogany"—and kept well polished with coconut husks. Furniture consists of beds, tables and low stools similar to those found in the Philippines. In the main room there are always a long bench, the family shrine and religious pictures on the walls. Often a second-hand American car is parked in the front yard.

In the days when church attendance was compulsory, most farmers built town houses and commuted back and forth daily, by bull cart, to work on their country farms. The hundreds of patient, plodding *carabaos,* or water buffalo, that did the pulling, performed the farmers' hardest work and sometimes provided steaks for fandangos and fiestas. The average Guamanian, content with his limited diet of rice, taro, corn, breadfruit, pork and chicken, all of which he raised easily enough in a small family plot, lived quite happily without money except for a few cents earned from copra for his church contribution, and a few more to bet at the cockfight.

By the end of the first two decades of American rule, over one-third of the Chamorro male population, lured by the many things a dollar a day could buy, were working in Agana for the Naval Government. Allowing their sound agricultural development to lapse, they adopted a false monetary standard based on Navy patronage. Farmers, fishermen and craftsmen became clerks and mess boys.

Lumbering to town in his creaking bull cart, the farmer boy who could offer his girl only life on a coconut plantation found that he must either remain a bachelor or hopefully get his name on one of the long waiting lists for government jobs. As one pert young American-Guamanian girl expressed it, she wanted "more out of life than love in a thatched hut." Her attitude is better understood when one realizes that in the country girls were expected to do much of the farm work.

With the advent of Guam's modern era, the simple life has fallen so low in prestige that more than half of the population of the island live in Agana, copy American ways and already have or hope to get a job as a clerk, teacher or Naval employee. While obtaining ice cream on a stick, banks, cars, electricity, radios, telephones, beauty parlors, canned foods, air conditioned theatres and flush toilets, the islanders lost some of their freedom and most of their self-sufficiency. Now they are, directly and indirectly, almost total dependents of American taxpayers more than five thousand miles away.

Breadfruit and yams can still be found easily enough growing wild in the hills. It is still possible to live in the country districts in a palm leaf house and, with the aid of a carabao, raise an ample supply of rice, corn and other vegetables. Supplemented with papayas, mangos, breadfruit, coconuts, fish, chickens and pigs, one can live fairly well with a minimum of work. But few Guamanians want to, any more.

The United States Department of Agriculture has worked toward making the islanders less dependent on a service economy. Blooded Brahma bulls were shipped to Rota and Tinian to improve the local stock. Pure-bred cattle, hogs, poultry, and a wide variety of new fruits have been introduced, including oranges, lemons, mangos, papayas and pineapples. Advice and free seedlings have been made available and there has been a decided effort to interest young farmers in developing the possibilities of modern progressive farming. Most of the former rice lands have now been taken over by the military forces. Recently, because of the high cost of imported rice, many islanders have been returning to taro, yams and corn, and a number of commercial farms are in operation.

The delicious island fruits, vegetables and fresh sea foods would make the fame of a New York or Philadelphia restaurant, but the islanders invariably prefer a can of American sardines or a jar of strawberry jam to anything the island produces. If a traveler is invited to a Guamanian dinner party, unless he lets it be known beforehand that he is allergic to canned foods, he will quite possibly be served American canned salmon, canned peas, canned peaches and other imports instead of the local products, as modern islanders consider canned goods a fine treat for any special occasion.

In the postwar build-up the military command concentrated on the development of harbors, landing fields and nuclear installations. Mountains have been cut in two and nearly four hundred miles of hard coral and tar surfaced highways constructed. The island's scenic Route 1, along the west coast, has been widened to a modern, four-lane superhighway that now goes completely around the island. Once a lonely port of call for Spanish treasure galleons, Guam has become America's number one forward base in the Pacific; a machine-age island with more modern sea and airport facilities than any island in Oceania other than Oahu.

Although Guam has had its face lifted by modern bulldozers for its new role as the Gibraltar of the western Pacific, it is still the "Pearl of the Marianas." The lush tropical vegetation has obliterated the jagged scars of modern warfare. Old Agana, Agat and most native villages have been rebuilt and the young people again play Pepino-Pepino on the village greens.

Caroline Islands

From one end of the vast, east-to-west-reaching Caroline Archipelago to the other is almost as far as from New York City to Venezuela in South America. Because of the great distances involved they are generally divided and referred to as the Western, Central and Eastern Carolines.

Most of the total land area of about eight hundred and thirty square miles is taken up by Palau and Yap in the west, Truk in the central area, and Ponape and Kusaie in the east. These, however, are not individual islands but are names applied to groups of islands. Including the above four there are over forty individual island groups in the Carolines. About these main groups are generally a large number of lesser islets and atolls.

Five distinct languages are spoken by the people of Palau, Yap, Truk, Ponape and Kusaie. Each of these groups has a different culture varying from stone to modern age, and they have long maintained divided social strata.

Palau

High, green, and entirely surrounded by blue lagoons and coral reefs, the Palau Islands have remained the least known of Micronesia's island groups, although they are the largest group of islands in the Carolines and have, on several occasions, loomed large in world events.

Located seven hundred miles southwest of Guam, they are a ninety-mile-long slight crescent of more than two hundred islands once widely referred to as the Singapore of Japan.

Containing one of the best natural harbors in Micronesia, the fertile, heavily wooded Palaus are often spoken of singularly as Palau, because they are for the most part a large central cluster of islands enclosed on the west within a sixty-mile-long reef and lagoon that is never more than twenty miles wide.

The central island group contains eight large and eighteen small islands. Beyond the central group, to the northwest, lies Kayangel, a small circular atoll; to the southeast, two-and-a-half by two mile Angaur, formerly—because of its phosphate—the richest island in Micronesia.

Most important of the central Palaus is Babelthuap, twenty-five miles long, and tiny Koror, the capital island. Looking like a tropic paradise from the air and from the sea, Babelthuap, the second largest island in Micronesia, contains two-thirds of the total land area of the Palaus. Often rising abruptly from the sea, it outlines in hilly green contours more than six hundred feet above the deep blue lagoons.

Within a five-mile radius south of Babelthuap lie five islands of which Koror, the capital and the administrative center, is most important. A horseshoe-shaped island, Koror is unique in that it is part volcanic and part coralline. It is the most developed of the central group and contains the main town, modern docks, warehouses, large schools, hospitals and administration buildings. Densely-populated Koror is the most Americanized island in the Trust Territory. Rock 'n' roll music is heard there and the town supports several night clubs complete with hostesses and juke boxes. Local Palauans wear modern western clothes and live in houses similar to those in many small United States agricultural towns. Many own some sort of a gasoline driven vehicle and have electric stoves and telephones. There are also taxis, pool halls and juvenile delinquency problems.

A mile long bridge from Koror connects with Arakabasan, a hilly two by three-quarter mile, well-cultivated island. At the southern end of the long central reef lies Peleliu, a fertile island with a narrow, irregular coast line and a steep, forested ridge of raised reef. Meaning "under house," Peleliu derived its name from the fact that at one time its warriors were always defeated in battle.

The climate of the group is damp but healthy, averaging from seventy-six to eighty-five degrees. However, two hundred and sixty-five days of the year are rainy days, and the fierce west and northwest swirling typhoons that devastate the coast of Asia from the Philippines to Japan are born in the Palaus. The seas around the

Carolines cradle as many as twenty typhoons each year, most of them in September.

Yap

There are few groups in Micronesia as lovely as the strangely shaped islands of Yap, three hundred and twenty-six miles northeast of Palau. Meaning "the land" in Yapese, they are a circling cluster of four heavily wooded islands and ten lesser islets that extend sixteen miles in a north to south direction.

Called by early travelers the Venice of the Pacific, Yap, Map, Tomil and Romung, the main islands, are separated by narrow waterways and all are entirely surrounded by a long shallow green lagoon and a great barrier reef that is two miles wide in many places. The fragrances of crotons and pungent wild ginger mingle with the scent of fresh sea tangle along the fringing reef when the wind is right. Except during the typhoon season the climate is excellent and generally moderated by the prevailing easterly winds.

The people of Yap, often described as the "Irish of the Pacific," are a proud, sensitive race. Before the Spanish came they were the most skilled artisans and the cultural leaders in a vast island world reaching as far east as the Marshalls, nearly fifteen hundred miles away. They were also the greatest traders and the most daring navigators. Superior dyes, the best weaving, the finest earthenware and the most advanced architecture and boatbuilding came from Yap. It was on Yap that the oldest customs prevailed. From there the arts of navigation were handed on to others.

Today, American currency is in wide use and, of course, desired. But the traditional stone money of Yap is still money to the Yapese. The island's roughly round stone "coins" vary from a few inches in diameter to as much as ten feet high and some weigh as much as five tons. A stone "coin" four inches in diameter and of the right material, shape, and color formerly could be exchanged for a fat pig. A stone five feet high might, on the proper occasion, purchase a whole village! Just as the careers of famous jewels, such as the Hope Diamond, are widely known all over the world, on the island of Yap the name, history, and ownership of each large stone is known to all and plays an important part in prestige and tradition.

Most of what passes for modern life in Yap centers around picturesque Colonia, on the shores of Tomil Bay. Colonia, like other administration centers, has its water reservoir, wireless station, power plant, reefers, schools, hospital, dental clinic, wharves, warehouses, trucks, tractors, jeeps and motor boats. Yet, only a short distance away from the administration headquarters the verdant jungle and old-time Yap prevails.

Most of the native houses are still of wooded posts and beams set on stone terraces or walls with thatched roofs of nipa palms. Often they are located on damp lowlands in dense, shadowy jungles. The people, for privacy, prefer to live in the semi-isolation of small villages widely scattered around the coasts. Their houses, used mainly for sleeping and storage, are hidden among flamboyant shrubs and trees. Most family living—cooking, weaving, entertaining and relaxing—is done in the coral-graveled garden area.

Generations of foreign influence have made little impression locally. The people, as their features clearly show, have mixed little with Europeans, Japanese or Americans. Most islanders still dress much as they did a half century ago and the men still build their outrigger canoes to designs that have been used for generations. Today colorful outrigger canoes and former Navy whale boats with native sails race side by side in Tomil Bay.

Yap could easily produce several times the amount of copra it markets. But, where one or two hours' work a day is ample to keep a man's family fed and sheltered, the men remain skeptical of the latest forms of agriculture and prefer to have little to do with modern commercial production.

The people of Yap possess a complex social system and are proud enough of their time-honored ways to want to preserve them. They are willing to co-operate and accept changes providing they are first completely convinced that the changes are worth while and not "just something new." After being told what to do in turn by the Spaniards, the Germans, the Japanese and now the Americans, perhaps some of the reserved and aloof Yapese feel that another war may drive out the Americans and bring still another race to tell them what to do.

Truk

Sailing a thousand miles east of Yap, through a long maze of atolls and reefs, one comes to the great basaltic islands of Truk, a group of high volcanic and low coral islands that comprise the largest population group in the Carolines.

Truk offers one of the best anchorages for ships in the western Pacific. It sheltered much of Japan's battle fleets and was considered by the Japanese high command to be impregnable. A coral ring entirely surrounds its huge lagoon, forming a rough circular necklace of reefs and atolls that are nearly one hundred and fifty miles in circumference. Northeast Pass, the best of four ship passages, is the entrance to Moen, now the principal island and U. S. Trust Territory Administrative Headquarters for the Central Carolines District. Modern dock and harbor facilities are under construction.

Truk, meaning "mountain" in the native language, contains fourteen volcanic islands and over thirty coral islets varying in size from several that are only three or four feet above sea level to four of the main islands that rise in dark green volcanic peaks more than a thousand feet high. Tol, eleven by three miles, is the largest; other high islands include Dublon, Udot, Moen, Fefan and Fala.

Honeycombed with lovely little islands, Truk has the largest lagoon in the world and the best for canoe and small boat sailing. There is almost always a breeze blowing and its iridescent waters are filled with myriads of pink, lemon-yellow, emerald and white coral trees, masses of blue moss, yellow and purple sponges, ultramarine starfishes and other strange living shapes in fiery rainbow hues.

The Truk District is one of the largest in the Trust Territory. Its 1960 population was approximately twenty thousand. Many Trukese people prefer to live in isolated villages remote from the administrative center. In recent years native life has been little disturbed in many of these areas, including Tol, a densely populated island, and Pis Island, a small motu on the north side of the barrier reef. Here most of the people live quiet, almost primitive lives in scattered settlements near the shore. Their canoes are of traditional design and their houses are mostly of thatched roofs and woven pandanus construction. The long bush knife and the primitive digging stick are still being used.

As in other island groups, life is much different in the administrative center. Moen has the largest trade emporium in the Trust Territory. Its three trading firms sell everything from Japanese canned fish, "aloha" shirts and soda pop to radios and kerosene refrigerators. In exchange it accepts cash, sacks of copra, trochus shell or handiwork. The town's movie theatre runs continuously from 10 A.M. to

11 P.M. Wild west pictures are popular and *The Bombing of Truk* is still shown on occasion to Trukese fans who never seem to tire of the picture although they have seen it a score of times.

Ponape

Four hundred miles directly east from Truk, on a clear day, the looming blue peaks of Ponape can be seen merging in the clouds from a distance of thirty miles or more. Its Mount Tolocome, rising 2,579 feet above the sea, is the highest mountain in the Carolines.

Ponape, containing one hundred and forty-six square miles, is a nearly circular island group made up of one large island thirteen miles in diameter ringed by twenty-three small islands and many tiny islets, some of which are mere fragments of sand and reef rock. Indented by long translucent bays, it is entirely surrounded by a wide lagoon and coral reef. Ronkiti, at the southwest end, and Ponape Harbor on the north side are the two best anchorages.

The rugged mountains and the valleys are thickly wooded and in some places almost inaccessible with ferns, orchids and creepers. In many places on the lower slopes bougainvillea, hibiscus and gay flamboyants run riot.

Because of its large land areas Ponape has remained an agricultural center. Life is comparatively easy because of the amazing fertility and the highly productive areas that have made it a heavily wooded tropic wonderland. Almost alone of Micronesia's many islands it has an abundance of fresh water from many rivers, picturesque waterfalls and lovely upland lakes. Few islands in the world have a heavier rainfall. Precipitation over much of the higher levels of the main and surrounding islands is as much as two hundred and fifty inches a year.

Most of the people of the main island live on separate farms and holdings along the coast, in homestead settlements and in Kolonia, the central town and headquarters for the district trust administration.

Today, rice, flour, tea, sugar, western clothing—and outboard motors for those who can afford them—are considered necessities of life in Kolonia. Paddling a canoe is almost a thing of the past to modern Ponapeans. Day and night the intolerable *putt-putt* of outboard motors is heard from all parts of the bays and waterways. Almost everyone who lives near the shores of Kolonia owns an outboard motor and looks forward to the time when he will be able to get another one with more horsepower than those of his neighbors.

Local islanders are a strong-willed, independent people. In Ponapean, "democracy" is translated to mean "do as you please." Most of the local government is in the hands of the islanders and, as in other districts, village and municipal officers are elected by popular vote. The local Congress is composed of two chambers, a House of Nobles which represents the ranking chiefs, and the People's House whose members are elected on the basis of one for every three hundred people.

In October, 1959, Micronesia's largest seat of learning, the Pacific Islands Central School, opened its new, typhoon-proof building at Ponape to the largest student body in its history. Training in practical agriculture is stressed at the school, with resident students growing much of their own food.

The main Agricultural Experiment Station of Micronesia is close to the new PICS campus. Here, in an area planted and pioneered by the Japanese, American agriculture experts have developed extensive gardens of tropical food trees, many of them brought in from all over the South Seas. They also are endeavoring to improve the Territory's subsistence foods. They would especially like to establish an additional cash crop for the Micronesians—such as, perhaps, cacao—and are carrying out experiments to that end.

Taro and yams, besides being favorite food staples on Ponape, can be big factors in a man's prestige. The person who grows the biggest taro or yam in a season is looked up to as the most accomplished individual in the community. A socially ambitious Ponapean secretly nurtures his prize yams in concealed areas with much care until they weigh perhaps two hundred pounds or more. Success in yam culture is considered proof not only of a man's ability and industry but also of his generosity and respect for others, as the prize is always donated to the chief.

Kolonia, which was almost completely destroyed during the last war, is being rebuilt in line with the administration's homesteading program. The plan encourages rebuilding on lots that are large enough for home subsistence gardening. Under this long-range program Ponape is becoming a melting pot. In fertile sections new farming communities have been established for many hundreds of people from other, overcrowded islands.

In the extreme south of the Ponape area are the atolls of Kapingamarangi and Nukuoro. Both of these overpopulated islands are inhabited by Polynesians who are much larger than most Micronesians in physique and quite different in demeanor. They are somewhat of a nomadic people and scores of them sail back and forth through the islands. Several hundred of these people have built their own Polynesian village on homestead sites in a small section of Ponape known locally as Porokheit Village.

Kusaie, at the easternmost end of the Caroline chain, three hundred and seven miles from Ponape, consists of a large island, seven by eight miles in size, an important but tiny adjoining island, and eight low coral islets on a fringing reef that almost encircles both islands. The little island of Lele lies just off the northeast coast of Kusaie and at low tide one can walk from one to the other. The town of Lele, on the west side of Lele Island, is the principal settlement of the group.

Kusaie is the second largest of Ponape's municipalities and it has been an educational center for Micronesia for more than a century. Most of the approximately eighteen hundred inhabitants live in small villages along the coasts and in the large main valley. At the Mission Training School in Lele, which was established by New England's Boston Mission in 1880, native teachers are trained and sent out to teach in various islands of the far-flung Caroline and Marshall Groups.

In addition to its fine climate and high productivity Kusaie is one of the loveliest and most remote islands in the central Pacific. Palms, tree ferns and a wealth of luxuriant vegetation color its slopes in great mantles of living green, from crescent white beaches to the highest mountain peaks.

It is known that a great race of daring navigators, warriors and artisans from the East ruled the Carolines in prehistoric times and erected their stupendous monolithic capital of Nan-Matal on the southeast side of Ponape. Fully as awe-inspiring as the pyramids of Egypt, and as mysterious as the great stone faces on Easter Island, these ancient remains of Nan-Matal are the most remarkable prehistoric ruins in the South Seas. On his historic voyage in the *Beagle,* Charles Darwin remained at the Carolines to explore many of the great masses of stonework and marveled at the skill and ingenuity of the early builders.

Ancient stone platforms, pillars and other relics long covered with

70

lichen and fern mosses are found in many places on Yap. Large pre-historic structures are located near Lele, amid the deep, shadowy palm groves of Kusaie. But neither compare with the remains of the deserted stone city of mystery, Nan-Matal.

Meaning "in many openings," Nan-Matal was a South Sea Venice of more than five square miles in area constructed on a group of small islands. Complete with long waterways, forts, castles, and large sun temples and altars, this ancient city was built by skilled engineers out of great stone beams and slabs, many of which are more than twenty feet in length.

How did this great city of stone arise? How were the countless tons of great stone pillars and blocks quarried, transported and constructed by a people who so far as is known had only shell tools to work with? Why was such an advanced metropolis erected in an isolated island group thousands of miles from the early civilized centers? Such questions have baffled archaeologists for ages.

A native legend says simply that Nan-Matal was built by the two brothers, Oleosiba and Oleosobo. Geologists suggest that the massive stones may have been quarried from huge prismatic blocks that became separated by fissures—others that they were quarried with the aid of levers, fire and steam, to be brought to Ponape on great rafts and there chipped, shaped and put into place.

One thing is certain: it must have required from twenty thousand to fifty thousand workmen to complete the great edifices. Many of the stones that remain today weigh from twenty to forty tons each. Massive, well-shaped and well-placed, they are but fragments of a South Sea kingdom that flourished more than a thousand years ago, a civilization that has vanished.

The Marshall Islands

In physical contrast to the widely scattered variety of the Caroline Groups, the low, windswept Marshall Islands form a compact archipelago. However, the geographical conditions, the products, the language and the ways of the people are largely the same.

Located midway between Hawaii and New Guinea, astride the direct routes from the United States to Australia and to the Philippines, they are the nearest of the Micronesias to Honolulu.

There is not a single high or volcanic island in the Marshalls. They are made up of thirty-four coral atolls and single islands, and more than eleven hundred narrow reefs and motus extending in two parallel rows approximately one hundred and thirty miles apart.

The easternmost row, containing fourteen atolls and two islands, is the *Ratak* (toward the dawn) chain and the westernmost row, with fifteen atolls and three islands including far westwardly Eniwetok and Ujelang, is called the *Ralik* (towards the sunset) chain.

While the actual land area of the group is but seventy square miles, or less than one-fourth the size of New York City, the total sea area occupied is eight times the size of New York State, extending about seven hundred miles north and south and approximately seven hundred and eighty-four miles from east to west.

The difference in formation between an atoll and a single coral island is usually due to the circling reef of the latter, which is so much smaller than that of the atoll that the coral debris is washed in from many sides until the lagoon is completely filled. Most Marshall atolls are made up of a number of long, narrow islets forming roughly oval or circular coral rings with one or several channels through which the tides flow into the inner lagoon. The widths of these passages vary from a few yards to several miles and are generally located on the leeward side.

Likiep, the highest atoll, rises only thirty-four feet at its maximum elevation and Wotje, the widest island in the archipelago, is less than a mile across. Most are less than the height of a man above sea level. Normally the beaches are protected from the breaking surf by the outer reef, but during typhoons and large storms the sea breaks far up and washes completely over the lower islands, destroying the coconut, breadfruit and pandanus trees and drowning the people. In the worst typhoons men lash their women and children to the strongest trees to keep them from being swept into the sea.

Long, narrow, thirty-five mile Jaluit was formerly the capital and trade center for the Marshalls. Fifty islets circle its beautiful, two hundred square mile lagoon. In 1958, during Typhoon Ophelia, the whole island of Jaluit was under three to four feet of water. Screaming winds reached one hundred and thirty-five knots and sixteen people lost their lives in the long-pounding seas. All homes and subsistence plants were swept away and eighty percent of the coconut trees were destroyed. "All that was left was misery and destruction," one report stated.

After the immediate havoc of a typhoon passes, the scarce soil of an atoll is so inundated with salt water that no crops can be grown for a long time. On smaller islands much of the topsoil is washed completely away and new earth has to be brought in. Long after a typhoon passes, as well as during droughts, when fresh water is lacking, whatever food scraps are available have to be cooked in sea water from the lagoon.

Warfare has proven even more destructive than the worst typhoons to some of the Marshall Islands. Only seven coconut trees survived the 1944 American conquest of Kwajalein, one of the largest atolls in the world. Later Kwajalein became one of the most vital Naval and Air Force Bases in the Pacific. Like Eniwetok, it is an important steppingstone linking Pearl Harbor and Guam. Its ninety narrow, flat islands and islets encircle a lagoon with an area of nine hundred square miles, that has on occasions held a whole armada of battleships, cruisers, destroyers and other vessels. It could, if necessary, hold all the navies in the world. Today space age missile facilities take up most of its land area.

Majuro, the only international trade port in the Trust Territory, is the main trans-shipping port for copra. It is also the Territory's administration center and most important island. The fifty coralline islands of its atoll are ringed around ninety square miles of lagoon. Most of the people live on the south side of Majuro Atoll on the island of Majuro, a twenty-one mile long finger of land that is only a few hundred yards wide in most places.

Among the most important of the other Marshall Atolls are Ailinglapalap, Ebon (or Boston) Atoll, Namu, Namorik, Arno and Mille.

In the light of past events the Marshalls now occupy a significant place in the future of the Pacific. Having cost the United States over six billion dollars to capture during World War II, their chief value lies in their strategic location. The Navy considers them its first line of defense beyond Pearl Harbor.

Today Bikini and Eniwetok, the home of the big thermonuclear testing base, are probably the most widely known islands in the Marshalls. Before the Atomic Age came to Bikini, Chief Juda and his one hundred and sixty-six subjects were informed that a man-made "monstrous thing" would soon blast their island home and perhaps destroy every living thing. Made fearful in the face of an impending disaster over which they had no control, the bewildered islanders agreed to give up their lifelong homes and gardens and begin anew on Rongerik Atoll, one hundred and nine miles to the southeast.

73

Queen Lijamer, Majuro, Marshall Islands. (Tattooing on neck and shoulders indi-cates she is of royal blood.)

To atoll dwellers, who have deep spiritual ties with their homes and historical ties centuries old with their home island, this was like going to another continent. Bikinians believe that the soul of their departed ones return to keep a loving and protective watch over the living. The uprooted people felt that their loved ones would never be able to find them so far away from the only island with which they were identified. Every tree and every rock on his three to five acre home has real value and meaning to a Marshallese. To be exiled is to be condemned to die a little.

After an unhappy year on Rongerik the Bikinians were transferred to distant Kwajalein. After another unhappy year at that atoll they were moved en masse to Kili Island in the extreme south of the Marshalls.

What has happened to the Bikinians would be comparable, in the Marshallese sense, to moving a whole California town of grape growers to the Nevada desert, then to Pennsylvania and finally to Canada.

When the hydrogen bomb got out of control in 1954 all the people of Rongelap were uprooted from their homes and moved to Majuro for three years of exile and treatment for burns and radiation sickness. The United Nations report of the accident stated, "About ninety percent of the people affected developed skin lesions. . . . No assurance could be given that cancer would not develop at the site of skin lesions."

Despite assurances from the government that better safeguards

Marshallese spokesman Dwight Heine told the United Nations of the suffering of his people from nuclear explosions and petitioned the United States to stop all further tests.

against radiation fallout would henceforth be taken, the Marshall Islanders are not convinced. They are especially worried about how to protect their coconut trees, the fish in their lagoons and their drinking water from radiation contamination.

The President of the Marshall Islands Congress appealed in person directly to the United Nations Trusteeship Council for aid for their people in settling land claims. The islanders pointed out to the Council that not only had their land been taken from them but their best fishing grounds had been destroyed. In conclusion they held that unless their land rights were respected according to their own free will they felt that Trusteeship should be given up and the Marshall Islanders returned to their "former freedom."

Before the advent of the bicycle, the refrigerator, the Sears Roebuck catalogue and the modern trade emporium, the average Micronesian got along very well on his local island diet and had an ample amount of what was considered freedom. Today, aside from Naval employment, the people of the Marshalls are dependent almost entirely upon copra for the money to buy flour, pork and beans, rice, sugar, biscuits, tea, coffee, clothing, building materials and other "necessities of life" to which they have recently become accustomed. The term "King Copra" applies to no other archipelago so much as it does to the Marshalls where the number of coconuts on an island is the largest single factor determining its population and living conditions. To add to the problems of the islanders, in late years Japanese copra buyers have demanded certification that the copra was not radioactive.

To offset to some extent the reduced land area, scientific farming has been introduced and other industries are being developed, including fishing on a larger scale, and the making of shell and coral by-products. The local lagoons are rich in bivalves and marine life and have often been called a "shell collector's paradise." Many of the most valuable sea shells are discovered in the more isolated areas. Among the rare species, "orange cowries" valued as high as one hundred dollars a pair have been found.

Learning to become like Americans, Marshall Islanders have become accustomed to a number of things that they never heard of before. Medical care and facilities have been effective in winning their interest and esteem and certain health measures such as inoculation injections against disease have proven popular. At first when an islander was given his "shoots," a remarkable psychological change took place. His optimism was unbounded, for he felt that at last he was free from any and all ailments, including accidents and bad luck.

Marshallese have always taken flies and mosquitoes for granted. On one island, during an intensive public health campaign, the naval doctor set up an enlarged three-foot model of a fly and a mosquito in order to demonstrate their dangerous features and arouse the people to an anti-insect campaign. While greatly impressed by the sight of the "big bugs," the islanders hastened to assure the doctor that there was little to fear at the present time, as such "big American bugs" had not yet been seen in the Marshalls. Despite a century and a half of Christianity, island magic "doctors" are still occasionally called upon to prescribe for stomach-aches and love sickness.

The villagers today have a far different idea of the outside world from what they once imagined it to be, derived partly from illustrated New York magazines, radio programs and motion pictures. At first shocked and deeply embarrassed upon seeing their first Hollywood love scene, they soon became jubilant motion picture fans. Except for "Springtime in the Rockies," the only outside songs they knew were "The Old Rugged Cross," "Onward Christian Soldiers" and other missionary hymns, many of which were memorized and sung in their own language. Such well-known American songs as "You Are My Sunshine" and "Song of the Islands" soon became popular on many atolls and the girls picked up jitterbugging and in some instances an American version of the hula.

More than a few servicemen have been distinctly disappointed to find that the gay sarong styles, so widely in vogue on islands farther south, are not to be found on the light copper-colored girls of the Kwajalein or Majuro Atolls—nor, for that matter, are they to be found anywhere in the Marshalls. Since that early day when "all natives put off their heathenism and put on clothing" the girls of the Marshalls, usually barefooted, have worn high-necked, ample-length "Mother Hubbard" gowns over two or more petti-coats.

Up until recent years, except for the good work that has been done by service personnel and by the Trust Administration, the missionaries were almost the only whites to give the Marshall Islanders reason to think well of Caucasians and to convince them that there were many Americans with interests other than cheating them, taking their land or molesting their women.

Most Marshallese belong to their own independent Christian Church of the Marshall Islands, a Protestant organization. Austere in their devotion to New England Protestant principles, they observe the Sabbath with far greater reverence than many places in the United States. There is no smoking or swearing and no working on Sunday. On numerous occasions they have refused double wages to unload ship cargo on the Sabbath, preferring to go to jail if need be.

The Marshallese, like the Polynesians in racial characteristics, are a gentle people widely known throughout Micronesia for their inherent courtesy and generosity. "*Yokwe yok,*" meaning "Love to you," is their traditional greeting to a stranger. It is often accompanied by a garland of fragrant flowers, and when an islander comes to call on a stranger for the first time he will invariably bring a hand-woven fan, a mat or some other small gift.

Even today, after a century and a half of white depredations, to call a Marshall Islander miserly or to say that he is "one who grants sparingly of food to others" would wound him deeper than anything one could possibly say.

"Is he kind?" is the first question the Marshall Island people ask about a stranger, for in Marshallese eyes the three most important qualities of a man are kindness, generosity and a low voice.

Young Marshallese are eager for improvement. Having always been more interested in the achievement of prestige rather than monetary wealth, they have taken readily to education to achieve skills and develop new talents. While many speak Japanese and a few know German in addition to their own native language, everyone has taken up the study of English. Having long experienced bureaucracy, islanders are now learning about democracy and for most purposes are already self-governing, especially on the outer atolls. The old authority and influence of chiefs and nobles is slowly diminishing. Today chief, nobleman and commoner eat alike, dress alike and have one equal vote in island affairs.

An entirely new society is evolving, based on the skills and knowledge being introduced by a dedicated small group of Americans in aloha shirts who administer the islands. The leaders of tomorrow who will take the place of the nobility will be young

Marshallese doctors, teachers, businessmen and American-trained students of island government.

American medical programs have almost entirely eradicated venereal and other diseases introduced by early whites. Recently the Marshalls, with the exception of the Bikini area, were rated among the healthiest islands in Micronesia. New gardens are blooming on many atolls. The skeleton coconut trees are green again with new fronds and the once withered breadfruit and pandanus have regained their shapes and colors.

Seen today, it is almost impossible to realize that only a few short years ago many of them were utterly desolate, battered areas pitted with the remains of shell-smashed rubble. As a permanent reminder, less than six miles from Kwajalein, at the north end of a small palm-clad island, a stand of green coconut palms fronts the lagoon where hundreds of tiny white crosses once bore the names of young boys from American cities, towns and farms.

Chapter Four

FRENCH OCEANIA

Tahiti Today

Just as Hawaii came into national prominence slightly more than fifty years ago, the jet age has now brought Tahiti and French Oceania into popular travel focus as the "new" island world of the Pacific. But Tahiti today is not at all like Waikiki, and Honolulu's highly civilized version of Polynesia does not compare with the offbeat charm of Papeete, the capital of French Polynesia. In spite of a relatively large cosmopolitan population, Papeete has remained Parisian in tone and manners and Polynesian in spirit. It is often said that "the French have the authority, the Chinese have the profits, while the Tahitians have all the laughter."

If a popularity contest were held tomorrow among world travelers, Tahiti would outdistance Bali, Capri and other famous islands more than two to one. Its nearby islands of Moorea and Bora Bora would probably tie for second place. If whole archipelagos were included, French Polynesia would win there too.

The one hundred and ten islands and numerous islets of French Oceania, located about halfway between Australia and South America, reach out over a million square miles to make France the dominant power in the east-central Pacific. Geographically and for administrative purposes they divide into a number of archipelagos known as the Tuamotus, Gambiers, Marquesas, Australs and the Society Group, with the administrative and trade center located at Papeete on the classic island of Tahiti.

Today the whining jet planes unloading one hundred and twenty-five tourists at a time onto the coral reef strip that extends into Auae Lagoon are doing as much to change Tahiti as Captain Samuel Wallis and the crew of the H.M.S. *Dolphin* did when they discovered the island nearly three hundred years ago. The effect of this once remote land's being linked up with the rest of the world can be seen and heard all over the island.

Local French officials, long known for their red tape and bureaucracy, have had a change of heart in recent years and have now joined hands with a small group of eager Americans to exploit the island's possibilities on a scale certain to relieve France of a major share of its colonial burden.

"Tahiti needs tourist dollars more than Hawaii," an official of the largest trading firm said a few months ago. "*Sacre Bleu!* Hawaii has its sugar, pineapples and coffee. Here the copra trade is diminishing and our phosphate will soon be gone. This beautiful island costs France four hundred million francs a year. The jets will save our economy. We will have bigger hotels. Next year we hope for fifty thousand tourists."

If the trade executive's hopes are realized it will be a tremendous increase for an island that had only nine hundred visitors four years ago.

"Most of all we want the luxury trade," emphasized an employee of the French travel agency. "We want tourists with ample money to spend—not your dreamers or beachniks."

"What the French really want," said an American poet who had to leave for lack of funds after two visa extensions, "is for the American tourists just to send them their trip money via airmail and stay at home."

Carpenters, masons, plumbers, laborers, truck drivers and the weavers of pandanus and split bamboo were never so busy. The former what-difference-does-a-day-or-two-make pace of working is gone. Pressures have arrived. A job that took a week to do five years ago now is done in three days. The maid who formerly took a few days off, spontaneously and without notice, whenever she felt the urge, now must show up steady or else. Nearly every type of employment is unionized. Islanders have demanded and obtained paid holidays, pensions, medical care and accident compensation.

New hotels, bungalow style, have been completed along the shores of the lagoon. New cars are arriving, and town traffic on peak tourist days is a conglomeration of whirling bicycles competing for space with putt-putting motor scooters, motor bikes and tiny French cars. Lotus Village, the first motel to be built in French

Polynesia, recently opened its parking stalls about six miles from Papeete and there will soon be more.

The island's picturesque "Tahitian-style" thatch villas that have been built of coconut, pandanus, bamboo and stone are not owned by Tahitians. Most have been built or are owned directly or indirectly by wealthy Americans or world-weary Europeans. The majority of Tahitians live in simple thatch shanties with "civilized" corrugated tin roofs.

What do the Tahitians think of the new prosperity? is one of the first questions an outsider asks. How do they feel now that the tranquil, undisturbed days are gone?

"*Aue!*" a large group of Tahitians exclaimed when the first huge jet liner whined down over Auae Lagoon. *Aue*, pronounced "ah-way" is the Tahitian word of emphasis for almost any occasion. It means nothing in particular. "*Aita peapeau*"—"It doesn't matter" —replied one of the oldest tiki carvers on the island when asked what he thought about it all. He accompanied the remark with a characteristic Tahitian shrug of the shoulders.

Tahitian nationalist leaders object strongly to the build-up and glamorizing of local color and "native life." "We resent," they say, "seeing our people making monkeys of themselves for the entertainment of tourists."

It would seem that everyone is concerned about the jet strip except the average Tahitian. Having survived the early explorers, whalers, missionary rivalries and World War II, most Polynesians feel that the jet era will have little effect on their basic way of life except in Papeete. There the Tahitian cab drivers think the strip is a good thing. All the taxi drivers can sing and most can play a guitar or left-handed ukulele, and they will with the slightest urging join a party at any time. As they see it, there will now be more fares and bigger and better parties.

Above all things, Tahitians believe that life is made for happiness and for love. Sometimes it is said with flowers. A *tiare Tahiti* (flower of love) or a hibiscus blossom behind the right ear denotes a free heart, while one behind the left means the wearer already has a loved one. When they sing and play the guitar or thump the hula drums the music is about love. When they dance it is about love. By Western standards the Tahitian hula is surprisingly bold, but by Tahitian standards it is simply an honest part of their culture and way of life.

Love to the Tahitians comes naturally and is as simple to them as any of the other wonderful things of life such as breathing, laughing, sleeping or singing. All children are loved regardless of their background or parental status. Old people are loved and respected. Despite much storied publicity to the contrary, marriage and fidelity to a truly loved one is as highly regarded in Tahiti as anywhere else.

Some early Polynesians, unable to understand the eagerness of white seamen for the favors of island girls, concluded that the white race must be composed of men only and in order to enjoy the company of girls it was necessary for them to travel to the South Seas. Otherwise, they asked each other, how could one explain the high value they placed on *vahines* (girls) and the great need that made them return again and again.

Children are loved and happy in French Polynesia regardless of their background.

The physical beauty of the pure Polynesians has been over-praised. The men are strong and well built according to Western standards but girls with slim, shapely figures, good teeth and good health are rare. Most have golden brown soft skin, straight limbs and bluish-black hair that often reaches to their knees. But they don't look like Dorothy Lamour or Brigitte Bardot any more than the average American girl does. The typically heavy-featured Polynesian girl is something else again if she is part Chinese or European. Tahitians of mixed ancestry, called demis, are of smaller stature and generally of finer features. Girls of mixed Chinese, French and Tahitian descent are among the most beautiful in the South Seas.

Many girls come in from the out-islands for a few months in Papeete before settling down to marriage and family life. Some become professional dancers, but mostly they enjoy life and may be seen most any afternoon or evening strolling about the esplanade or under the flamboyant trees along the Quai Bir Hackeim, the colorful waterfront of Papeete. More than a few former dancing girls have discarded or packed away their grass hula skirts and married Americans. The more sophisticated girls wear form-fitting skirts and tight-bodied dresses Parisian style—barely to the knees. The majority wear the Polynesian *pareu,* a large rectangle of gay print cloth worn as a snug wrap-around held on by folds and tucks.

The pareu, which is called a sarong or lava-lava in other parts of the Pacific, is also worn by the men. At a staged dance men wear flowered loincloths, but much of the time they wear a T-shirt, pandanus hat and shorts or the pareu worn as a waistcloth or folded and tucked to make swim trunks.

Men of Tahiti work at what they enjoy most: fishing, building a boat, harvesting a little copra, building a house. They especially like to ride motor-scooters or drive a car or a truck. Most of the dull, hour-after-hour routine is left to the Chinese, who never seem to mind it.

Today, as do the Indians in Fiji, French Polynesia's seven thousand Chinese control the retail trade. They are the butchers, bakers, bankers, tailors and shopkeepers. They have reclaimed swamp areas and introduced rice cultivation and truck gardening. They dominate the vanilla and copra trade and own the best trading schooners. The frugal Chinese, living simply, working from dawn until after dark, always ready to take advantage of an opportunity, have extended their influence to the remotest islands and atolls. By acting as moneylenders and by encouraging Polynesians to accept goods on credit they have gained control over the lives of many native islanders. The Chinese of Tahiti maintain their own schools and clubs but they pay higher license fees than the French and are subject to other forms of discrimination.

Unlike the native Hawaiians, most Tahitians own a few acres of land and raise much of their own food. They usually own a bicycle, a canoe, a dog or two, a cat, a few chickens and a pig or two. With an excellent climate and a plentiful water supply from numerous rivers and mountain streams, the rich earth of the valleys and coastal areas yields a wide variety of agricultural produce in abundance.

In the country districts waterfalls cascade from high peaks and lively streams tumble seaward. Lagoon beaches, though small, are surrounded by palms and breadfruit. Taro patches abound in the lower areas; higher up, valleys are green with coffee and vanilla plantations. In the lower mountain slopes thickets of *fei* (wild plantain) hang with bunches of red bananas.

Despite the jet age build-up, the life of an average Tahitian, close to the land, the reef and the marine life of the lagoon, is still a life of calm simplicity. To a sophisticated, nervous Westerner it might seem monotonous.

Typical Tahitian families living in the districts rise at about 5:00 A.M., shortly before dawn. For breakfast they usually eat a loaf of French bread, bought from the nearest *Tenito* (Chinese) store for about eight cents, and consume large bowls of coffee sweetened with raw brown sugar. The coffee is hand-picked, dried, husked, shelled and roasted. It is inky black and very strong. Some islanders add a bit of vanilla bean to the coffee as it is brewing. After breakfast the men go fishing or perhaps split coconuts to make copra. The women do washing and may weave a few palm leaf baskets or hats. Water is free and Tahitians often let the faucet run because they like the sound of running water. After the clothes are washed and the girls have bathed and perhaps fished for an hour or so they change to a clean, dry, pareu that often has an orange, blue or red floral design.

At about 11:00 A.M. (and no one uses a clock to tell when) lunch, the main meal of the day, is started. A fish is laid out on some red-hot stones, together with bananas and peeled breadfruit wrapped in banana leaves. Perhaps there is a lobster or two or, if

Tahitian "coconut radio station." All the village news and gossip is gaily exchanged on wash day.

no one went fishing, then a chicken and breadfruit will do. Ordinarily Tahitians depend on the daily proteins supplied by seafood. Unless *popaas*—white visitors—are present very little is said until the main part of the meal is over. Then the latest news from the coconut radio (gossip) is exchanged.

After lunch everyone enjoys a siesta in his favorite spot. Even the dogs, cats and mynah birds observe the quiet period. Between 2:00 and 3:00 P.M. the family slowly emerge from the shadows of wherever they have been napping to go fishing again, to hunt for pahua clams inside the reef, or to work on a boat, or repair thatch, or lay out some split coconuts to dry into copra. Supper at twilight consists of bowls of steaming black coffee and large chunks of bread with perhaps a few bananas or a piece of breadfruit left over from lunch.

At a *tamaaraa* (native feast) fish is filleted, cut into small pieces and placed in a bowl of fresh lime juice to marinate for two hours. The acid of the limes does the "cooking." If available, onion and tomato slices and coconut cream are added. Poi is for dessert. Very different from Hawaiian poi, Tahitian poi is made from crushing the bananas, pineapple or papaya into a fine paste. One part of taro flour is added to two parts of fruit and baked together with a stick of vanilla. Coconut cream squeezed from grated coconuts is added and the exotic dish is eaten while still warm.

Early islanders asked the first whites, "Have you coconuts in your far away land?"

"No."

"Have you breadfruit?"

"No."

"Have you yams?"

"No."

They then concluded that white men must live in a sparse land that abounded only in iron and hatchets and were forced to sail to the South Seas out of sheer hunger.

More than half of the total population of Tahiti reside in and about Papeete on the northwest coast and the rest live in or near the small villages at the foot of blue-purple valleys east and northward toward Arue and Papenoo, west and south along Broom Road to Punaavia and Papeari.

Most American and European residents live miles out of town and those who look on the jet strip as a tragedy consider moving farther out. A few permanent residents admit freely that they once were weary individuals who came to Tahiti to escape their pressurized home world. "One of the unspoiled, fine things about the island," some say, "is there are no televisions present or contemplated." Others who came seeking beauty and quietude were surprised to find a world where human beings are natural, kind and gracious, and later found it impossible to return to watching a clock instead of a mountain or a reef. One way or another *l'ambiance Tahitienne* touches even the most hardened Westerner. Be he professional exporter, anthropologist or writer, whether he operates a soap factory or a honky-tonk, he will invariably pause to watch the vivid glow of sunset spread across the jagged peaks of Moorea and experience deep joy.

Papeete is the liveliest capital in the South Seas, a town where Parisian sophistication and Tahitian simplicity mingle strangely. On a Sunday afternoon you may see a rooster fight at one end of town or a wild west thriller at the cinema. A few blocks away, along the esplanade where bicycle riders swerve around Chinese peddlers carrying wares on bamboo poles, it is not unusual to see a replica of a Dior original or another Parisian couturier's style being worn by a chic young French or mixed Tahitian vahine. In a backstreet restaurant you can enjoy a platter of gigots or escargots. In another, a block away, shrimp and octopus curry is featured. In a Chinese emporium you can buy perfumed blue soap made in Tahiti, a fly swatter, a tin of New Zealand butter, a flacon of Feme de Rochas or Chanel Five direct from Paris.

Some of today's visitors lament the sad spectacle of the king-sized bottle of Benedictine that sits irreverently atop the tomb of King Pomare V who abdicated to the French in 1880. Some find Tahiti too "uncivilized"—meaning that they resent the tackiness of Papeete, the shanties, the slums and the cluttered, narrow streets. Much of the town is ramshackle, and for some that is part of its charm. A riot of multicolored hibiscus, poinsettias, crotons and showers of brilliant purple and red bougainvillea festoon the wide verandahs and do much to hide the general shabbiness and lack of paint. On the unattractive side are the island's vast population of rats (as big as coconuts), cockroaches and mosquitoes, and its high percentage of tuberculosis. The lagoons are wonderful but the black and brown sand beaches are scarce and don't compare with those in Hawaii and California.

Many modern Tahitians grow weary of having their island pointed out as a center of romance and say that beach "boys," dancing girls and other entertainers are but a small part of their population. They point out that many Tahitians are in small businesses, own fishing boats and taxis, work as stevedores, teachers and craftsmen, hold many responsible positions and in 1960 elected their own Polynesian candidate into the country's highest elective office.

The island of Tahiti roughly forms a figure eight. Its two ranges of mountains, connected by a narrow isthmus, are thirty-three miles long by about sixteen wide and entirely surrounded by a barrier reef from one to two miles offshore. Its approximately six hundred square miles of land is divided into seventeen districts, of which the loveliest is Tautira at the southeast end, where Robert Louis Stevenson lived and wrote *The Master of Ballantrae*.

All life in Papeete, economic, cultural and social, centers along a two-block-long crescent of waterfront which is the most picturesque in the Pacific. Far-famed as a rendezvous for small boat sailors from around the world, Papeete is now the only town left in Polynesia where the major commerce is still carried on in grand old sailing schooners such as the *Vaitere, Tiare Taporo, Tagua, Tamara,* the *Denise,* the *Tamarii Tahiti* and many others. Large trading schooners sail in from the Marquesas, Tuamotus, Gambiers or the Iles Sous le Vent with copra, vanilla and mother-of-pearl shell. Scores of yachtsmen arrive yearly in everything from small blue-water sloops, yawls and ketches to large motor sailers and luxurious private liners.

Weather-beaten copra cutters beat in from the Tuamotus so heavily loaded that their lee rails are but a few inches from the water. Mooring stern-first to old sunken cannon barrels on the waterfront, they unload pungent cargoes of copra and, for the return voyage to their lonely atolls, take on a few sacks of rice and flour, perhaps a drum of kerosene and some fruit, coffee and vegetables. The cutters are often owned communally and on each voyage different islanders crew the vessel, thus giving a number of them a chance to visit Papeete, the only town they ever know.

Despite the new transportation speed-up it is still possible to board a copra vessel and visit some of the remotest and loveliest islands in the Pacific, islands that can be reached only by trading schooner. Sailing schedules are listed on blackboards outside of Chinese stores. No matter how full the schooner is, her captain or the Chinese supercargo will always make room for more cargo or another passenger or two. The cost of such schooner travel averages five to six dollars per day, including meals. The food is plain; there are no frills. Quarters, which are shared with strangers, are small, cramped and hot, and smell strongly of copra. Schooner skippers are not the gold-braid type. Most are Polynesian or part Polynesian with a lifetime of experience in local waters. They navigate largely by dead reckoning: by noting a point of departure and thereafter calculating time, wind, drift and average speed of the ship. When caught in fierce storms these aged vessels take a terrible beating and sometimes limp into port with all of their deck cargo gone and perhaps their weather railing and bulwarks smashed in. Some end up on a treacherous reef or coral strand.

One can sail about eight miles south of Papeete inside a beautiful blue lagoon. North of the town the lagoon runs about four miles and then opens out onto broad Matavai Bay where Captain

Le Truck. Bus of all service. Papeete, Tahiti.

Bligh first anchored the *Bounty*. At the northern end of the bay is Captain Cook's famous Venus Point lighthouse.

Behind Papeete, falling back into the foothills, are the residential sections. The land rises steeply behind the red roofs of the town. In the background, above the mottled green hills, the jagged thrusts of misty mountain peaks reach upward to seven thousand feet and can be seen on a clear day from a distance of seventy miles at sea.

Within walking distance east of Papeete is the valley of Fautaua, the scene of Pierre Loti's pathetic idyl *Rarahu* and the source of the town's water supply. In its way, there is nothing more enchanting.

French naval officer Loti met the little Tahitian Princess Rarahu in tears with a dead songbird in her hand. From his next visit to San Francisco he took back twenty goldfinches and linnets and together with the charming Rarahu set them free to sing near Fautaua Pool, now called Loti's Pool. Thus began a love later described in his classic *Rarahu.* Today a monument stands there dedicated to the memory of the sailor-writer who captured the gay-sad spirit of Polynesia.

At the first big pool, eternally shaded by hanging guava, buroa and great tree ferns, the water of Fautaua Falls cascades from such great heights that it disappears in veils of mist before reaching the cool green valley below. From Loti's Pool, a small river tumbles slowly to the sea, its banks overhung with exotic plants and an earthy fragrance that penetrates everywhere.

In Tahiti, an hour before dawn, one may awake to the great stillness of the Polynesian night, a stillness that is part of the deep silence of the mountains. But when the first orange glow of daylight reaches the mountain peaks, islanders are already astir, roosters crow and mynah birds engage in family arguments. Sleepy fishermen who have fished part of the night have left their bonito boats and are bringing fresh-caught tuna to the Papeete market place. Chinese merchants, housewives and maids are pedaling to the square. Tahitians who have come in forty miles or more on "Le Truck"—an island bus—and spent the night sleeping on mats on the sidewalk, are up and walking to market.

At 5:30 A.M. the gates are opened and everyone rushes in to vie for the best cuts of beef, the choicest fruit and the best vegetables.

"That bonito is mine," shouts a man who has come in from Pirae. "*Aita!* No! It's mine," laughs a hefty housewife, grabbing the fat, iridescent tuna by the tail and handing the fisherman a bank note.

Strings of orange, deep blue, yellow and scarlet fish, frails of fresh limes and whole dressed pigs glisten in the bright early light. The scents of fresh fruit, bakery goods and raw and cooked meats mingle with the smell of clean ocean fish. Guavas, mangoes, bananas, papayas and avocados that weigh as much as two pounds each are plentiful and cheap.

A gay exchange of banter mingles with the excitement of buying a cackling hen, a still-live octopus or a fatted pig on a tether. Between laughter and sales the *parau api* (local news) and the latest "coconut radio events" (gossip) from around the island are exchanged in a babble of French and Tahitian with an occasional English word or phrase. Before the sun is an hour high the best of everything has been carried away in coconut leaf baskets.

By 6:30 A.M. the drivers of Les Trucks, the gaily-painted Tahi-

Tahitian poses uneasily in old burial cave seven miles from Papeete.

tian buses-of-all-service, have left the market place for the country top-heavy and overloaded with fish, poultry, and dozens of personal shopping items they have bought for suburbanites who live along the ninety miles of winding road that circle the island. By 8:00 A.M., so far as the Tahitians are concerned, the day is almost half over and it is time for *petit dejeuner*—breakfast rolls and coffee.

Though there are now over a hundred taxis the main transportation for most people are Les Trucks. These rumbling, open-sided buses ramble and honk their way from village to village with chickens, bicycles, boxes and perhaps a pig or two on the roof, shiny tuna, with maybe a string of parrot fish dangling from the rear, and fifty to eighty islanders squeezed inside on wooden benches built for thirty. Someone along the line who is waiting for the bus, perhaps a traveler sleepy from a night of merrymaking, places a palm frond on the road and rests under a coconut tree until awakened by Le Truck driver's horn.

There is a movement on to keep Tahiti as it is. Some want it "as it was." "Who knows?" they say, "Perhaps tomorrow will be too late."

It is true that the island's remoteness is gone, but the mystique remains. Tahitians may be interested for a short while in the fanciful things Americans dollars will buy when changed into French francs but they definitely are not interested in the American way of life. They still love best the simple things. On nights when Venus rivals the moon there is the clickity-clackety-click of sticks against bamboo blocks and the thump of hula drums. The rhythms of the *otea* and the *aparima*, dances which captivated the crews of Captain Wallis and Captain Cook, are still heard. The spirit that entranced the *Bounty* mutineers is still present and very real. And when the high winds blow strange, fluting sounds through the coco fronds the older Tahitians say it is the whistling of the Sea Gods.

Despite the raucous honky-tonks, the rasp of brassy bands and the new fling of American dollars—despite all these things and many more—Tahiti remains essentially Tahitian and will always retain a special meaning, a magic mysterious something that seems to elude the efficient-minded traveler and illumine those who least expect it.

It has been said that the spirit of Tahiti is in her mountains. Some see it in the cool of the late afternoon when great pageants of clouds gather about the peaks of Orohena or when the blue light in the mountains grows deeper and the first bright stars appear. Others hear it in the chant of a Tahitian stomp, in the compelling rhythm of island drums or in the creaking of blocks as a Tuamotuan copra cutter hoists its three sails and stands out through the pass to sea. It is not necessarily in any of these things. It may be in the scarlet of the flamboyants, in the haunting cry of the blue-throated vini vini birds or in the smell of copra and vanilla along the Quai Bir Hackeim. Whatever it is, no one vision can tell it all.

French Polynesia

Although French Oceania contains many of the most beautiful islands in the world, it was one of the last parts of the globe to be inhabited by man. From the beginning of the Christian Era the first settlers, a proud, freeborn branch of the Caucasian race, moved eastward from island to island "toward the dawn." During their epic migrations they brought food, plants and domestic animals in their mighty deep sea canoes and added to their knowledge of handicrafts, while living in the archipelagos of Micronesia. (Top authorities discount recent westward-from-Peru drift theories.)

When the long-wandering Polynesians finally dropped their stone anchors in the tranquil blue lagoons of the Society Islands they were surprised to find the great, haze-purple valleys and the verdant mountain lands totally uninhabited. Coconut trees were planted and later taro, breadfruit, bananas, yams, sugar cane and other food plants were introduced.

As the population increased, Polynesian settlers, led by Rata, the outrigger Viking and other great navigators, sailed on colonizing expeditions east to the Tuamotus, south to the Australs, southeast to Rapa and southwest to the Cook Islands. During one of these voyages the Marquesas were discovered and by 1000 A.D. settlers from Tahiti had reached most of the archipelagos now known collectively as French Oceania.

At a time when Latin civilization was disintegrating the Polynesians' culture was in its ascendancy and their great navigators were making voyages unexcelled by any race. It is generally believed that at least one of the early sea kings reached Peru and returned with the first sweet potatoes. Native history reveals that Ui-te-rangiora, a Polynesian, sailed south in the tracks of the Southern Cross until he reached the icebergs of the Antarctic. In the tenth century a Polynesian visited New Zealand and reported finding no inhabitants other than "a fantail flitting and a bell bird singing in the forest." And it was a Polynesian who ventured thousands of miles north to Hawaii long before the Norsemen discovered America.

Guided by a simple knowledge of the sun, moon, and stars and often by sea birds, exploring parties remained at sea for months at a time. For shore sighting they often used the long-winged frigate-birds. On being released, these powerful birds would fly in ever-widening circles and then take a course toward the nearest land. Between Tahiti and Hawaii Polynesians followed in the tracks of the Pacific golden plover, and it was the long-tailed cuckoo bird that led them south to the "land of the long white cloud" (the North Cape of New Zealand).

Mythology was the most important influence in early Tahitian society, and island chiefs were believed by the people to be direct descendants of the gods. The highest ranking chiefs and spiritual leaders settled on Tahiti and at Raiatea, where the first great House of Learning was built and where many of the great gods of Polynesian mythology were believed to have been born. Located at the hub of a wide area, the two islands became the seed center and spiritual headquarters for all Polynesia. Leaders from distant archipelagos made long, periodic sea voyages to Raiatea for feasting and consulting. And during the Golden Age their island world became the nucleus for the dissemination of learning throughout the central Pacific.

A century after the last of the great Polynesian migrations the best navigators of Europe were still afraid to venture beyond the Pillars of Hercules and out into the "Green Sea of Darkness" (the Atlantic).

· The first white vessels to make a landfall in French Oceania were Spanish galleons from Lima and Peyta, Peru, commanded by Alvaro de Mendana.

"Behold the glorious sight of land!" shouted Mendana's Portuguese pilot Pedro de Quiros on July 21, 1595. "Sound the call. Let us pray God to guide us to a safe anchorage." The pious but unreliable pilot believed that they were arriving at the Solomons, which are over three thousand miles away.

A week later after a solemn High Mass, prayers and the firing of royal salutes the islands were named the Marquesas to honor the wife of the Viceroy of Peru. "Long live our high and mighty monarch King Philip, sovereign of Castile, Leon and Aragon," proclaimed the old and weary Mendana as the brilliant red and yellow standard of Castile was raised over the land.

Stouthearted Willem Corniliszoon Schouten, a Cape Horner from the Zuider Zee, was the first to bring the flag of Holland into these lonely seas and he was followed nearly a century later by Jacob Roggeveen on the last of the great Dutch voyages.

The Honorable John Byron, better known as "Foulweather Jack" (grandfather of the famous poet), was the first of the Britishers to arrive in the Tuamotus. Two years later, in 1767, Tahiti was discovered by Captain Samuel Wallis, together with Moorea and a number of other islands in the Leewards and Tuamotus.

While at Tahiti the handsome Captain Wallis was ardently courted by Queen Oberea, and at the advice of his physician he retired to the Royal Palace to recuperate from the long voyage. The able-bodied seamen of H.M.S. *Dolphin* spent so much time withdrawing spikes and nails from the vessel to exchange with island maidens for romantic favors that a notice was posted that any seamen caught withdrawing objects from the ship would be severely flogged with nettles. However, each morning additional spikes and nails were missing. After five weeks at Tahiti the boatswain reported that every cleat on the twenty gun sloop was gone and the crew were sleeping on deck for lack of nails to hang their hammocks.

"Men, you are wrecking my ship," thundered Wallis to a muster of the *Dolphin*'s entire crew. "And for what, I ask you—for what?"

"For love," someone muttered in a low voice. The sheepish grins left their faces quickly enough when Pinckney, a seaman who had been caught withdrawing spikes from the mainsheet cleat, was flogged round the ship three times with nettles.

Fearing for the safety of his ship, Captain Wallis bade the weeping queen a touching farewell, presented her with a Union Jack and sailed on to the west.

French interest in the South Seas dates from the tales told by the many French sailors who accompanied Magellan's expedition; but little was done until a number of daring buccaneers entered the Pacific by way of Cape Horn and made the French pirate colors known to the residents of treasure-laden Granada, Guayaquil and Paita as the flag of terror. During the reign of Louis XIV hundreds of French buccaneers from Tortuga and Port Royal turned the King's Islands near Panama into a rendezvous for freebooters. As filibustering became increasingly difficult, many Frenchmen returned home with a knowledge of the Pacific that again stirred the interest of the French Crown toward the South Seas.

Less than a year after Captain Wallis left Tahiti Louis Antoine de Bougainville, a gentleman and philosopher, brought the Tricolor to the island at the truck of the swift little frigate *La Boudeuse*. Unaware of British discoveries, Bougainville took formal possession of Tahiti in the name of Louis Philippe, the "citizen king." The gallant Frenchman entertained the islanders with music and nightly displays of witch quills and skyrockets. Before leaving he planted wheat, barley and onions, and left pairs of turkeys and ducks and a large supply of cloth and tools. For exceptional ability Bougainville ranks high among early explorers, and as a man of honor and respect for the rights of native people he stands beside Captain James Cook and Otto von Kotzebue.

Captain Cook, discoverer of the Society Islands, was a superb seaman and a man of vision and scientific curiosity. Rarely before or since has any one navigator possessed those qualities to such a degree. On his first voyage to Tahiti he discovered the Leeward Islands of Huahine, Tahaa, Raiatea, Bora Bora and Maupiti and named them the Society Islands in honor of the British Royal Society. Sailing south from Tahiti, the H.M.S. *Endeavour* was the first ship without an outrigger to anchor in the Australs.

After the publication of Bougainville's and Captain Cook's narratives a good part of England yearned to go adventuring in the Pacific. When the London Missionary Society announced plans for sending a vessel to save the souls of the indolent Tahitians, it was not hard to find missionaries willing to forgo their struggles amid the misery and suffering of the English working classes for the distant green isles in the South Seas.

Before departing from England, James Wilson, the missionary-captain of the gospel ship *Duff*, received implicit instructions from the directors of the Society that in approaching the native chiefs, "as an inducement to us to prefer their island they must give us a full title to whatever land we may have occasion for." On arrival at Tahiti, Captain Wilson promptly began landing negotiations, and on March 5, 1797, the mission flag bearing three white doves with olive branches was formally raised for the first time in French Oceania.

The gay Tahitians were plainly disappointed with the evangelists for not bringing anything more lively than a German flute to entertain them with. Remembering previous Scottish visitors, they had hoped for at least a bagpipe. Once the reception formalities were over and much of the best land obtained, including the whole district of Matavai, flute-playing and the presentation of gifts was dispensed with in favor of fiery sermons on the evils of indolence and gaiety.

It greatly annoyed the busy Londoners in their frock coats and top hats to see scantily-clad Tahitians basking idly in the sun, singing, laughing, and relating folk tales much of the day. They were determined to replace every last vestige of levity with a solemn air of piety. According to their Calvinist precepts, "an idle brain is the devil's own workshop," and they believed that those who loved the Lord could best prove it by diligent labor and by giving generously toward the propagation of the gospel.

Some dances were erotic, so all dancing was banned. Ordinarily the women went about unclothed above the waist and were proud of their form and figure, a state of affairs considered indecent by the missionaries.

At first the natives looked upon the men of Jehovah as strange but harmless and were inclined to feel sorry for the sad, pale-faced *popaas* (white men) who were always worried about something or other. Later, when the missionaries began to interfere with native love life and actively oppose their natural moral inclinations, the people of Tahiti turned, and on at least one occasion four missionaries were stripped and beaten. Just as the Maoris used the Forty-sixth Psalm as a battle chant when fighting the whites, the Polynesians adopted Calvinist hymns to far different purposes than the missionaries ever intended.

Chagrined and deeply affronted because "the heathen seem to hold themselves as civilized people as any beneath the sun and treat the customs and manners of Europeans with great indifference and contempt," eleven missionaries decided to leave the Tahitians to their sinful gaiety and sailed away on a whaler for more enlightened fields of endeavor. Contrarily, two others, finding the charms of the Tahitians irresistible, deserted the mission to take up residence with young native wives. One brother fell in love with the queen; another went insane trying to teach the islanders Hebrew. By 1803 when Pomare, the reigning chief, died and was buried according to pagan rites, the missionary outlook was decidedly low.

However, when Pomare's dissolute son acquired his hereditary rights and the reigning title of Pomare II, things brightened for the missionaries. The clever maneuvering of Henry Nott, a bricklayer-turned-evangelist, and his influence over the new monarch, did more than any other single thing to force the white man's beliefs upon the people of Tahiti.

A cruel, treacherous tyrant, Pomare II was eager to obtain white men's goods, and shrewd enough when sober to realize that his espousing the cause of Christianity would ensure a good supply of muskets to control the growing resentment of his people. Under this despot ruling with powder and muskets supplied by the missionaries the people of Tahiti were subjected to a reign of terror. In time Pomare's wanton slaughter of his fellow islanders in the name of Christianity resulted in a number of uprisings that were put down with much bloodshed.

After the "Christian victories" a new set of laws was promulgated to keep the islanders busy in the Lord's work. Those found not attending daily chapel service were severely punished at hard labor, and in their spare time they were all expected to keep the mission staff well supplied with pigs, fish, turtles, chickens, fruit and other contributions.

Woe to the unfortunate islander caught "Sabbath-breaking" or wasting time in dancing, singing, or any other pastime displeasing to the Calvinists! With the introduction of ludicrous bonnets and large cotton nightgowns, accompanied by stern exhortations on the virtues of keeping the body clothed, missionaries were soon able to report that the girls were "taking great pains to cover themselves with gowns that even keep their feet from being seen."

During his sober hours Pomare helped Nott to translate the Bible into Tahitian. Yet, sober or drunk, he slew his own people for the slightest disobedience as quickly as he did the island dogs. For minor infractions of the missionary code they were sentenced "to the reefs" and left to die slowly under the pitiless sun, without drinking water or any food beyond the shellfish that prolonged their agony indefinitely.

It was under the constant threat of such punishment that thousands of Tahitians were driven to labor on the huge Mission Chapel, an edifice seven hundred and twenty-eight feet long by fifty-eight feet wide containing three pulpits two hundred and sixty feet apart and with a five-foot mountain stream passing through the center. So many Bibles were translated into Tahitian during this period that the island's animals were almost completely exterminated to provide skins for bookbindings. By 1820 one hundred and five thousand copies were in circulation.

When Lieutenant Otto von Kotzebue visited the island he reported that "a police officer is especially appointed to enforce the prescribed attendance upon the church and prayer meetings. I saw him in the exercise of his functions, armed with a bamboo cane, driving his dejected herd to the spiritual pasture."

On numerous occasions the missionaries set aside their Bibles and tried their hand at a number of commercial ventures including shipbuilding, trading, sugar milling, and a factory for spinning and weaving cotton. In the latter enterprise, although "numerous quotations and passages of scripture were affixed to the walls of the factory," native interest in the backbreaking toil lagged and missionary dreams of a profitable cotton industry ended in failure.

At about this time the English Protestants were informed that a vessel was about to leave Bordeaux loaded with Jesuits and a cargo described by the Londoners as "all the paraphernalia of Popery. Crucifixes, crosses, shrines, banners and bells, together with all the apparatus for working miracles including a galvanic battery, electrifying machine, fireworks and a splendid organ so constructed that the person who plays it will be invisible." Recalling the effectiveness of their own cuckoo clocks and "spirit twisters" (batteries) in gaining converts, the Protestants hastened to forewarn Queen Pomare and the leading chiefs against the invasion of the "French Popists."

When Brother Columban Murphy arrived at Tahiti in 1835 to make arrangements for the establishment of a Catholic mission he was given a cool reception and allowed to land only on the assurance that he was bound to Hawaii as soon as a vessel was available. The presence of the Irish catechist in the "vineyard of the Lord" could not have been more distasteful to the Protestants had he been Beelzebub or the devil himself. They had no intentions of tolerating competition from Catholics of any nationality, much less an Irishman representing a French congregation.

The French government, fully awake to the political and economic value of missionary penetration, and considering the influence of the Protestants a sinister one, gave firm orders to its naval officers that they were to assure the rights of French Catholics to reside and proselytize in Tahiti and other islands.

The Polynesians, long accustomed to the sight of British and American ships, were duly impressed by the arrival of the *Venus, Bonite, Artémise, Astrolabe, Zelee, Heroine* and other powerful French warships.

George Pritchard, the Protestant leader and British consul, grew tired of hoping and waiting for the arrival of a powerful squadron of Queen Victoria's frigates and hurriedly left for Downing Street to protest directly to the Foreign Office. While he was gone, Admiral Du Petit Thouars set up a French Protectorate over the island.

Despite a long list of previous complaints against local authorities, including the harassing of missionaries, the actual incident which prompted a series of demands resulting in the raising of the Tricolor was a row between a local Frenchman and the native constable over a dog fight and the confiscation of several bottles of brandy.

The American consul at Papeete informed Washington that, inasmuch as it was his understanding that the United States would prefer to see Tahiti ruled by France rather than added to Great Britain's imposing colonial acquisitions, he had not opposed the raising of the French colors.

In discussing the French seizure, Lord Aberdeen maintained that "public feeling in England was deeply wounded by the proceedings

100

at Tahiti." But having just won the Opium War and hoping to act in concert with France against American aspirations in Hawaii, Great Britain refrained from protesting French action following assurances that British Protestants would be accorded the same treatment and protection as French Catholics. As Herman Melville put it, "for once in their brawling lives, St. George and St. Dennis were hand in glove; and they were not going to cross sabres about Tahiti."

After the cruise of the American sloop of war *Peacock,* followed by the Wilkes' expedition, American maritime traffic increased considerably in these waters. American vessels, mostly whalers, anchored at Tahiti for refreshing, carousing and taking on fresh supplies of hogs, yams and whiskey. Tahitian cotton, oranges and limes were soon being shipped to San Francisco, which, in turn, became the center for Polynesian coconut oil and pearling products.

After escaping from Typee Valley in the Marquesas Herman Melville landed at Papeete on the day the French Protectorate was declared and was promptly thrown into the Calabooza Coloniale. Later he roamed about Tahiti and Moorea as a beachcomber before writing *Typee* and *Omoo,* which laid the foundation of all South Sea literature and charted the course for Pierre Loti, Robert Louis Stevenson and Jack London.

Melville, Stevenson and Paul Gauguin, the three men of genius who have dealt with the South Seas, all wrote classic personal narratives from their experiences in Tahiti and the Marquesas.

Because Melville pleaded for forbearance and charity for cannibals, and because he stated that praise of missionaries was usually written by themselves, the London Missionary Society launched an attack against young Melville that attracted more readers than his publisher's advertising. They considered him vile because he had romanced with a charming young Typee lady named Fayaway. He was labeled a puritan who had "back-slidden," and it was stated in the *Living Age* that Melville was known to have "consorted with a reckless gang of seafaring creatures, known in the Pacific as beachcombers."

All of the major writers who visited the South Seas during the period of white expansion and the beginning of commercial ventures have affirmed that the white man spread death and destruction wherever he went. It would seem that throughout the nineteenth century most labor-recruiting vessels and all blackbirding ships left a sordid trail of blood in their wake. At the time that Melville wrote his classics *Typee, Omoo* and *Moby Dick,* most archipelagos had felt the impact of white civilization. The scourges of tuberculosis, syphilis and smallpox had wiped out entire villages. Thousands of natives in the great, lonely Marquesan valleys were already living in the shadow of death.

During the first part of Queen Pomare's fifty-year reign there were a number of serious uprisings against the French before the people of the outer islands resigned themselves to domination by a foreign power. In 1877, when the queen died, her son Pomare V came to the throne, but after less than four years as king he turned over the powers of his kingdom to France. Later he drank himself to impotence with the shameful memory of having sold his kingdom for an income of forty thousand francs per year.

All of the outlying archipelagos were brought under the administrator at Papeete and since that time French Oceania has been administered as a single colony. Subordinate administrators for the Leeward, Tuamotus, Marquesas, Gambier and Austral Groups are responsible to the governor at Papeete, who in turn, is under the French High Commissioner at Noumea, New Caledonia.

There is now a strong and growing movement among the non-French Tahitian people for self-rule. After more than one hundred years of French rule Tahitians claim it is about time that they be given whatever training is necessary to hold all local administrative positions. So far, the island's large police force, rigid control of the press and radio stations and the declaration of martial law on occasion have kept the movement in hand.

Tahiti has always been overburdened with French functionaries. In 1947, Tahitians, aroused at the high cost of supporting large numbers of French officials, picketed French ships and prevented newly arriving functionaries from debarking. Large groups led by war veterans of Tahiti's own Pacific Battalion threatened to deport all the French, including the governor.

The real crux of the situation at Tahiti and elsewhere in the French Pacific Empire is that despite a certain amount of democracy and self-rule all real power lies in the hands of a nonelective governor appointed direct from Paris. The governor is free to overrule proposals put forth by the elective bodies, and frequently has done so.

Pouvanna a Oopa, a Tahitian war veteran, revived the ancient Tahitian flag and established a nationalist political party in 1949.

He became the most outstanding and influential islander and in 1958 was elected to the Territory's highest office, representative of all French Oceania in the National Assembly at Paris. Soon after Oopa became head of the local government his party introduced a Tahiti-for-the-Tahitians policy which led to angry demonstrations by the local French colony and to intervention by the governor. Pouvanna a Oopa was arrested and held a year in jail without trial. Later, in the face of popular demands for his release, he was sentenced to eight years' imprisonment and late one night in strictest secrecy was taken aboard a warship and banished from Tahiti for fifteen years.

In the 1960 general elections Pouvanna a Oopa's son, Marcel Oopa, was overwhelmingly elected to represent French Polynesia in the French Chamber of Deputies in Paris—a result regarded throughout the South Pacific as a stinging defeat for the French administration and a strong mandate for Tahitian nationalism. Whatever the final outcome will be, the flag of the Tahitian people revived by Pouvanna a Oopa now flies alongside the French Tricolor.

Society Islands

The Society Islands include two groups known as the Windward Islands and the Leeward Islands or Iles Sous le Vent (Islands below the Wind). The Windward Group contains Tahiti, Moorea, Mehetia, Tubuai Manu and Tetiaroa. The Leeward Group northwest of Tahiti includes Raiatea, Bora Bora, Tahaa, Huahine, Maupiti, Motu Iti, Mopihaa, Scilly and Bellingshausen. Next to Tahiti the the three principal Society Islands are Moorea, Raiatea and Bora Bora.

While Papeete bears the main brunt of French Polynesia's travel boom, the outer islands—especially Moorea and Bora Bora—are welcoming those who seek a retreat that has more peace and quietness than the capital island.

Incredibly lovely, the island of Moorea, looking somewhat like a miniature Tahiti, lies twelve miles of lumpy sea northwest of Papeete. Except for a narrow coastal strip, its thirty-five square miles is almost entirely made up of rugged mountains with craggy blue peaks reaching nearly four thousand feet high, cut by steep valleys overgrown with wild green vegetation. Thousands of coconut

103

palms grow along the coastal lands and large groves of breadfruit, oranges, limes and other products are found in the valleys and on the lower mountain slopes. Scarlet and purple creepers wander everywhere.

Most of the residents live in or near one of the eight villages along the shores of a tranquil lagoon which entirely surrounds the island. When the sun sinks gradually behind the jagged outlines of Moorea it throws the fantastic peaks into silhouette against the sky and colors the waters of the lagoon with changing shapes.

Beneath the misty peaks of Tohivea, Rotui and Mouaputa, far below the wind-flung spray of waterfalls, lie two fiords and bays known as Paopao, or Cook's Bay, and Papetoai Bay.

More than any other coast in the Pacific, Moorea's north coast, indented by Cook's Bay and Papetoai Bay, symbolizes all that is loveliest in the South Seas.

Raiatea, the second largest island in the Society Group, is one hundred and eighteen miles northwest of Papeete. Extending about twelve miles in length by seven and one half miles wide, the island rises to an extreme height of 3,389 feet and contains thousands of acres of highly productive agricultural lands along the coasts and in the large fertile valleys.

Together with its adjoining island of Tahaa, two miles to the north, Raiatea is encircled by a barrier reef which provides one of the best lagoons in the South Seas for sailing craft. Vessels drawing three feet or less can go entirely around the island in the protected lagoon waters. Jack London preferred Raiatea and Tahaa to all other islands in Polynesia.

Uturoa, the port town and seat of government, is a modern town in many ways. It has a refrigeration plant and a radio station, electric lights, sound movies and many restaurants, department stores and hotels. With a large concrete pier and adequate port and commercial facilities, it has become second to Papeete in commercial importance.

A large section of Uturoa has the appearance of a tropical Chinese village for, as in Tahiti, the most profitable business ventures are in the hands of the Chinese. The older Chinese generally speak a hybrid Tahitian but many of the young moderns who have been to France, Hawaii or California to school speak excellent English, French and Tahitian. By acting as moneylenders and encouraging

Polynesian girl grating coconut.

the islanders to buy on credit, Chinese businessmen have obtained a local monopoly.

Almost all of the little unpainted, tin-roofed trade stores scattered through the Isles Sous le Vent are owned by Chinese. Fishhooks, lemonade pop, kerosene, nails, pork and beans and corned beef from Australia are among their main trade items. There are usually ropes of dried fish and perhaps an octopus hanging to dry. From the rear of the store there is always the smell of copra and vanilla.

Bora Bora, thirty miles northwest of Raiatea, is composed of several islands enclosing a central lagoon. The island of Bora Bora is the largest of the group and the second largest is uninhabited Tupua Island on the west.

A picturesque village road encircles Bora Bora, running parallel with the white sandy shoreline. Backed by 2,386-foot Mount Temanu, with its sheer spires perpetually wreathed in wispy clouds, the principal village of Vaitape rests at the edge of a deep, mile-wide lagoon that offers an excellent anchorage for vessels of any size.

The American World War II dollar prosperity that was so abundantly felt in New Caledonia reached Bora Bora and the Society Islands with the arrival of American ships throughout the war. Large sums were spent by the United States Navy in constructing an air and naval base at Bora Bora. Airplanes, bulldozers, juke boxes, baseball, Coca Cola and thousands of Americans became well known to the Bora Borans.

Alain Gerbault, holder of France's highest honors and one of the greatest single-handed sailors of all time, was buried at Bora Bora in 1948 with Naval honors. Gerbault, like Gauguin long before him, tried to awaken the people of France to what he called "the reign of mediocrity at Papeete" and to the breakdown of Tahitian health and morals in late years. The diminutive Frenchman severely berated local French officials for slum conditions and widespread venereal disease, for the continuing sale of French intoxicants to Polynesians and for encouraging the type of tourists "who bring only the gospel of gold."

Austral Islands

South of Tahiti the Australs form an eight-hundred-mile chain of seven islands reaching from Maria, Rimatara and Rurutu southeast to the craggy blue peaks of Rapa, formerly known as the Island of Women.

For many years these islands were declared by the French "forbidden either for access or sojourn to any and all persons not native of those islands," but the prohibition on travel has been lifted and now anyone may visit the group.

Four hundred miles south-by-east of Tahiti, Raivavae, two miles by five, is the most beautiful of the Austral Islands. Lofty and green-mountained, it is entirely surrounded by a broad lagoon abounding in shrimp, lobster, crabs, oysters and many types of fish. Luscious peaches grow well in its temperate climate and wild orange trees rise forty feet high heavily laden three times a year with sweet fruit. Scarlet flamboyants riot along the coasts and vie with purple bougainvillea and yellow oleander on the lower slopes. The nine hundred inhabitants of the island are a friendly, peace-loving people.

One hundred miles northwest of Raivavae, egg-shaped, six- by three-mile Tubuai is a fertile, well-wooded island completely encircled by a barrier reef. Its principal products are taro, coconuts, manioc and bananas; and wherever they have been planted mangos, guava, alligator pears and even grapes do well.

The mutineers of the *Bounty*, attracted by the luxuriant vegetation, the mild climate and the beauty of the women, attempted to make a settlement on Tubuai. When the natives refused to give up their best lands to labor for white masters, the mutineers dug trenches and erected a small fort with the intention of forcing their will upon the independent islanders. In the bloody battle that followed the men of the *Bounty* were forced back to the sea and finally had to return to Tahiti.

Nearly all of the eleven hundred Tubuai islanders are closely related to each other by blood or marriage. There are at present a number of natives who came originally from various islands as far away as the Society, Tuamotu and Cook Groups, but once settled they rarely if ever leave Tubuai.

The verdant island of Rurutu, three hundred miles almost due south of Tahiti, is the northernmost of the Australs. It is a high-volcanic island, similar in many respects to Raivavae and Tubuai. The energetic inhabitants are a strong, handsome people, and the most enterprising and independent of the Austral islanders. Co-operative groups have built large seagoing schooners for trading among the islands and for carrying their copra, vanilla, arrowroot and livestock north to Tahiti. It is largely because of efforts of the enterprising Rurutuans that the trading firms of Papeete have never been able to gain a foothold in Rurutu or elsewhere in the Australs.

Seventy-seven miles west and slightly south of Rurutu, the nearly circular island of Rimatara is the lowest of the inhabited Australs, rising but three hundred feet above the sea.

Less than twenty miles in circumference, Rimatara is entirely surrounded by a narrow, fringing reef, so close to the shore in most places that the incessant booming of the surf is heard from any of the three villages to the top of Oromana in the center of the island. Taro, bananas and breadfruit are plentiful and pigs roam through the villages and about the hillsides.

The people have remained little touched by progress. Living on an island without a single harbor and having few contacts with others, their simple village life is, for them, the ultimate in an island world.

Crescent-shaped Rapa, called by the natives Rapa-iti, is about twenty miles in circumference, with picturesque rugged mountains rising in places almost straight up to an altitude of two thousand feet or more. Horses and goats still roam wild over the remote districts and graze on the thousands of acres of verdant grasslands.

It was discovered by Vancouver in 1791, and long before the Tricolor was raised, the Union Jack flew over Rapa's large sheltered bay of Ahurei, the best harbor in the Australs.

The people of Rapa are of almost pure Polynesian stocks and distinctly different in many ways from other Austral islanders. Bold descendants of sea kings, the men consider no accomplishment greater than the craft of seamanship. Because their island is scalloped with deep bays and rocky, turbulent coasts, they acquire their skill at a very early age. Men of Rapa are sought after by schooner skippers, and many boys on reaching fourteen make plans to leave for Tahiti.

With most of the men away to sea, Rapa formerly became widely known as the Island of Women. Such tasks as the planting and cultivation of coffee and taro and the gathering of firewood, fruits and vegetables fell to the numerous girls who, in consequence, are more lithe and attractive than the women of other islands.

When a growing number of single white men began to arrive at Papeete with the intention of settling in Rapa and the other Australs, the French government issued an edict prohibiting them from doing

Dependent on the sea, Tehapi of Rimitara carefully hangs his nets to dry.

Copra cutters from the Tuamotus. These 30-foot vessels sail many hundreds of miles bringing copra to Tahiti and returning to their home islands with flour, sugar and coffee.

so in an effort to preserve what remained of native health and simple life. The population, once estimated at several thousand, had dropped to less than three hundred in 1960.

Tuamotu Archipelago

From two hundred to eight hundred miles northwest and southwest of Tahiti, the seventy-eight atolls of the Tuamotus, meaning "cloud of islands," contain numerous islets so small that they cannot be noted on maps by even a dot and so low that some are completely washed over by the long, rolling waves that sweep in from the southwest during the hurricane season.

A Tuamotuan looks first at the sea, at the line of the reef and at the sky when he emerges from his *fare* (house) in the morning. If it is the hurricane season—December to March—he looks twice. Raw colors are always there; raw smells, also, from the exposed reef at low tide; and there is always the sweep of the sea.

The fury and destruction of a major hurricane in this area staggers the imagination. One hundred mile an hour winds are accompanied by twenty- to thirty-foot seas that sweep clean across some atolls. Coconuts are whirled through the air like cannon balls. At Hikueru, the center of the pearl shell industry, five hundred lives have been lost in the vast fury of a single hurricane.

Life in the Tuamotus is always precarious and never much more than a struggle for survival. Fresh water and vegetation are scarce. There is not a blade of grass and few trees are to be found other than the coconut and the air-rooted pandanus. Small gardens are sometimes managed out of coconut humus, coral gravel and a few sacks of precious earth brought in from high islands by schooner. Chickens live on coconut and fish scraps and think nothing of flying over a housetop. Their toughness remains despite any manner of cooking. The main items of local diet come mostly from the rich harvest of the lagoons.

The approximately eight thousand Tuamotuans are a strong, hardy and—in spite of diet deficiencies—much healthier people than the Tahitians or Marquesans. Relatively the poorest islanders in French Oceania, the Tuamotuans share everything equally, and quite often in the stormy season "everything" is only a few fish scraps and coconuts.

Because of the swift, treacherous currents and the number of hidden reefs that are strewn over hundreds of miles, yet visible only from a short distance or not at all, scores of vessels have been wrecked in the Tuamotu Group and they have become widely known to mariners as the Dangerous or Low Archipelago.

The Tuamotus are the center of the pearl shell industry in French Polynesia and Hikueru has long been the headquarters and the most productive island. Each year during the diving season buyers come from all over the world to buy the black-lip pearl shell. The dark or cream-colored pearls that are found on rare occasions are eagerly bid for by dealers who in turn sell them to the New York, Paris or London market.

All shell diving is now under strict government supervision. Aqualungs and mechanical devices are no longer allowed. The season is a short one and each year different lagoons are opened up and others kept closed to prevent the shell beds from being worked out.

The pearling fleet of the Tuamotus attracts the finest divers in French Oceania, and the highest ambition of a Tuamotuan boy has always been to become a great diver. Young boys begin by diving to fifteen or twenty feet and gradually progress to greater depths as their lungs develop and they acquire the skill of retaining air. The average depth for professional divers is from thirty-five to one hundred feet. Some island women are very good divers and go down to one hundred feet. The best male divers reach one hundred and twenty-five feet or more and stay down for three full minutes.

Each day that the season is open the islanders go out in their outrigger canoes and locate the shell beds by means of a water glass. Then, massaged with coconut oil, the diver adjusts his goggles and before going down begins "taking the wind." It takes years of practice to acquire the difficult trick by which a master diver turns himself into a human compressor, strangely gulping, groaning, and wincing, as he works his jaws and face, pumping long deep draughts, until finally, forcing his diaphragm down, he succeeds in drawing the utmost of air into his lungs. Instead of diving from the side of the canoe he plummets down forty to a hundred feet by means of a heavy weight, thus preserving strength and reserve of air against the terrific constriction and pressure, which sometimes forces his head to thump and his nose and ears to bleed. Once on the bottom, keeping a respectful eye out for a conger eel or an octopus, he gathers as much shell as he can find, and when his two or three minutes have elapsed he returns swiftly to the surface. Occasionally the purple veins on his arms and face stand out as though his whole body might burst.

A sheath knife is the Tuamotuan diver's only weapon against octopuses, moray eels, poisonous-spiked scorpion fish, fierce barracudas and sharks, which he respects but does not fear. There is also the danger of nitrogen narcosis or underwater illusions during which a diver who stays under too long pays with his life. Scores of divers have been killed or mauled or had their limbs amputated by barracuda and sharks. Others have become suddenly deaf, crippled or paralyzed from the pressures of great depths.

After each haul, the shells are quickly and skillfully pried open with a large knife to avoid marring the inner skin. Most often there are no pearls at all; sometimes they are too small to be of much value; but, as in panning for gold, there is always the possibility of a big find. Meanwhile the value of the exported shell exceeds fifty million francs per year.

Makatea, a three-mile by five-mile "treasure mound" located at the northwest end of the Tuamotus, is the richest of the outlying islands in French Polynesia. Its large, high-grade deposits of tricalcic phosphate have been worked since 1908 by French and British interests. Normally hundreds of laborers are employed in its production and phosphate valued at more than two hundred and fifty million francs is exported annually.

Besides Makatea, the principal islands include Fakarava, which has the best harbor; Apataki, the administration headquarters; and in the northeast, Rangiroa, the largest island in the group. Many of the other islands are remote, uninhabited and visited only by the ghost terns and frigatebirds. It is now almost impossible for Americans or Europeans to obtain permission to live in the Tuamotus, as the government wants to keep them as they are.

Gambier Islands

It is far easier to find twenty people who have been to Vladivostok than one who has been to Mangareva—an archipelago even the mapmakers overlook on all but the most detailed maps.

To come on deck at sunrise and see the slate-gray ridges of Mt. Duff looming out of the blue, with fantastic peaks half in the clouds and the soft green slopes of Mangareva drenched in sunlight, is to know that there is no archipelago in the South Pacific that surpasses the beauty of the Gambiers.

Called by the French the Forgotten Islands, the Gambiers comprise four high, rugged islands and numerous islets enclosed within a barrier reef nearly forty miles in circumference. Located nine hundred miles from Tahiti, at the remote southeast end of the Tuamotu chain, the inhabited islands are Mangareva (the capital), Taravai, Akamaru and Aukena.

The ruins of Mangareva's once great center of Rikitea are as remarkable as those in any other part of the world. Their true history has never been written partly because so much of it is clothed in mystery.

Mangarevans have a dislike for most forms of arduous manual labor. Nothing is done today that can be done *ari' ana*—"by and by." How, then, did they become so industrious that they built in a comparatively short time an amazing religious city with sheer manpower, coral and stone? The answer is Père de Laval, mad priest, architect and engineer, one of the most remarkable characters in Polynesian history.

After escaping violent death by a hair's breadth for refusing to make love to King Maputeoa's daughter, Père de Laval soon brought the king and his subjects to do his every bidding with no other aid than the hypnotic power and driving force of his fanatic personality. In less than twenty years Laval changed an estimated six thousand happy people into weary, dying citizens of a fantastic city, and made Mangareva one of the strangest islands in the Pacific.

Immense squares of rock were quarried and erected into large summer and winter quarters with huge towers, arches, colonnades, courts, and gardens. Convents, jails, monasteries, schools, palatial stone houses, elaborate dikes, and fish traps all became part of Mangareva's magnificent capital of Rikitea. The crowning triumph of Laval's mad zeal was the great Cathedral of St. Michel, which stands intact today, one of the finest structures in the South Seas. The cathedral, once adorned with rare oil paintings and solid gold cups and vases imported from Europe, is as large as many of the greatest cathedrals of the world. Two imposing square towers are built entirely of cut stone. Thick white coral columns uphold a blue ceiling studded with stars of inlaid mother-of-pearl.

During a long investigation of his regime, Laval was finally asked by the French Governor, "What sort of government do you call this? Five thousand men and boys have died in the past ten years from this mad building plan of yours."

"True, Monsieur Le Comte," he replied, "they are dead, but they have gone to heaven the more quickly!"

Adjudged insane by the tribunal in Papeete, Laval was banished forever from the Gambiers and died in Tahiti a few years later.

The Mangarevans never recovered from Laval's relentless program. Their population declined until there are only a few hundred people left, as compared with the many thousands living there when Laval arrived. Today the great cathedral remains a forlorn sentinel. It has no bishop and there are only a handful of Polynesians to spread out and occupy its twelve hundred empty seats.

Mangareva was formerly the world's largest pearling lagoon. Its coves and inlets have yielded countless treasure troves of rare and lustrous pearls. Accounts of the first voyagers tell of children playing games with pearls. Small ones were traded for a plug of tobacco or a bar of soap and sometimes a brass bedstead was exchanged for a fine one. Shrewd dealers have sold the exceptionally rare pearls to jewelers in London, Paris and New York for as high as eight thousand dollars each.

One of the most popular pearl shells is the tiny pipi. Measuring only two inches in diameter, it yields large golden, pink, black and —on rare occasions—blue pearls that may weigh three or four carats. Previously found only in the Tuamotus, some have been found in recent years off one of the uninhabited and seldom visited Gambier Atolls.

With a rich soil and excellent climate, the valleys and fertile lowlands contain a luxuriant vegetation and produce an abundant supply of vegetables and fruit, including peaches and alligator pears. The distant location of the islands and their lack of transportation and commercial inducements have combined to keep them relatively free of outsiders. Beachcombers are unknown and the only foreigners are a few French and Chinese.

Mangareva today is an island of simple happiness over which hangs something of sadness. The notes of the rogo-rogo and the soft chanting hoo-hoo of the dance are no longer heard. The coral wharves are crumbling. Coconuts fall in the valleys and the cry of the blue heron echoes out over the pass when the wind is low.

With little outside intermarriage the stalwart islanders have retained the pure Polynesian blood to a surprising extent. People of immense kindliness and simple charm, with few wants and no worries, the Mangarevans live each day as it comes, for in their soft, melodious language there is no word for tomorrow.

Marquesas Islands

North of the Tuamotus, seven hundred and fifty miles northeast of Tahiti, lie the towering, slate-green peaks of the lonely Marquesas. They are eleven islands of unrivaled primitive beauty, remote, and geographically as undisturbed as in the beginning of recorded history.

Lacking barrier reefs, they have few beaches and almost no coastal areas. Most of the fertile land is contained within great, beautiful valleys separated by sharp mountain ridges and black volcanic cliffs that rise thousands of feet almost straight up from the sea. The six inhabited islands are Nuku Hiva, Ua Huka, Ua Pou, Hiva Oa, Tahuata and Fatu Hiva. Nuku Hiva, in the northwest, is the largest island, and Hiva Oa, the administration center, is second in size.

As an offshoot of the old China trade, Yankee vessels from New England began to call at Tahiti and the Marquesas in their relentless quest for sandalwood, bêche-de-mer and tortoise shell to exchange at Canton for teas and silks.

During the War of 1812 the U.S.S. *Essex,* the first American man-of-war to enter the Pacific, rounded Cape Horn without orders, under the command of Captain David Porter. After waging disastrous raids which all but destroyed the British whaling industry, Captain Porter made the three-thousand-mile voyage southeastward to the Marquesas for fresh supplies and to repair his ships.

Following upon long months of offshore voyaging and fighting, the Yankee sailors cheered with delight when the American fleet entered the beautiful bay of Taio Hae in Nuku Hiva and were even more enthusiastic at their first sight of the comely, well-formed Marquesan girls. As Captain Porter reservedly reported, "with the common sailors and their girls, all was helter-skelter."

Naming the new-found haven Madison Island and the large, well-protected harbor Massachusetts Bay, Porter set the men to building an American village near the shores of the bay with a strong fort for its protection.

Porter notified the Typees, fiercest of the Marquesans, that they must henceforth live in peace and must pay tribute to the Americans in coconuts and pigs. The proud Typees promptly replied they never had and never would pay tribute to anyone, much less to pale white men who were so weak and cowardly that they had to depend on "smoking sticks to do their fighting."

With a well-armed force Porter invaded Typee Valley but was outnumbered and roundly defeated by the Typees. The young American captain and his musketeers had to run for their lives down through the valley to the sea, hotly pursued by scornful Typees hurling spears and shouts of derision.

In the second attack against the Marquesans American arms and gunpowder prevailed against stones, clubs and raw courage. The handsome Typee people were slaughtered right and left, their villages, canoes and gardens were destroyed and the Stars and Stripes was raised over the valley. Captain Porter proclaimed: "Our right to this island being founded on priority of discovery, conquest and possession, cannot be disputed. . . . I do declare that

116

I have in the most solemn manner under the American flag taken possession of said island in the name of the United States." Soon after sailing from the Marquesas Porter was captured by the British and taken to Honolulu as a prisoner of war.

When Yankee warships began calling at most trade ports in the South Seas, Rear Admiral Du Petit Thouars received orders from Paris to take immediate possession of the Marquesas, by persuasion or force, as circumstances required. The French admiral, sailing from island to island in the *Reine Blanche,* soon obtained the signatures of a number of chiefs to a document ceding all of the islands to France.

Although the Marquesans greatly valued their independence as a free people, island chiefs could always be persuaded by the white man's rhetoric, by presents and other means to sign papers agreeing to almost anything. Usually they had only the vaguest sort of an idea of what the papers entailed, and white traders were quick to exploit native ignorance of the European laws of private ownership.

When the Marquesan race was in its ascendancy it added one of the great pages to world history. Outstanding in valor, the Marquesans were master craftsmen, and like the ancient Greeks they had the highest respect for physical beauty.

In Marquesan eyes their wealth, consisting of products of the land and sea, works of art and handicrafts, were of value only for the social prestige of giving away. Whole families vied to make the best gifts and to contribute the most to community feasts.

They were a race of tall, beautifully formed people. The strength and symmetry of the men and their prowess in athletics, as well as the loveliness of the women, gave the early Marquesans the reputation for being the most perfect physical types in the Pacific.

Highly skilled craftsmen, working in stone, wood and shell, they excelled in the most exacting types of carving and designing. To satisfy their innate aesthetic sense all objects of daily use, besides being extremely well-made, had to be beautiful as well.

Annual artists' conventions were held for the display of distinctive styles and the discussion of individual works of art. Art centers were maintained where tattooing, carving, the adzing of beautifully-shaped canoes from temanu logs and other crafts were taught.

In native guilds, under the keen direction of master craftsmen, tapas of the finest texture were made and finished in scarlet, brown, yellow and black dyes derived from the roots of plants and the bark of trees. Poi poi pounders were adzed from solid blocks of stone and painstaking designs carved in the hardest kind of volcanic rock by the use of tools with rats' teeth as a cutting edge.

The art of tattooing reached a higher development in the Marquesas than anywhere else in the Pacific. During its heyday, when tattooing was the national expression, a few outstanding artists became as famous among the Marquesans for their graphic genius as Da Vinci and Michelangelo were in Europe.

Like highly skilled, artistic people in other parts of the world the Marquesans dislike common labor and bitterly resented being made to labor on the roads or in the making of copra in order to pay government taxes. In the eyes of the administrators their greatest crime was their pride, dignity and extreme independence as a free-born people, which made it difficult to turn them into docile subjects of France.

The Marquesans have been repeatedly duped by whites and almost all of their political and religious contacts with Europeans have been bitter ones. To stimulate native production of copra and other local products, opium was introduced by the early traders and soon became the major medium of exchange. It was even fed to the children. For a forty thousand franc fee the French government licensed an opium farmer to sell the drug. Later, when opium was forbidden, laudanum and cheap rum took its place as trade lures.

Vessels arriving in the Marquesas for refreshing allowed their crews full license. Generally they comprised the sweepings of the waterfronts of the world. Besides syphilis and gonorrhea, they introduced raging epidemics of influenza, tuberculosis and measles. Thousands of islanders were wiped out in a single month.

In 1863 a shipload of husky islanders, previously blackbirded as slave labor for the Chilean mines, contracted smallpox from crew members and were dumped back onto the beaches of Taio Hae Bay. They were welcomed into the homes and hearts of their unsuspecting loved ones and within a few weeks entire families were stricken. Soon once-populous villages were completely wiped out and whole valleys became silent, inhabited only by hundreds of unburied dead.

A few missionaries waged a relentless campaign against the depredations of white sailors and, on occasion, protested directly to home governments against the abuses of administrators who took too large a view of their authority. They translated the Bible into Marquesan and conducted mission schools and, although mission facilities and supplies were pitifully inadequate, they helped the sick to the best of their ability.

For their part, the Marquesans were deeply confused by the contradictions of a new religion that was totally unsuited to their spiritual and material needs, and were quick to realize that the missionaries lacked the power to enforce the spirit of brotherly love on their own white countrymen. Faced with the early destruction of their native culture while experiencing in bewilderment the worst of ours, they were soon convinced that existence under white missionaries and administrators had little to offer in comparison with what they had lost.

With the sudden cessation of all their natural means of expression, with their traditional code of morals misunderstood, with the beautiful, figurative language of their chants and epics gone and their deepest faiths harried by ridicule and mockery, the spirit of the Marquesan people was finally broken and a malady of sadness settled over what were formerly the happiest islands in Polynesia.

Told of the attractions of Heaven while living in the wake of tragedy many could see no good reason for postponing the voyage to the next world any longer. In the latter half of the nineteenth century hangings and other means of suicide became frequent. An aimless state of maladjustment spread to every inhabited island.

In slightly over a century the population of the Marquesas dropped from one hundred thousand healthy people to less than two thousand listless inhabitants. Great valleys that once held three thousand to six thousand islanders today have less than a hundred. A few have only three or four, and some none at all.

While in recent years there has been an increase in births over deaths, at the present time it would be extremely difficult to find twenty completely healthy Marquesans.

The art of Paul Gauguin did more than the efforts of any other man to interpret the primitive spirit and the mysterious, somber beauty of the Marquesas to the civilized world. "Here poetry is liberated by its own power," wrote the great modernist from the Marquesas.

Towering with disdain of smugly respectable people, Gauguin, while living in Tahiti, heard that he could hire models for a stick

119

of candy in the Marquesas and sailed for the island of Hiva Oa with a whole sackful of sweets and an organ to play on lonely nights.

"I have traveled ten thousand miles to find a spot on earth where I can be free," Gauguin said after arriving at Hiva Oa. Later from his *fa'e* (house) in Atuona he heard the wracking cough (rapid consumption) of the islanders echoing sometimes all day and all night through the valley and knew that he had come too late. The apathy of sadness had thinned the ranks of the Marquesans to a shadowy remnant of a once-great people. Some were already digging their own graves. Half blind and wracked with pain, Gauguin with infinite love and compassion immortalized the somber, brooding Marquesans against a background of raw, primitive beauty.

In the Vale of Atuona, valley of flowers, Gauguin died in agony and abject poverty attended by Tioka, an ex-cannibal sorcerer. "*Mata, mata, mata,*" wailed Tioka, trying to bring his white friend back to life. "He was one of us. Alas, now there are no more men."

Other tattooed islanders who had loved the thin artist took up the cry, "*Ua mate Koke, ua pete enata*"—"Gauguin is dead. We are lost."

"Koke was good to us" said Tioka, as he and three other Marquesans carried the artist up a steep trail to be buried above Atuona. "He was poor but he gave what he had to men poorer than himself."

Gauguin had hardly been buried before the French gendarme who took over his place made a huge bonfire of "the madman's rubbish," burning priceless paintings and strange carvings of incredible gods, trees and human beings that, a short while later, could have made him one of the richest men in France.

Gauguin's last canvas, painted while he sat huddled with fever and pain on his lonely *paepae upe* (veranda) in the Marquesas was of the roofs of a Breton village blanketed under the snow.

Melville's Typee Valley and the background scenes of Gauguin's paintings remain today almost unchanged from the way they were a century ago. Beyond a few villages, the ruggedness and the vast loneliness of the Marquesas still linger in the isolation of their deep valleys.

New Caledonia

Early voyagers attempting to persuade their sovereigns to back an expedition to the South Seas usually emphasized that "rich minerals might be found," yet for several decades no one bothered much about New Caledonia, the one island that provided such wealth in vast amounts. The production of nickel, a key mineral of the atomic age, has greatly increased the island's importance and today it is France's most valuable colony in the Pacific.

Located halfway between New Zealand and Guadalcanal, about seven hundred and fifty miles northwest of Brisbane, Australia, New Caledonia is the second largest island in Melanesia.

It is an island of high rocky coasts and bare headlands, of deep fertile valleys with numerous rivers that are fed by torrents from a central chain of mountains. Reaching two hundred and fifteen miles in length, and thirty-one miles wide, it is entirely surrounded at a distance of three to twelve miles by a vast barrier reef.

In 1774, Captain Cook brought his flagship, the *Resolution,* accompanied by the *Adventure,* to anchor in Balade Bay, at the northeast corner of New Caledonia, and because the mountains reminded him of Scotland he named the island New Caledonia (New Scotland).

During the thirty-year period beginning in 1864, when the *Iphigenie* sailed from Toulon loaded with two hundred and forty-eight manacled galley slaves, the French government transported twenty thousand criminals and more than four thousand political prisoners to New Caledonia. They were thrown into heavy iron cages and kept like animals in the dank, fetid holds of the prison ship. Those who survived the voyage were placed on the Isle of Pines and on Ducos Peninsula, where there was less chance of escape than on the main island. A few who incurred the displeasure of the local authorities were thrown into Noumea's infamous *"Cachot Noir"* (Black Cell) where humans were confined for years in total blackness. Those who came out alive were frequently blinded for life.

The first French settlers in New Caledonia were a hard, ruthless element bent on getting rich off the island as quickly as possible. They swiftly deprived the native owners of their lands and herded them into the interior where they remained practically in isolation.

M. Jules Garnier, sent out from Paris to survey the island's natural resources, wrote, "Strangely enough, it is fortunate that the natives do get up to mischief from time to time, for their confiscated land increases the public wealth and helps the colonists. Without that, let's admit it openly, one would be obliged to act with brutality in driving them back into the mountains."

121

The native people of New Caledonia, while basically Melanesian, are a curious mixture of the black, small-statured Melanesian and the brown, relatively-advanced Polynesian. Despite the prolonged hostility of the early Melanesians to the French and their tenacity in clinging to their ancient traditions, European rule gradually brought about the complete destruction of island culture. Examples of their architectural carvings and sculptural forms, many of them unique in South Pacific art, are to be found today only in the museums of France and the United States.

Foreign capital, attracted by the local French laws permitting the indenture of cheap labor from French Indo-China and Java, undertook the exploitation of the island's mineral resources on a large scale. Today the three largest chrome mines are owned by American, British and Australian interests. The colony shares with Canada a world monopoly of nickel which has been largely responsible for its prosperity.

"New Caledonia is a solid ball of minerals," colonials will tell you. Although enormous amounts have already been removed, much of the island's fabulous wealth is still untouched. In addition to nickel, chrome and iron there is cobalt, zinc, gold, silver, platinum, copper, cinnabar, mercury and coal.

Next to mining, the raising of pigs, sheep, cattle, goats and horses is the island's most important industry. On the lower slopes between the Caledonian mountains and the sea there are beautiful plains with nearly a million acres of green pasture land well adapted for stock farming. Thousands of wild deer are exported annually and venison steak is as common to Caledonians as beefsteak is to Texans.

Coconut palms line the beaches along the coastline and in the more fertile valleys coffee, manioc, corn, tobacco, cotton, rice, vanilla, pineapples, bananas and many other products are produced, including such mild-climate fruits as peaches, apples and grapes.

The Colony's 1,700,000 acres of timber contain many valuable stands of ebony, sandalwood, kauri, rosewood, ironwood and other exotic wildwoods. Much pine is found in the Loyalty Islands and the Isle of Pines.

In late years a number of new industries have been brought forward in an effort to relieve the island of too large a dependence on mining. They include tobacco, flour milling, the processing of a local vegetable oil and the manufacture of soap products.

It is estimated that the island could easily support well over a million people. The total population in 1960 was 70,747, about twenty-three thousand of whom were living in the capital of Noumea, a typically French coastal town.

The fact that most of New Caledonia's wealth is controlled by absentee owners has developed a "draining economy" principally concerned with supplying raw materials for the cartel monopoly and large dividends to a small group of absentee stockholders. This has severely affected local economy and social development. No large-scale transportation, irrigation, education or health program has ever been put into effect. In turn, the social rights and welfare of the native Melanesian people have long been a neglected issue. Those wishing to reside in or near the various European centers must first make application and obtain permission from the administration.

Under French rule the native population has fallen from seventy thousand to an estimated thirty-seven thousand at present, most of whom are relegated to inland reservations where they subsist mostly on taro and yams. In less than a century, well over ninety percent of the native lands have been taken over by the government and private interests have acquired large areas to exploit the natural resources. While religion has made but slight spiritual gains among the Melanesians, over one hundred thousand acres of their best lands have come into the hands of the mission stations.

As a holdover from the old penal days when free convict labor was supplied to French colonists, almost any type of manual labor is considered beneath the dignity of white residents. The delightfully mild, dry climate is ideal for white labor. Yet most small farmers, of the type that in France or the United States would work their own farms by tractor and cultivator, in New Caledonia insist on having a large number of low-paid coolies to do their farming and housework.

The fall of France in 1940 had tremendous repercussions in New Caledonia. While most of the colonial empire clung tenaciously to the Vichy Regime, the majority of Frenchmen in New Caledonia, armed with guns and iron railings, poured into Noumea, overthrew two pro-Vichy governors and rallied to the blue fanion with the red cross of Lorraine (De Gaulle's standard).

On the economic side, American dollars brought New Caledonia the greatest wave of prosperity it had ever known. Tens of millions were spent on airfields, docks, fine roads and other permanent installations and Noumea became the most important Allied base in the Southwest Pacific. At the end of the war most of the permanent installations that were built by the American armed forces were converted to peacetime uses.

The blunt facts of World War II convinced many people in New Caledonia that their ties with France are primarily sentimental. Some feel that their real military, economic and social ties lie logically with Australia, New Zealand and the countries of the Pacific world.

Wallis, Futuna and Other Dependencies

The Isle of Pines, a geological continuation of New Caledonia located thirty miles to the southeast, is a popular tourist and holiday resort for people from Noumea. Other groups with few, if any, permanent inhabitants include the Huon Islands, tiny Belep Archipelago, the Chesterfield Group and Walpole Island. All are low-lying and of coralline formation, mostly of value for their guano deposits.

Of New Caledonia's adjacent dependencies the three Loyalty Islands of Mare, Lifu and Uvea are the largest. Located seventy miles off the east coast, they contain eight hundred square miles and support a native population of fourteen thousand.

The colony of Wallis and Futuna, New Caledonia's most distant dependency, is located between Samoa and Fiji about three hundred miles northeast of the latter Group. Most of the ten thousand Polynesian inhabitants live on the three high, thickly-wooded islands of Uvea, Futuna and Alofi which together with a number of lesser islets have a combined area of seventy-four square miles.

Clipperton Island

Far to the northeast of Tahiti, tiny Clipperton Atoll is France's most isolated Pacific possession. Located eighteen hundred miles due west of Panama, it is a low, barren, lagoon island, roughly circular in shape and about two miles in diameter.

The island obtained its present name, in 1705, from Captain John Clipperton, the leader of a band of notorious pirates who cruised about the eastern Pacific in a small, heavily-armed bark and used the remote atoll as a hideout base.

124

Primarily of significance because of its strategic position in relation to the Panama Canal, Clipperton Island was used as a seaplane
and air base during World War II. At present it is uninhabited.

New Hebrides and the Condominium

The twelve large and about eighty small islands and islets of the
New Hebrides including the Banks and Torres Groups comprise a
fertile archipelago located northeast of New Caledonia about four
hundred and seventy miles west of the Fijis.

These islands, especially Espiritu Santo, Efate and its centrally
located harbor of Vila became well known to thousands of Americans based there during World War II, although the group saw no
actual combat beyond the continual quarreling of British and
French residents.

Less well known is the fact that the New Hebrides are one of the
richest though least developed of the big archipelagos in the southwest Pacific. Much of the land area is covered with almost impenetrable mountain jungles where millions of orchids bloom unseen and
where countless thousands of teak, sandalwood, mahogany and
catalpa trees grow wild.

The early contacts of local islanders with the white whalers, sandalwood seekers and labor recruiters was the usual sordid story.
White traders and sandalwood seekers increased the practice of
cannibalism by establishing a steady demand for smoked human
heads, an export business that brought large profits from European
curio dealers. Later, when the human head trade was outlawed,
the New Hebrides became the center for the native slave trade, or
blackbirding industry.

From a once political no-man's-land the New Hebrides came
under a joint administration by France and Great Britain known
as the Condominium. Under the Babel-like machinery popularly
known throughout the South Pacific as the "Pandemonium" there
are three sets of laws and three currencies (French, Australian and
British), two kinds of police (British and French), two systems of
weights and measures (British and metric) and other cumbersome
absurdities.

After nearly sixty years of the Condominium the fifty thousand
native people of the New Hebrides still cannot become French or

British citizens and still have no national status of their own. While both sides are still endeavoring to save the islanders' souls and bring them into the French or British fold there is still no joint Condominium education department. What education is available is handled separately or by the missions. Although the New Hebridean is still without political standing or status he is free to become a Catholic or Protestant, and many have, since the mission leaders have been almost the only ones to stand up consistently for native rights and welfare.

In some affairs the officials of both powers have acted together for the common good, but on the more important issues their attitude has been determined according to the best interests of their own nationals. Because the New Hebridean people are squeezed between the rival interests of the two ruling powers, their general welfare and advancement has been seriously retarded. As the renowned Dr. S. M. Lambert of the Rockefeller Foundation has expressed it, "The natives of the New Hebrides have had the hardest experience of any island race in the Pacific."

The abuses of native land rights in the New Hebrides are exceeded nowhere in Melanesia except in New Caledonia. Disputes resulting from early land grabbing have been going on for several decades and at the present time Europeans are claiming about two-thirds (well over two million acres) of the most promising land in the islands. Most titles are based on claims to early "purchase" or barter from the natives and, as is usually the case, such deals were tremendously in favor of the white buyer. Quite often the purchase price was simply the exchange of a mouth organ or a few yards of cotton print for "all the land from here to there and as far back as I can see."

With a rich, fertile soil and abundant rainfall, coastal planters are able to raise a wide variety of tropical and many semitropical products including cotton, maize, bananas, vanilla, rice, sugar cane, pineapples and many kinds of vegetables.

Some New Hebrideans have attained moderate wealth and are taking a leading position in money and trade. Most are looking toward eliminating the European trader by doing business direct with the shippers. Beyond that, the modern New Hebridean is now thinking politically and asking what his future status is to be.

France and Great Britain are both dissatisfied with Condominium joint rule and it is certain that some sort of an adjustment will soon have to be made.

126

Chapter Five

FIJI, THE KINGDOM OF TONGA
AND BRITISH PACIFIC ISLANDS

British possessions in Oceania include Fiji, Tonga, the Solomons, Ellice and Gilberts, certain Line Islands and joint control of the New Hebrides.

Fiji Islands

In less than one hundred years the Fiji Islands have advanced from a cannibal stronghold where "long pig" (roasted humans) was an important part of the national diet to a world shipping and aviation center only twelve hours by jet plane from San Francisco. More than Hawaii, Fiji is the true crossroads of the Pacific.

Modern Fijians, many of whom have been to universities and hold responsible positions, like to boast that any plane that flies can land at their international airport, with its new air-conditioned terminal building, larger than those in many of the world's major cities.

It was in Fiji that the Melanesian and Polynesian races met and the present-day Fijians, a tall, healthy, well-formed people, have many of the best characteristics of both races. Normally they are a happy, spontaneous people. During a festive *Taralala* (shuffle-dance) or on almost any occasion, if a young Fijian girl likes you, she will smile warmly and shout *"Kasine,"* meaning "What a fine thing you are!" If deeply moved, she will make the neck-slicing gesture that signifies "I'd cut my throat for you!"

Labeled by Darwin as a "people forever lost to civilization," the Fijians have proven, to the contrary, to be a highly intelligent, adaptable race. Today in many rural villages the huge drums that sounded the call to cannibal feasts now sound the call to church services. The Fijian Choir, heard in Suva's Methodist Church on Sunday nights, and the aplomb and blare of the Royal Fijian Band

127

Christmas morning in Fiji finds churchgoers attending services, then celebrating the day with feasts.

are unexcelled in the Pacific. The conversion of the islanders to the attractive people they now are is one of the outstanding achievements of missionary work. Had the Fijians been other than intelligent and adaptable by nature the changeover might have taken centuries.

Some Fijians are thoroughly Westernized. A few are in business for themselves. All are proud of their ancestry and traditions and disinclined to envy European or American ways. The ever-smiling Fijians of the travel posters can be vastly different fellows when the occasion warrants. On Guadalcanal they became the terror of Japanese jungle fighters. They are among the gentlest and—if need be, the toughest—islanders in the Pacific.

Green and mountainous, Fiji is an archipelago of three hundred

and twenty islands astride the date-dividing line of today and tomorrow. On any map one can see that the one hundred and eightieth
meridian, which is the boundary between Melanesia and Polynesia,
passes directly through Fiji.

It is widely known as the "Little India of the Pacific," because
more than half of its population are East Indians. Actually it is a
small united nations of five communities: East Indians, Fijians,
Europeans, part-Europeans and Chinese, the majority of whom live
on the two main islands of Viti Levu and Vanua Levu.

Visitors who dress for dinner and dine on English roast beef and
Yorkshire pudding at the stately Grand Pacific Hotel, who see turbaned Moslems, tall bearded Sikhs, a Hindu with his dhoti and
gaily dressed Madrassis women with their yards of muslin and filmy
saris in downtown Suva, can't help but wonder how it all came
about. Invariably they ask first about the background of the smiling
jet-age Fijians who play cricket and rugby barefooted in skirted,
wrap-around sulus.

The high points are easily told.

After the discovery of Fiji by Tasman, Cook and Bligh there was
a long period of warfare between island chiefs and their white advisors, some of whom were more cruel and barbarous than the worst
Fijians. Enemies defeated in battle were always cooked and eaten.
Ordinarily only Fijian males feasted on *bokolo* (man-meat). Cooking,
usually oven steaming or boiling, and the act of eating one's fallen
enemy was believed to endow the eater with the *mana* (power and
prestige) of the dead foe. Whites were not looked on as a delicacy,
as they were considered too badly tainted with tobacco and salt.
On some islands warriors were instructed to kill only fat enemies
with shiny, healthy skins.

"Terrible" Thakombau of Viti Levu, and Ma'afu, a Tongan
rebel, emerged as the most powerful and ruthless leaders in the islands. The wily and ambitious Thakombau became embroiled in
white machinations and almost wholly dependent on British support to maintain his influence and position as the self-styled Tui
Viti—King of Fiji.

In 1849, while the American consul was celebrating the Fourth
of July with a magnificent display of fireworks, he managed to burn
down the consulate. The following day, sobered and aghast at his
predicament, the consul claimed that it was all King Thakombau's
fault for not having any means of fire protection on the island. In

due process of law the consul, Mr. J. B. Williams, totaled damages done to the consulate, together with previous claims made by several American cotton planters, and presented the king with a bill for forty-five thousand dollars damages! The impudence of the consul stunned the king.

To enforce the claim, Commander Boutwell arrived in the U.S.S. *John Adams* "to demand and insist upon reparation for wrongs committed upon the property of American citizens."

Worried over his inability to raise the forty-five thousand dollars and at the same time fearful of attack by his powerful rival Ma'afu, Thakombau offered his "kingdom" to Queen Victoria on the condition that she would pay the American claims and that he would be upheld as the king of all Fiji.

The official British attitude expressed by Lord Carnavon, the Colonial Secretary, was that "It is painful to refuse but there must be a limit somewhere to our protecting and governing duties especially when we gain nothing by the acquisition."

Thakombau next offered the Fijis to the United States, but coming at a time when the nation was recovering from the Civil War, the offer was ignored by President Abraham Lincoln.

In 1874, despite the opposition of a number of lesser chiefs, King Thakombau, Ma'afu and other leading chiefs signed a deed granting Fiji to Great Britain. The British representative declined to agree to the cession until it specifically stated that all of the lands in Fiji were to be considered henceforth as property of the British Crown.

Britain's decision to annex the Fijis was hastened by the demands of powerful interests in New South Wales and the consideration of strategic factors, including, as Lord Granville put it, "the risk of the United States assuming the protectorate."

The establishment of the promising sugar industry created a large demand for cheap labor. The Fijian would gladly work hard building a house for a friend, or a canoe, or in the communal coconut grove or taro patch; but he could see no sense in toiling long hours in the cane fields to make a few white men rich, especially since the share he was offered in the prosperous plans was only a few cents a day, the lowest wages in the world.

The white planters insisted on cheap, docile labor—brown, black or yellow. Their persistent demands were accompanied by a certain amount of influence with the Home Office. In the following thirty-eight years the steerage holds of British vessels transported over sixty-four thousand indentured coolie laborers from India to the Fijis.

Sugar soon grew to be an important export and in time became the economic backbone of the islands. Eventually, as the smaller planters were forced to the wall, the entire industry came under the direct control of the giant Colonial Sugar Refining Company.

The immigrant laborers, accustomed to working from sunrise to sundown for three annas a day in India, were bitterly disappointed by the unsanitary huts into which they were herded and the intolerable conditions of their indenture. Numerous suicides are recorded among these earliest arrivals who were faced with almost hopeless prospects for the future. Those who survived eked out the barest sort of a daily existence.

In late years the average employees of the Colonial Sugar Company still have received such low wages that over eighty-five percent remain insolvent so long as they are in the employ of the sugar company. Another thing that has kept many Indian peasants in debt is the laxity of laws regarding usury. A law known as the Crops Liens Ordinance in effect protects the moneylender and his high interest rates. The peasant farmer who finds he must borrow on his crop often remains forever in bondage because his small income is only sufficient to pay the interest.

By American standards the sugar farmers are very poor. Many have little more than the barest necessities in their shanty villages along the highways. In 1960 about two-thirds of Fiji's total wage earners were receiving approximately eight dollars per week. Over twelve thousand Indian children in the six to fourteen age group were unable to attend school, according to the last census report.

All of the Indians in Fiji are not peasant farmers. Many, after completing their indenture, remained in the islands and leased small holdings from the native Fijians. Others arrived to enter the mercantile or transportation business, and today the town of Suva has a large number of tailors, merchants, lawyers and other small business men among its many Hindus, turbaned Moslems and bearded Sikhs. About ninety percent of the Colony's Indians are Hindus.

The routine of the Indian farmer, who rises shortly after 5:00 A.M., breakfasts on *roti* (Indian bread) with milk or tea and works from 6:00 A.M. to 5:00 P.M., differs vastly from the irregular Fijian way of life. The good-natured Fijian has never been able to understand the plodding, thrifty Hindu who is content to labor from sunup to sunset for a mere existence. The dull routine of sugar farming and the fact that the land which once belonged to Fijians now belongs to an Australian corporation has made regimented tenant farming unpopular with the Fijians. They have made but little attempt to compete against the shrewd, canny Indians.

The government and the Sugar Company, in an effort to develop a peasant laboring class dependent on yearly crop money, have made repeated efforts to lure the islanders away from their communal and co-operative ways of life. Modern training farms and agricultural schools are maintained by the government and by the mission schools. Except for a few model farming settlements the plan has not worked out. Most Fijians still adhere to subsistence farming in or near their home villages, much preferring to raise such native staples as sweet potatoes, taro, tapioca, yams and bananas.

"If we could only instill in them the full spirit of competition for profit," is the lament most often heard when colonials gather to discuss what's wrong with the Fijian farmers.

It has often been repeated that the Fijians are inherently lazy and refuse to labor because they have little use for money. The modern Fijian, while not caring to compete on a subsistence level with cheap labor, is remarkably adaptable to changing conditions and quite willing to work hard whenever good living and working conditions are provided. In the gold mines and other industries many hundreds of Fijians are successfully employed—many at the hardest kind of labor, operating mechanical conveyors, excavators and pneumatic drills. Most have been employed steadily for many years and are content to remain because they receive fair wages and attractive social and health conditions.

Fijians who go to Suva usually work for the government as clerks and in minor administrative posts. But the majority prefer to live along the coasts or beside the many rivers in ancestral thatched-roof, high-beamed *bures* (houses). Food production for subsistence is still their main occupation and communal methods are at the center of all village life. Fijians are naturally good agriculturists and each settlement has its pigs, fowl and gardens of yams, taro and tapioca.

Indian-owned motor buses, locally called "wog-waggons," roll east from Suva on King's Road or west on Queen's Road carrying everything, including as many humans as can be squeezed in with bundles of meat, taro, bunches of bananas, baskets, crates and per-

*A Fijian house of bamboo and thatch withstands gales and heavy rains and is
pleasantly cool in the hot season.*

haps a live goat. Wog-waggons regularly honk their way around the
island to the hilly interior where few Europeans are seen and island
life remains much the same as it was fifty years ago.

In Suva where there are far more Indians than Fijians the latter sometimes hire an Indian taxi driver and order him to drive about the island. Sitting back in comfort and at ease the Fijian receives deep satisfaction from being able to give orders to his economic superior for a brief hour or so.

The average Fijian looks upon the Indians as encroachers and would like to see them sent back to India. Besides the peasant farmers and leaseholders, he finds Indians in control of most dairies, transportation and nearly all small stores in the well-populated districts. If a Fijian buys a pair of shorts, a quart of milk or a pound of tobacco, or attends a motion picture theatre, he invariably must do so at an establishment owned by a Hindu or a Moslem, and he will perhaps be directed on his way by a Sikh policeman.

Many Hindus and Moslems, not forgetting for a moment that their religion and civilization are among the oldest in the world, look down upon the Fiji Islanders as eaters of pork and beef and consider them a lazy, unenlightened people but slightly removed from jungle savagery.

British administrators have worked hard to give the Fijians a fair government. Though beset with problems that sometimes call for Solomonlike decisions, they have built up a tradition of justice based on local conditions. It is to the credit of the administration that the Fijian population has continually increased under British rule and that they have among other things encouraged the use of the native language and brought forward an educational program well suited to the principle "Fiji for the Fijians." Unlike the French, the British have banned the sale of intoxicants to Fijians and encourage them to drink the nonharmful yaqona.

To see a handsome eighteen-year-old black boy from the Solomons stand barefooted in front of a class and draw detailed pictures explaining functions of the human heart is to realize at once that Suva's Central Medical School for the training of young island boys as medical practitioners is one of the best things that Westerners have ever done for the native people of the South Seas.

The plan started with a small number of Fijians. Through the efforts of Dr. S. M. Lambert, funds have been provided by the Rockefeller Foundation for enlarging the school, which now includes students from nearly every major island group in Oceania.

Students for the five-year course are selected primarily for their intelligence and desire to become medical men. They are taught to be proud of their home islands and of their own people. Attending

A Fijian chief poses proudly with his necklace of whale teeth.

school barefooted, barelegged, dressed in simple sulus, they are given the white man's medical knowledge but are protected from acquiring his habits so that they will return to their own people as simple in manner as when they left. Some graduates have become medical men of extraordinary ability, especially in surgery, and have saved the lives of many people in remote areas, including more than a few Europeans. Articles written by native graduates have been quoted in medical journals round the world.

The Central Medical School deserves much credit for the presently increasing population on nearly all South Pacific archipelagos and is unique in that it brings together different native races and governments in a common cause.

In the last few years the British have made a strong effort to bring the Indians and Fijians into closer cooperation through social and political channels.

Fijians are extremely loyal to the British. As a part of his traditional allegiance to the tribal chief, the Fijian looks to Great Britain with a degree of respect and loyalty that is not entirely shared by the approximately two hundred thousand Indians who now represent more than half of Fiji's total population.

Suva's Indian leaders, strongly in favor of having a government similar to Hawaii with electoral equality for all, are always able to remind white officials that they were invited and transported to Fiji by the British and then denied a truly representative part in their own government.

"There are many thousands of acres of land not being used," a young Indian member of Fiji's Legislative Council recently pointed out. "As British subjects we want the right to buy or lease this land at a reasonable price. We also want the common roll with equality and real democracy for all people. Is that unreasonable?"

A new generation of intelligent, progressive-minded Fijians and Indians has come forward. Many realize that the respective rights of both communities—Fijian and Indian—must be more thoroughly understood and somehow combined if Fiji is to move forward cooperatively.

Most Indians are young people born in Fiji who naturally look upon the islands as their only home. Everyone agrees that without the Indians to do most of the hard work Fiji's whole economic structure would collapse overnight.

With much of the Colony's productive wealth going out of the

136

country to Australia, Fiji's number one problem for the future is how to feed her rapidly expanding population on her limited resources. New industries have to be established and new lands brought into use very soon if the Colony is to be saved from a major crisis.

On the premise that the present Fijian way of life has to change or perish, most experts agree that the Fijians must forego their ancestral ways and quickly become a community of independent farmers. Local Indians are increasing twice as fast as all other races and Fijians have little choice but to develop modern methods or find themselves relegated to reservations like the American Indians.

Suva, Viti Levu and Vanua Levu

Cosmopolitan Suva, the largest town south of Honolulu, is Fiji's capital and the seat of administration for the British Governor, who also exercises supervision over Tonga and Pitcairn Island.

From the stately banks and busy offices on Victoria Parade to King's Wharf and beyond, a babel of voices is heard speaking English, Fijian and Hindustani. Fijians speak their own Bau dialect and most Indians speak Hindustani. Though English is the official language, it is not compulsory, and colonials from their Olympian tea tables have learned the Fijian language.

Along Cumming Street and Renwick, strange music is heard in bootmakers' shops. The traveler is offered filigree silver from Thailand, ivory and silken saris from India, teak from China, war clubs, "cannibal forks" and blocks of Fijian tapa cloth. In the Indian shops, where men huddle all day stitching garments, a new suit can be made up to order and delivered in two days. Mr. Fong Wing Fook of the Chang Sing Loong Company, specialists in Chinese delicacies, offers fat, well prepared *sucu walu* (sea slug or bêche-de-mer) and if the buyer can afford it, a pound of processed sharks' fins can be had for six dollars.

While Englishmen at the Fiji Club drink tea or sip gin and tonic Indians drink milk or buttery ghee and the Fijians drink their yaqona, an earthy-tasting nonintoxicant made from the root of a pepper-family plant. A number of businesses with Fijian employees have a midmorning and an afternoon yaqona-break.

Suva, with its pomp and tradition at Government House, its Venicelike canal, teeming market places, its Indian section smelling of curry and garlic, and its winding, crowded streets is a metropolis of forty thousand inhabitants run on colonial standards. Unlike Tahiti and Honolulu, it shutters-up early and after the witching hour of nine the lights and sounds are few.

Substandard housing is the rule for a large percentage of the population. Some of the Colony's worst wood and tin shacks, fire-traps and blighted slum areas are found in urban areas behind the capital town. A late census report showed that only about forty-seven percent of all families have their own separate living quarters. Some are separated only by a partition of sacking.

Ninety-mile-long Viti Levu—which means "Greater Fiji"—contains more than half the Colony's territory and most of its population. Economically an island of sugar, gold, copra, bananas and tourism, it is divided by a four-thousand-foot mountain chain which no road crosses.

Modern hotels are being built on both sides of the island to attract a larger share of tourist dollars. Some have swimming pools, East Indian food and de luxe thatched bures, with rates at twenty-six dollars per day and up. "Old Pacific hands," planters, traders and many seasoned travelers prefer Suva's small hotels with their easy ways and authentic color for five to ten dollars per day. These older hotels have tradition and charm but much of the plumbing is politely referred to as "communal"—meaning down the hall and to the right.

The yellow-green cane fields of Viti Levu's dry leeward coast and the dense jungle green of the eastern shores are almost like separate countries. All of the northern and western lowlands where most of the sugar is grown is relatively dry. Palms flourish along the shore-line below the many miles of cane fields. Along the graveled Queen's Road to Korolevu there are tapioca fields, paw paws, mangoes, huge fig trees and many coconut and banana groves.

On Korolevu's half-moon of white sand beach tourists can see a *meki-wesi*—head-hunters' war dance—re-enacted, or can take part in an ancient *kava* (yaqona) drinking ritual. Here the island's most exclusive hotel, built like a Fijian village, summons its guests to dinner with the *lala,* a tree-trunk drum formerly used to sound the call to cannibal banquets.

In the center of the island the land and vegetation change abruptly to a wet, verdant area where moisture-loving flowers, trees and jungles of tropical plants abound. On the windward side there is no month without rain. Every valley has abundant streams, many of which are used to irrigate large cleared areas of taro. Banana plantations do well. The warm climate and rich soil will produce almost anything that the Fijian people want to eat.

Northeast of the main island, Vanua Levu is Fiji's second largest island. Its one hundred and forty-six miles of broken coastline provide many harbors and sheltered bays with small towns and settlements. Lambasa, with its modern sugar mills, warehouses and sprawling cane fields, is the center of life on the western coast. Sometimes smoke from the sugar factories darkens the sky. Those who like quietude and the old colonial way of life live on the beautiful coconut (eastern) coast of Vanua Levu along the scenic, little-traveled Hibiscus Highway.

For those who prefer places more remote than the two busy main islands, the Colony has over three hundred islands of little economic importance but of much interest and beauty. The fifty-seven islands of the Lau Group and the twenty scenic atolls of the Yasawa Chain are among the best. On the little island of Mbengga, off the southernmost point of Viti Levu, the ancient art of firewalking is performed. During the *Vilavilairevo*—"Jumping into the Ovens" ceremony—people of Mbengga jump onto white hot stones and walk slowly around on them without being burned. Doctors and scientists are still unable to explain how it's done.

Kingdom of Tonga

East of Fiji and five hundred miles south of Samoa, the tiny nation of Tonga is the last of the South Sea monarchies. Ruled by Her Majesty Queen Salote Tupou, a direct descendant of the world's oldest reigning dynasty, Tonga's slightly more than two hundred islands and islets comprise the smallest kingdom on earth.

Most of the queen's sixty-four thousand subjects live on the three main island clusters of Tongatabu, Haapai and Vavau, which extend about two hundred miles from north to south. Nukualofa, the capital, is on Tongatabu, an island shaped like an irregular crescent that contains about half of the population and much of the best land in Tonga.

From the deck of a copra schooner coming up to Nukualofa from Eastern Passage and the Narrows the turret of Tonga's wooden palace and the royal chapel come first to view. As the boat approaches the jetty the neat, flower-lovely town with trim turf-covered streets

139

and cedarlike Avava trees looks more like a sleepy New England village than the capital of a modern copra-and-banana kingdom.

Although Tonga has a small airstrip there is no regular air service. Those who would see the beauty and grace of the Polynesian race unspoiled by modern hotels, honky-tonks, bars, slums and brassy bands must go down to Nukualofa by ship from Suva or come up from New Zealand. Normally an unscheduled passenger plane flies down from Fiji about once a month, taking three hours for the flight. There are no hotels, but accommodations may be had at Beach House on the waterfront road, a clean, congenial boarding house that serves excellent meals at nominal prices. Nukualofans do not encourage tourists or permanent settlers but are friendly and hospitable to travelers, especially to those who do not expect to find a carnival atmosphere of native performers, jazz and hula drums.

Tongans who never heard of Epicurus know better than the Greeks ever did how to be happy. Under the wise leadership of a queen who is the widest known and most universally respected Polynesian in the South Seas they have developed a society well adjusted to the modern world and well adapted to their own needs.

With their slight admixture of Fijian blood the handsome Tongans are the most progressive of Polynesian people. They have no real poverty and no unemployment. The government has prevented the development of any large, European-owned plantations with their usual native serfdom. No one can buy Tongan land and no more than two hundred acres is ever leased to a European; consequently there are no white-master-brown-boy social standards. The kingdom gives every Tongan a farm of his own. This prevents poverty and promotes equality, independence and an effective system of social security in keeping with the dignity of free men.

The outlying islands of Niuatobutabu, Tafahi and Niuafoou (Tin Can Island) are included within the queen's domain and about fifty miles northwest of Nukualofa the disappearing jack-in-the-box island of Falcon has become Tonga's contribution to the natural wonders of the world.

In 1865 Falcon Island was reported by the British warship H.M.S. *Falcon* as a shoal reaching barely above the surface of the sea. Twenty years later a submarine volcano produced an island two hundred and ninety feet high that extended several miles in area. During the next ten years the island, called by the natives *Fonua Foo* (New

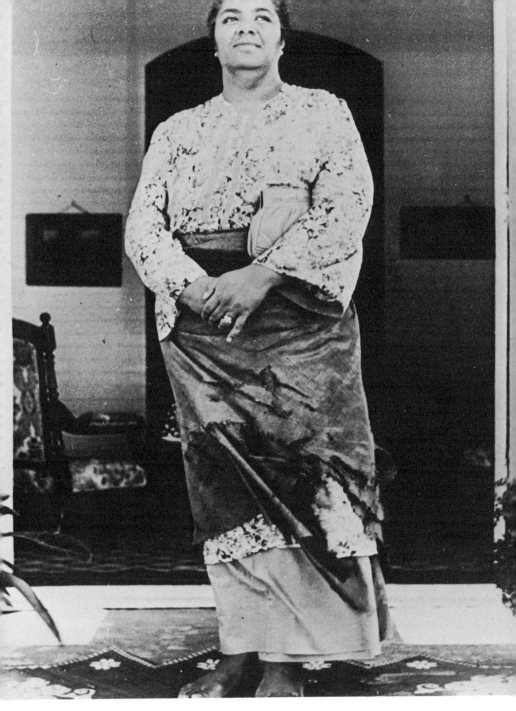

Queen Salote of Tonga, known and respected by royal families around the world, rules an independent ocean kingdom of about 150 islands.

Place), subsided to one hundred and fifty-three feet, and in 1895 the British Admiralty reported it to be only forty feet above the surface. Three years later it disappeared completely!

In 1900 Falcon stood ten feet above the sea, but by 1913 it had completely disappeared again. After violent eruptions of steam and sulphur during 1927 and 1928 the island reached an elevation of three hundred and sixty-five feet and one and a half miles in length. A party of alert nobles from Tongatabu quickly planted the red and white flag of Tonga on the highest peak and proclaimed it a part of Queen Salote's domain. In a few years the sea again eroded the pumice island to below sea level. It appeared again in 1955 and the Tongan government once more annexed it but in 1959 it had disappeared from sight.

The first Tongans came from Samoa during one of the final waves of the great Polynesian migrations. Excellent seamen and boatbuilders, they sailed widely among the archipelagos of Central Polynesia and brought many hundreds of outside islands under their control. For several centuries they made slaves of the Samoans.

The Dutchmen Willem Schouten, Jacob Le Maire and Abel Tasman visited Tonga in the seventeenth century and were followed more than a hundred years later by Captain Wallis and James Cook. Because of his hospitable reception Captain Cook named the group the Friendly Islands. Today in the palace grounds there still wanders a giant, scarred turtle which Cook presented to a Tongan noble in 1773. Tongans honor this aged, blind creature as they would a chief, presenting it with food and kava, the ceremonial drink.

When the first evangelists disembarked from the gospel ship *Duff* "to labor in the Lord's vineyard" Christianity was looked upon with a cold eye by the Tongan priests and chiefs. Unimpressed by descriptions of the glories of Heaven or the horrors of Hell, they strongly believed that all rewards for virtue and punishment for vice were bestowed in this world. Although the English missionaries were well armed with cuckoo clocks and electric batteries—"spirit twisters"— they failed, at first, to lure the sinners into the fold.

In the first part of the nineteenth century all of Tonga was involved in civil warfare. A number of chiefs who were against war succeeded finally in restoring the islands to their former peaceful state. Outstanding among them was young Finau Ulukalala, who was bitterly determined to maintain the ancient beliefs but was opposed to the warring policies of his famous father, a fearless leader whose insatiable ambitions had often made him shout, "Oh—that the Gods would make me King of England!"

Young Finau, on becoming the leading chief of Vavau at the death of his father, made an impassioned plea to the assembled nobles:

"Listen to me, chiefs and warriors! I have seen with sorrow the wide destruction occasioned by the unceasing war carried on by the chief [his father] now lying in the malae. The land is depopulated; it is overgrown with weeds, and there is nobody to cultivate it. Had we remained peaceful it would have been populous still. What madness! Is not life already too short? Is it not a noble characteristic in man to remain happy and peaceful in his station? What folly, then, to seek for war, to shorten that which is already too short!

"Not that we ought to banish all thoughts of fighting. If any power approach us with the front of battle and attempt to invade our rights, our bravery shall be more excited in proportion as we have more possessions to defend. Let us confine ourselves to agriculture, for that is truly guarding our country."

A virile, capable people, successful in their wars upon neighboring islanders, the Tongans were inclined to look upon white traders, adventurers and other would-be exploiters in anything but a subservient light.

Captain Croker of H.M.S. *Favorite* landed a force on Tongatabu in an attempt to aid a group of native converts and Wesleyan zealots who were determined to impose Christianity on the pagan Tongatabuans. Undaunted by the superior arms of the invaders, the valiant pagans decisively defeated the British forces, killed Captain Croker and a number of officers and forced the party to flee ignominiously back to sea leaving their guns, ammunition and field pieces on the shores of Tongatabu. British prestige suffered from the encounter.

Progress in Tonga dates from the rule of Taufa'ahau—widely known by his Christian name, King George Tubou I, and long considered "the greatest Tongan." After half a century of civil warfare, Taufa'ahau pacified and united his people under a single rule, encouraged them to become Christians, revived their agricultural pursuits and advised them wisely in all things. In recognition of his outstanding qualities of leadership he was acknowledged as the ruler and accorded the full honors of a king by the United States, Great Britain, France and Germany.

143

The Reverend Shirley Baker, a Wesleyan missionary, played a major role in establishing Christianity throughout Tonga and in helping the king to establish the foundation of a modern government.

Wesleyan missionaries stimulated giving to the point where a Tongan would contribute everything he had, including the clothes he wore, to impress fellow worshippers with his generosity. Wash basins were placed in front of the pulpit and the entire congregation marched round and round dropping a coin each time in the big basins. A family fell out when their money was gone. Those who had saved up enough money to last longest were hailed with much acclaim and honor.

Eventually King Tubou became aroused over the large sums that were being sent to the Wesleyan headquarters. He felt that the directors in Australia were dipping too deeply into the tiny kingdom's contributions and leaving too little for the Lord's work in Tonga. The king protested directly to the Wesleyan Conference and was strongly supported by Reverend Baker.

The Wesleyan Conference immediately excommunicated Baker. Incensed over the removal of Baker and the refusal of the Wesleyans to give an accounting of Tongan money, King Tubou appointed Baker to the position of Prime Minister and together they organized The Free Church of Tonga.

The Wesleyans, having traded their rights to preach in Samoa to the London Missionary Society in exchange for exclusive proselytizing privileges in Tonga, had no intention of giving up the latter field of endeavor and an intense rivalry developed between the two factions.

During a series of fairly frequent volcanic eruptions on Niuafoou Island, the Wesleyans informed the natives it was a sure sign of Jehovah's wrath directed against the Free Church. When the island of Tofua erupted, the deacons of the Free Church pointed out that Divine anger was aroused against the Wesleyans.

As Prime Minister, Baker induced King Tubou to end his absolute rule and extend a constitutional form of government to the people of Tonga. With the abolishment of serfdom and the establishment of civil rights every Tongan was guaranteed a plot of ground and a state system of education had its inception.

During the remainder of his reign, wise King Tubou refused to sell a single foot of Tongan soil to any outsider, and fortunately for

144

the islanders there were no minerals and no forest resources in their kingdom to attract the white man's warships and political ambitions.

The power behind the throne of Tonga is in the hands of a British Agent. While the Tongans regard and speak of him as an advisor, actually he has large powers over the royal purse strings and is able to veto expenditures. In addition he has control over white residents and full charge of the tiny nation's foreign relations. As a result of wise financial management the kingdom has no public debt and now invests much of its surplus money in Australia and New Zealand.

Tongans have retained their own cultural integrity and are still the most independent native people in the South Pacific. Unlike the Fijians, they are governed by a democratically elected parliament and have their own flag, passports and postage stamps and a well-backed currency.

Every male Tongan upon reaching the age of sixteen is free to take up an allotment of eight and a quarter acres of country land, plus two-fifths of an acre in a nearby village for his living quarters. Thereafter, to retain this land, he pays the nominal sum of about two dollars yearly and is required to plant two hundred healthy young coconut trees during the first year and maintain adequate food crops for the support of his family. Farm implements are rented on a nonprofit basis. About four days' work a week is found easily sufficient to maintain a local farm and supply the farmer with staple foods, housing materials, tobacco and native soap. This plan has proved a great success and has prevented European exploitation, usury and unemployment.

A Tongan plants bananas, yams, corn and tapu trees on his best land. Taro and tapioca do well on his poorer soil. He also raises excellent citrus fruit, melons and pineapples; and grows pandanus for mats, sugar cane for thatch and shrubs for scents and dyes.

Money is of relatively little importance to the average farm family. Tongans are willing enough to buy such imports as cloth, tinned meat, tobacco and kerosene, but are restricted by very small cash incomes. The fluctuating price of copra determines with finality how many Tongan dollars a family has for yearly extras.

A co-operative agricultural group known as the Local Producers' Association stimulates cultivation and enlarges the extent of Tonga's participation in the marketing of her own products. Special departments, such as the Copra Board and the Banana Board, concentrate on ways and means to improve the quality of exports. Copra shipped from Nukualofa, once the worst in the Pacific, is now among the best.

Every boy or girl is entitled to free elementary and advanced education in any one of Tonga's government-supported schools. In native colleges the boys grow all of their own food on college-maintained plantations, thus relieving their parents of the burden.

Tongan men as well as women wear skirts called *valas*. Of uniformly fine physique, they enjoy better health standards than other Pacific islanders. The kingdom has modern medical and hospital facilities by which every Tongan is entitled to free medical attention from the islanders' own well-trained doctors without any of the restrictions and reservations that are usually tacked on to socialized medical plans. As a result of health education and increasing adjustment to modern conditions the traditional thatched-roof, reed-walled, earthen-floor *fales* (houses) are being replaced by small wooden cottages with glass windows and metal roofs.

Through the initiative of Premier H.R.H. Prince Tungi much attention is presently being given to the development of a tuna-fishing industry and to the education of young Tongans in modern vocational techniques. The premier refuses to contract with any of the big trading firms for his kingdom's total copra output and seeks each year for the highest prices and for new ways to process a larger amount locally.

In opening the 1960 Legislature Prince Tungi said, "we should value more and retain firmly our peaceful way of life, as that is the only means by which a poor country like ours can survive. Let us not imitate questionable examples set from the outside, but let us hold on to our unity with renewed vigor."

On December 4 of that year Tonga had completed one hundred and sixteen years of progressive rule under a monarchy that might someday lead to a mature Polynesian democracy. A nation without poverty or riches, the frank and easy-mannered Tongans are in step with the times. Their confident way of life is opening up new horizons and higher standards of living. They are far ahead of much of the world in social legislation and it is doubtful whether there is a happier, more self-reliant people anywhere in the Pacific.

Solomon Islands

At the time Japan controlled the entire Pacific Ocean west of Midway to north of the Coral Sea and Tokyo Rose was demanding,

146

"Where are the United States Marines hiding?" Americans at home were finding out that the Solomons are a double row of large, lofty islands reaching out over nine hundred miles and looking like a convoy headed northwest.

Even the least informed of the several million Americans who were in the South Seas during World War II knew that there were no Sadie Thompsons or Shangri-Las in this area. But few realize even now that more lives and equipment were sacrificed by both sides for the control of the Solomons than ever before were lost in the history of modern warfare.

The Solomons are nearly twice as large as Hawaii, the fiftieth state, and their ten large islands and island clusters are still more primitive than much of Africa and one of the most hauntingly wild and beautiful places in the world.

The average GI who served in that area remembers above all Guadalcanal, an island considerably larger than the state of Delaware. He also remembers the Slot, a long narrow body of water that divides these islands. To tens of thousands of Americans Guadalcanal means mainly the northern slopes of the island with its Henderson Field, Bloody Ridge and the crocodile-infested Matanikau River. To seamen it usually means Savo Sound where Allied leadership miscalculated and an enemy assault force destroyed the backbone of Allied sea forces in less than an hour, inflicting the worst defeat in U. S. Naval history.

To others the Solomons could mean the Santa Cruz Group where cerebral malaria all but completely wiped out a large Army Engineers party sent to survey the area for airfields. Thousands remember the smoking volcano in Empress Augusta Bay and Piva on Bougainville Island where U. S. Forces were barraged into their only full-scale retreat of the war.

When the Solomons burst into world history few Americans knew of the decided differences between the Solomons, the New Hebrides, New Guinea and other Melanesian archipelagos. At the start of Operation Shoestring even the admirals and generals had faulty charts and information. Guadalcanal's first land battle was fought on the wrong river. Hard-bitten marines fought on the Ilu River which the top command thought was the Tenaru River.

Some of the finest assault troops in the world—the U. S. Marine Corps' First Division—learned how it felt to faulter under fire, to be left without supplies, to be reduced to eating captured enemy rice.

The U.S. drive from the Solomons up through New Britain and the Admiralties gets under way.

Several times in the long, bitter campaign Allied Forces averted complete disaster by the narrowest margin.

The decisive Allied victory known as the Battle of Guadalcanal was the greatest naval surface action since the Battle of Jutland in the first world war. Two weeks later in the final sea battle of the Solomons the Japanese were again defeated in a last desperate effort to maintain their sea lines to Guadalcanal. The long-embattled marines were finally relieved by fresh army units and on February 9, 1943, American forces completed the capture of Guadalcanal, bringing to an end the longest, most bitterly fought campaign of World War II. Naval losses on both sides were staggering, as were air and land casualties.

By the end of June the long-heralded Allied drive up through the Solomons began with the invasion of Rendova Island and New Georgia and the interception of the sleek destroyers of the "Tokyo

148

Express Line." It was near Rendova Island that President-to-be John F. Kennedy was nearly killed when his PT boat 109 was cut in half by a speedy Japanese destroyer. Despite serious injuries, Lieutenant Kennedy swam and towed injured members of his crew to the half of the PT boat that remained afloat, and later swam out into the strait with a torch to summon help.

At Munda U. S. forces were landed too far from their objective and had to fight unnecessarily through dense, fever-infested jungle, flooded rivers and the steel-jacketed enemy. Despite the miscalculations of their generals American GIs grimly fought their way up the Slot, jumping finally to Vella Lavella and Empress Augusta Bay. To gain two hundred and fifty miles in the Central Solomons it took nine months of the toughest fighting in the Pacific.

To aid the "Big fella-white-master" countless Solomon Islanders gave services beyond reckoning. "Boys belong bush"—primitives out of the Stone Age—saved hundreds of Americans from almost certain death. They built roads and landing strips and even helped erect palm-thatched churches for American troops. Their canoe transport, bush lore and ability to track through impenetrable jungle was of the greatest value.

Many brave, outstanding leaders like Solomon Sergeant Vouza refused under repeated torture and bayoneting to reveal American secrets to the enemy. More than a few paid with their lives for their staunch loyalty to the Allied cause.

Differing greatly in physical appearance, the people of the Solomons range in size from the tiny pygmies of the southern islands to the huge black Malaita men of Bougainville Straits. In color they vary from the isolated brown Polynesians of Rennell, Sikaiana, Tikopia, Ontong Java and the Reef Islands through the darker people of Guadalcanal, Malaita, Santa Cruz and Ysabel to the handsome, blue-black New Georgia, Choiseul, and Bougainville Straits Islanders. More than thirty different dialects are spoken throughout the Group.

Only a small percentage of islanders are mission, government or plantation "boys." Most of the people continue to live in coastal or jungle villages and are indifferent to outside activities. Luck and "magic" to a large extent control their whole life. After their conversion to Christianity many continue to propitiate the old and numerous evil spirits just to keep on the safe side all around.

Stone-Age economics and rituals are little changed even in lowland outposts where calico, iron tools and Christianity prevail. The growing of yams, taro, plantains and coconuts, fishing and the raising of pigs are still the bases of the Solomon Islanders' economy.

Paid employment is not generally regarded as a means of livelihood, but as a temporary way to acquire the means of social prestige in home communities. The "finish-time boy" in his calico lava-lava who has completed his labor indenture returns proudly to his home village with a small wooden chest filled with tobacco sticks, several clay pipes, colored calico, a blanket or two, knives, matches, peroxide, bracelets and curios—a "sophisticated" individual.

A few miles of lowland or mountain comprise the area of a tribe. Some villages are separated by dense brush pierced sparsely by narrow paths or by streams which after a sudden deluge of tropic rain become flooded and impassable. A village of low huts with bamboo walls and thatch roof is generally enclosed by jungle.

In bush villages one's garden is sacred and taboo to outsiders. Pigs root and snuffle in the damp areas. It is now a criminal offense for islanders to allow pigs to sleep in their houses. Rough fences have to be continually built to keep wild pigs from newly cultivated areas. The soil is quickly depleted and each year new plots of jungle forest have to be cleared and yams, sweet potatoes and bananas newly planted. Weeds must be constantly tilled. There is no season of leisure. Such a life is not conducive to easy laughter and most Solomonese subsistence farmers are quiet, serious-minded and often brooding.

The rich soil and heavy rainfall have blanketed parts of the larger islands with rain forests and large swamp areas where millions of orchids and screaming cockatoos are found. Many smaller islands are a mass of dense, parasitic rain jungles and shrubs with an occasional glistening white sand beach. With the oppressive heat and torrential rainfall in the southern and central Solomons, malaria, dysentery and blackwater fever continue to take their toll.

Alvaro de Mendana discovered the Group in 1567. Naming one of the largest islands Ysabel after his young wife, he called the archipelago "The Islas de Solomonis," hoping that such a title would entice future Spanish settlers into the Group on the supposition that they were the fabulous land where King Solomon obtained his wealth in gold and jewels. Because of the uncertainties and inaccuracies of early navigation, other Spaniards failed to locate the main Group and even Mendana was unable to find the islands again twenty-seven years later.

Mendana's ruthless expedition left a wake of blood that was taken up by whalers and blackbirders. White traders seeking trepang and sandalwood aided and encouraged head-hunting, often favoring one head-hunting chief against the other and supplying him with better arms to do the job. More than sixty thousand Solomon Islanders were shanghaied, blackbirded and later recruited in shipload lots to work as virtual slaves in Queensland until the human labor traffic was stopped in 1903.

Nearly half of the Protectorate's present population of about one hundred and twenty thousand live on Malaita, a torrid, weirdly-beautiful island that was formerly the most dangerous in the Pacific for head-hunting rivalries and cannibalism. Today in a day's walk on dark, brooding Malaita one can still pass through three or more different village areas speaking languages as different and as little understood to each other as Korean or Hindustani is to the average American.

At the time Japan was invading the islands Solomon Islanders were amazed to see their former white masters fleeing for their lives before the Japanese. They also were surprised to see them desert their Chinese neighbors—including women and children—at Tulagi. They never forgot those first impressions even when the situation was reversed. Later when they saw American Negroes driving jeeps and bulldozers they quickly learned to become good truck drivers and offered their services wholeheartedly. They also became aware of ideas and outside standards through close contact with liberal-minded American GIs. American humor, generosity and material things impressed them more in one year than fifty years of colonial rule ever did.

After 1945, with their views of white superiority greatly altered, the rugged Malaitaians and other islanders organized a strong anti-European movement called the "Marching Rule." They refused to pay taxes or take orders from the British and threatened to keep them off their land. As a result of their repeated defiance a destroyer was sent to the Group, but it was not until 1959 that the authorities were able to report that the "Marching Rule" (called by some wags Marxian Rule) influence was gone.

Taking the view that it is better to be too early than too late, the administration late in 1960 took the first step along the path toward self-government for the Solomons with the establishment of a local Legislative Council that included six Solomonese members. At the present rate of progress in the Group it is expected that full self-rule will take another half century or more.

In 1955 gold was discovered at Gold Ridge on Guadalcanal only twenty-two miles from Honiara. Since that time the lure of gold has continued to draw outsiders to the Solomons. After nearly four centuries there is a good chance that Mendana's prophetic title may yet come into its own.

Regardless of mineral wealth or its major exports of copra, trochus shell, timber and green snails, the Solomons and Guadalcanal in particular will always remain one of the most remembered names in American history. Over a hundred major warships lie rusting at the bottom of Iron Bottom Sound, including several aircraft carriers and nineteen heavy cruisers. Many brave members of their crews remain there too.

New air service direct from Fiji is expected to open up the Solomons as an entirely new travel route and an up-and-coming tourist attraction.

"We have a lot to offer here," says A. C. Blair, vice-chairman of the Honiara town council. "The war history alone will bring people in." Honiara plans a tourist bus to some of the wartime sites, including a few of the wrecks piled up along the Guadalcanal coast.

Today the Quonset-hut look is gone from the clean, attractive capital, and well-designed buildings are appearing. With its beautiful flame trees, scenic ridges, prevalent sea breezes which keep the mosquitoes away and a fine spirit of hospitality, Honiara may soon become a tourist stopover. "Do you know where the Solomons are?" will be a popular travel slogan, according to the plans of Honiara businessmen.

Larger aircraft can now arrive at Munda and Henderson airfields, and it is expected that the whir of turbojets will soon be heard over villages where today surplus U. S. Army helmets are still being used as cooking pots.

The Gilbert and Ellice Islands Colony

The Gilbert and Ellice Islands Colony is the only territory in the world that sits astride both the equator and the International Date Line.

Three hundred miles northeast of the Marshalls, the sixteen Gilbert islands and atolls form a five-hundred-mile connecting arc between Micronesia and Polynesia. Two hundred and fifty miles farther south, the five atolls and four islands of the tiny Ellice Archipelago complete the southern and easternmost end of the Micronesian chain.

Composed of narrow sand and coral land strips five to more than fifty miles in length, both Groups are dominated by the green and white world of the atoll. There are always the pounding surf, the living reef, the stretch of sand, coco palms, corrugated tin roof shanties and the big, whitewashed churches. Inside the shimmering lagoon are tiny *motus* (islets), coral gardens, sea birds, reflections of clouds and unnamed greens and blues.

The gay and exuberant Polynesians of the Ellice Islands are very different from the reserved Gilbertese. As a result of the fusion of Samoan and Tongan invaders the gentle Ellice Islanders are a large, light-skinned people, while their more numerous Micronesian neighbors, the Gilbertese, are a lean, vigorous race smaller in stature and speaking a language closely related to Melanesian.

Although light skins have darkened with each generation, there are still many traces of early American and British paternity scattered throughout the Ellices and Gilberts. On Funafuti, a few years ago, there were several dozen native O'Briens among the island's small population.

Forty-five thousand people now crowd these narrow strips of coral that are never more than fifteen feet above the sea. With most islands heavily overpopulated, the struggle for sufficient soil to produce the barest essentials of survival is a continual one. Except for coconut and pandanus trees nothing grows easily in the two main Groups. The islanders depend almost entirely on coconuts, pandanus, taro, fish and shell food. On those islands containing a few breadfruit trees the soil has to be carefully tended and mixed with powdered pumice. One of the most esteemed foods of the sporting Gilbertese is the red flesh of the tiger shark, and esteem usually rises in proportion to the shark's ferociousness and the attendant danger of getting it.

In the northern Ellices and southerly Gilberts, overpopulation is especially acute in relation to the available food-producing land area. The people have frequently suffered from hunger and dire thirst when prolonged droughts have killed all sources of food and drink, including the pandanus and coconut trees.

The first white man to live among the people of the Gilberts was considered a god and carried about on the shoulders of the natives for the first few months. Later, he introduced them to the use of firearms, encouraged warfare and—with the arrival of other whites —fell from grace via the "coconut toddy road."

Native warfare was incited and prolonged by reckless whites, many of whom were fugitives from American and British prisons. By the middle of the nineteenth century these renegade beach-combers were so actively engaged in fighting and promoting murderous attacks among rival groups that the native name for a white man became "the killer."

After the islands had been held in part by natives, missionaries and white beachcombers for nearly a hundred years, Great Britain obtained possession of what is now known as the Gilbert and Ellice Crown Colony by a long series of protectorate proclamations and "Orders in Council," all of which eventually amounted to the same thing: outright annexation. As Rosamond Rhone, an early British writer, expressed it, "A protectorate is the camel's nose in the tent. When he gets his head in and his hump, it becomes a colony."

As missionary influence spread throughout the Group there was more than a little resentment among the island women against wearing that singular missionary-designed garb, the Mother Hubbard gown.

Robert Louis Stevenson stated, while residing in the Gilberts, that "the mind of the female missionary tends to be continually busied about dress. She can be taught with extreme difficulty to think any costume decent but that to which she grew accustomed on Clapham Common, and to gratify this prejudice the native is put to useless expense, his mind is tainted with the morbidities of Europe and his health is set in danger. He is told no song, no dance, no tobacco, no liquor, no alleviative of life—only toil and church going."

Contrarily, one of the early missionaries declared, "It is wonderful what the Gospel does for them. In their heathen state they have few wants; nature is bountiful and they gather the coconuts, eat, sleep and have a good time. When they become Christians, they want clothing, and there is only one way to get it, that is, to go to work. The coconuts must be gathered and dried to sell to the traders. The teachers encourage them to plant taro and other foods, and thus much work is done. They buy all their books, and these must be paid for; so little by little they learn to work, and there is nothing like work to keep a man or woman out of sin."

At least two of the native kings, fearing that missionary influence would undermine their own powers, refused to allow missionaries to enter their island kingdoms. When one of them insisted on landing, King Tem Binoka, "the terror of the Gilberts," quickly learned how to read and gleaned as much information as he could about Christianity. Then, after obtaining several copies of the Bible, the wily king took care of what he considered two evils at once: ordering the missionary to leave his own kingdom, he persuaded him to go to the islands of his bitterest enemy.

In explaining the Bible to his subjects, King Tem Binoka mentioned only passages that were likely to inspire them to produce more copra and to look to him as an oracle of wisdom and supreme advice.

Hearing of the many evils and the strange things of the outside lands, the king of Kuria, one of the lesser monarchs under Tem Binoka, set forth on a voyage "around the world." After sailing for several months to all the islands of the Gilberts, the king returned home a disillusioned monarch, convinced that the Bible "had lied" and the world was "all the same."

When Robert Louis Stevenson sailed aboard the chartered schooner *Equator* for the "kingdom of Abemama, Aranuka and Kuria" he went amply supplied with gifts of beads, mouth organs, colored ribbon, umbrellas, blue spectacles and five-cent cigars for fat King Tem Binoka.

Dreaded and feared by all men, white or brown, His Majesty Tem Binoka discouraged outsiders from setting foot within his domain and made friends with but two white men in his lifetime. They were Robert Louis Stevenson and Bully Hayes, whom he called the "Big Captain."

Stevenson wrote, "There is but one great personage in the Gilberts: Tembinok' of Abemama; soley conspicuous, the hero of song, the butt of gossip." A ruler "with a beaked profile like Dante's in the mask and a voice that matched it well, being shrill, powerful and uncanny, with a note like a sea bird's."

Distrustful of white men and of the rotting hulls of most South Sea trading schooners, Tem Binoka always had his men lash a large, outriggerlike structure to the hull of a foreign ship before he would go aboard to inspect the trade room. He weighed four hundred pounds and became so fat he was barely able to walk and on occasion, when a ship was in, or during inspection, it took from six to ten men to carry him about.

When told by a captain one afternoon of Columbus's and Magellan's great voyages of discoveries, the king spent almost the entire night perusing the Bible by candlelight. At the break of dawn, having found no reference to either explorer in the New Testament (translated in Gilbertese), he felt certain of his facts and declared that the captain had "lied again."

A firm believer in hard work for commoners, King Tem Binoka kept his subjects constantly employed making copra and coconut oil and fishing for bêche-de-mer in order to maintain a favorable trade balance and keep up his wholesale purchases.

The welcome mat was always out for supercargoes who brought something new. Naval uniforms, music boxes, dress suits and black alpaca coats were purchased in large quantities. The king's vanity never permitted him to stint in anything, regardless of the poor condition of his people. When confronted with a new object he never considered any price too high, but would simply order his subjects to work harder until the thing was paid for.

When in the right mood Tem Binoka would distribute a large share of his purchases among favorite subjects, always certain of winning them back at poker on the following day. Since one of his kingly prerogatives was the privilege of dealing himself two hands to the other players' one, he never failed to win.

In addition to handling all the official affairs of the kingdom, Tem Binoka managed all trade and shipping matters, was judge and executioner, acted as island architect, kept an historical journal and devoted a considerable amount of time to composing island songs and poetry about "sweethearts, trees and the sea." The local choir performed his works.

There were a number of colorful monarchs in the Gilbert and Ellice Groups besides Tem Binoka. Long after the islands came under white domination they retained much of their distrust and a good deal of suspicion of the white man's veracity.

Old King Karaiti of Makin, upon hearing about the first airplanes from a trader, set about making himself some huge wings; and when they were finished he strapped them to his shoulders and launched himself out over the end of the local pier. He fell ignominiously into the sea and several of his wives had to swim out and rescue him from nearly drowning in a tangle of wing lines. Upon

156

reaching shore the king rose to his full height and bellowed to all his subjects that the "damn white trader had lied again," since flying was obviously impossible.

News of such local antics spread widely, and in time both Groups became facetiously known as the "Gilbert and Sullivans" among the officials and foreign consuls of many tropical ports.

Several of the kings—men like Tem Binoka and Tebureimoa— were capable, outstanding leaders. While on occasion their antics seemed and were ludicrous, as Robert Louis Stevenson has pointed out, they were no more so than those of a good many whites, including more than a few prominent European officials.

In 1897, a supercargo in the employ of the Pacific Islands Company visited the Gilberts and on his return to Australia took back a large piece of island rock "because of its strange markings." The rock was found on the German island of Nauru, which later became part of the Ellices and Gilberts and is now a United Nations' Trusteeship under Australian rule.

Placed in a corner of the company office, the rock remained for many months gathering dust and in the summer was used as a door prop. Albert F. Ellis, a man of wide experience with island guano, noticed the rock one day while employed in the company laboratory and remarked that it certainly looked to him like phosphate.

Others scoffed at the idea, but the young chemist persisted and the door prop was finally broken up and analyzed. The test revealed that the rock contained eighty percent pure phosphate of lime, the richest ever known.

Sailing at once for Ocean Island, because of its closeness and similarity to German-held Nauru, the "discoverer" surveyed the island and found that it too was entirely composed of almost pure phosphate!

The isolation and fresh water lakes on these two high coral atolls once attracted great flocks of sea birds and in time both islands became sanctuaries. With billions of birds nesting in the crevices and ledges, after thousands of years their leavings filled the vales and rose above the highest pinnacles forming large guano plateaus. When the last of the fresh water pools and lakes were filled the birds went elsewhere. The phosphoric acid of guano and the coralline lime in time became a phosphate of lime rock, one of the most valuable fertilizers known.

Mr. Ellis and his associates, quick to realize that they had stum-

157

bled onto millions of tons of high-grade fertilizer, made an agreement with the island chiefs for the sole right to remove the phosphate and a British warship was dispatched to raise the Union Jack over the "billion dollar island" two hundred and fifty miles west of the Gilberts.

Ocean Island and Nauru are for their size the richest islands in the South Pacific. It is estimated they have over a hundred million tons of the highest grade phosphate of lime valued at well over a billion dollars. Nominally both islands are still under native ownership and the Nauruans and Ocean Islanders, called Banabans, are paid a few cents royalty for each ton of superphosphate.

Immediately after the Pearl Harbor debacle Japan occupied Apaiang, Marakei and Butaritari, the most northerly of the Gilberts. Later they took Tarawa and Abemama. Their planes repeatedly bombed Nauru and Ocean Islands, and late in 1942 both of these "billion dollar" phosphate islands were occupied, as was Christmas Island.

It was feared Japan might extend its conquests through the Ellice and Phoenix Islands to Samoa and the Fijis. Such a move would have effectively prevented the American convoys from getting through to Australia and New Zealand. As it was, Japanese planes and submarines based in the Gilberts were in an advantageous position for forays against Allied convoys. It was imperative that their advance be stopped at the Gilbert end of their eastward penetration.

Early in 1943 Funafuti, the capital and principal port of the Ellice Group, became an American advance base; and toward the end of the year American sea and air power was marshalled in sufficient strength to begin the long-heralded Central Pacific offensive. With the Gilbert Islands first on the list of strategic objectives, Tarawa Atoll—especially Betio Island—was subjected to severe pre-invasion bombardment.

On November 21, 1943, the first wave of marines from the Second Division fought their way ashore over the coral flats on the lagoon side of Betio at the southwest corner of Tarawa. But tidal calculations were wrong, H-hour was missed, and the marines were caught between a devastating enemy cross fire as they struggled across the reefs. Despite the previous naval bombardment Japanese resistance was so tough that few got through. By nightfall of the first day the marines were still fighting waist-deep in water toward a beachhead that remained a twenty-foot-wide toe hold. The invasion had to be postponed until heavy naval gunfire had further reduced enemy strength.

While the marines on Tarawa were experiencing some of the hardest fighting of World War II the 165th Infantry swept ashore in Amtracs at Butaritari on Makin Atoll and quickly dislodged the Japanese defenders there.

The enemy commander at Betio Atoll had boasted that his narrow island couldn't be taken in a hundred years; all of the Gilberts were taken in less than a week. But the price was high. In the desperate seventy-six hour struggle for Tarawa three thousand American lives were lost.

Where hundreds of thatched Gilbertese homes had once been, thousands of tents and Quonset huts arose. Airstrips were cleared through coconut groves. Plantations became large athletic fields, open-air theatres and supply areas. New piers and hard-packed roads were built. Most of the things that go to make an American standard of living were brought in and Tarawa became one of the most powerful naval and air bases in the Central Pacific.

The islanders soon learned how to drive jeeps and steam rollers, and how to take care of water purifiers and operate motion picture machines. In addition to working for the occupation forces they set up their own laundries and went into mass production of curios and handiwork.

Co-operative societies now operate on every island and on occasion effective boycotts have been maintained against British trading firms. Previously, islanders sold their copra output to the local white trader, who in turn sold to the shipper, and from the shipper it was bought by the various foreign buyers. By handling the direct sale of their own copra and eliminating the relatively large profits of the middlemen, the Ellice and Gilbert Islanders receive a worthwhile incentive toward getting the maximum production from their plantations.

Strong family and community ties lend themselves readily to co-operative trading societies. These societies, having had a hard struggle during the formative years, when the price of copra was extremely low, emerged successfully and now handle practically all of the copra produced as well as retail trade goods. Thus, native enterprise has eliminated most of the white traders from both Groups.

At present the population of the Colony is steadily increasing and severe problems of overcrowding are being met by moving and re-settling large groups of Gilbert Islanders on distant islands, including the Fijis and the Phoenix Islands. Late in 1958 a settlement of Gil-bertese people were resettled on Gizo in the Solomons.

The Gilbertese and the Ellice people have evolved an advanced and very successful form of government requiring a minimum amount of British supervision. Both Groups are encouraged to re-tain their own material culture and have been given a large measure of self-rule. It is the professed aim of the administration to grant them eventually the right to govern themselves entirely.

The airstrips built by the United States in the Ellice and Gilbert Islands have all been planted over with coconuts, except one on Tarawa, the commercial center of the Colony. And although is-landers remember, a bit wistfully, the steam rollers, GI rations, chocolate bars and American dollars, all know that they are vastly better off today with a copra and pandanus economy so long as their windswept atolls remain a tranquil world of reef and palm.

Besides its two main archipelagos, the Gilbert and Ellice Islands Colony includes Ocean Island, the Phoenix Group and the three detached islands of Fanning, Washington and Christmas.

The Phoenix Group, about five hundred miles northeast of the Ellice, are eight low coral islands—most of which were discovered by Americans—situated on the direct route between Hawaii and Fiji. The development of transpacific aviation brought these land specks into international importance in a dispute between the United States and Britain over their use as bases for commercial air lines.

In 1939 a settlement was reached placing Canton and Ender-bury Islands under a fifty-year joint American-British control. Since 1958 long-range aircraft fly past Canton but the island remains of importance because of its emergency landing facilities. The remain-ing islands, Hull, Gardner, McKean, Birnie, Sydney and Phoenix, are governed by the British.

Fanning, Washington and Christmas Islands are east of the Gil-berts and directly south of Hawaii. All three have large coconut plantations worked by Gilbert Islanders.

The Abbé Rougier of Papeete, Tahiti, who was sent out from France to save the souls of South Sea Islanders, organized a syndi-cate that controlled for many years most of Fanning, Washington

160

and Christmas, where he made a large fortune in copra. In 1947 Britain canceled the lease held on Christmas Island by the estate of Father Rougier.

Six-by-twelve-mile Fanning Island was discovered in 1798 by Captain Edmund Fanning, of the American ship *Betsy*. It was also named American Island by Captain Mather, a Yankee whaler. Seventy-four years later the island was declared a British possession, and in 1902 it became an important connecting link in the long British-owned cable extending from British Columbia to Fanning and to Fiji and the Antipodes.

Washington Island, which was once called New York Island, is about seventy-five miles northwest of Fanning. It was discovered by Captain Edmund Fanning in 1798 and named by him after George Washington. Nine miles in circumference by less than ten feet high, Washington is owned by Fanning Island Plantations Ltd., a British concern which also owns Fanning.

Christmas Island, so named because it was discovered by Captain James Cook on Christmas Eve, 1777, lies slightly over a hundred miles north of the equator and eleven hundred and sixty miles south of Honolulu. Extending one hundred miles in circumference, with a forty-four-mile lagoon, it is by far the largest island in this area.

Often visited by New England whalers, Christmas was first occupied and later claimed for the United States by Yankee guano diggers. In 1859 it was bonded by the government as an American guano island. Commander Meade of the U.S.S. *Narragansett* visited the island in 1872, and finding three Americans in occupation, took formal possession for the United States. Sixteen years later, Great Britain claimed Christmas Island in disregard of American claims and protests, and in 1919 the island was declared a part of the Gilbert and Ellice Colony.

Located on the direct airline between Honolulu and the Antipodes, Christmas Island's large protected lagoon became increasingly valuable as a seaplane base with the development of transpacific air travel. In 1936 the United States sharply questioned British claims. A few months after the American protests Britain, refusing to relinquish its claim to Christmas, sent a warship to the island and placed a permanent resident-observer ashore.

In 1956, after one hundred and eighty years of relative obscurity, Christmas Island came into world prominence with its sudden build-up as a modern British naval air base and nuclear testing station. The harbor has been greatly enlarged by dredging, as has the channel leading to the sea. A large steel piling dock and piers for small craft have been constructed. As part of the extensive nuclear project a seven-thousand-foot airstrip with twenty-five miles of roads have been built with all the facilities of a small modern town, including quarters for two thousand men.

Malden Island

Malden Island, which was of some importance during the British nuclear tests in 1957, is at present uninhabited, as are the other four British Line Islands of Starbuck, Caroline, Vostok and Flint.

Pitcairn Island

Ironically, the first British settlement in the South Seas on what might properly be called an island was made by the *Bounty* mutineers in 1790. Today lonely Pitcairn, located about halfway between Australia and South America, is Great Britain's smallest and most remote inhabited possession.

Pitcairn and nearby Oeno, Henderson and Ducie comprise what is known as the Pitcairn Island District. These four small islands and Chile's mystery island of Easter, farther east, are almost the only bits of land in the entire western half of the Pacific Ocean.

Late in 1960 a 250-watt modern radio station was activated and manned by young Pitcairner Thomas Christian to maintain contact with administration headquarters for the District which are at Suva, Fiji, three thousand miles away.

After the well-known mutiny of Fletcher Christian and his men against the tyrannical Lieutenant Bligh, the mutineers sailed to Tahiti where Christian discovered, in the ship's library, an account of the discoveries made by Captain Carteret. Among them was considerable mention of an isolated, mountainous island two square miles in area and about a thousand feet high that Carteret had named Pitcairn after the midshipman who first sighted it.

Fearing retaliation and capture by a British warship, Christian and eight of his followers, with six Tahitian men and twelve island girls, sailed from Tahiti for distant Pitcairn in H.M.S. *Bounty*. Finding the island even more inviting than Carteret's description had led them to expect, they removed everything from the *Bounty* and she was run onto the reef and burned.

The settlers could hardly have chosen a more appropriate spot anywhere else in the Pacific. In addition to its isolation, the island was without a harbor, lagoon, or any means of safe anchorage, and therefore unlikely to attract other settlers or white vessels. For nearly two decades they remained completely cut off from the rest of the world.

They divided the island into nine portions, one for each of the mutineers, but after two years of peace and happiness fighting broke out among the men, occasioned by drinking and jealousy over the Tahitian girls. Eight years later, at the end of a reign of terror, all of the native men and all but one of the mutineers were dead, most of them killed during fighting.

In 1800, John Adams, the sole survivor, finding himself alone on Pitcairn with twenty-five young women and children, underwent a remarkable reformation. Deciding that his only hope of salvation lay in saving the souls of the living, he brought forth from his sea chest a long-forgotten copy of the *Book of Common Prayer* and used it as a textbook to instruct the children in the rudiments of reading and writing. Later he taught them simple songs, and aided by the lonely Tahitian widows, convinced them of the advantages of sobriety and peaceful living. From the time of John Adams' reformation, the colony prospered and multiplied. The Bible and prayer book taken from the *Bounty* by the original mutineers is still used today on the island.

Contrary to the general belief, inbreeding has not resulted in physical or mental degeneration here. Today's descendants of the *Bounty* mutineers are a very healthy, fine people. As a result of over-population and resettlement, about six hundred former Pitcairners now live on Norfolk, an island territory of Australia that lies half-way between New Zealand and New Caledonia.

Though formally under the British High Commission, the island-ers have been left to control their own affairs through a local council with a president and vice-president. The former also acts as chief magistrate. Under their self-governing, partly communal way of life, boatbuilding, salt harvesting, house construction and farming are co-operative enterprises. About half of their twelve hundred moun-tainous acres are cultivated. Goats and poultry are plentiful and the fertile soil with a fine climate produces excellent yams, melons, sugar, oranges, bananas, pineapples and coffee.

This lonely island was one of the first places in the world to have compulsory education. Pitcairn boys in khaki shorts with shirts and young girls in green pinafores with white blouses now go to a completely modern school paid for by the sale of postage stamps depicting the mutiny on the *Bounty*.

Adamstown, with its seventy corrugated tin roofs and weatherboard houses, has a present population of about one hundred and fifty, all of whom are Seventh Day Adventists.

Chapter Six

AUSTRALIA'S TERRITORY OF

PAPUA AND NEW GUINEA

In 1960 when Premier Nikita Khrushchev called upon Australia to give immediate independence and self-government to the nearly two million people of New Guinea few Americans were aware that a human head was still a coveted trophy in several parts of New Guinea.

Thousands of former GIs who fought on land and sea to save Australia by saving New Guinea know that this second-largest and least-explored island in the world is about as long as from New York City to Denver—a land of great beauty and riches, of billions of mosquitoes, countless crocodiles, leeches, green tree pythons, and bumblebees that can drill holes larger than a man's thumb through wooden posts.

It cost the United States thousands of lives and billions of dollars in air and naval power to recover the Territory of Papua and New Guinea embracing the eastern half of the main island (the western half is Dutch New Guinea) and including eight hundred nearby islands, most important of which are Buka, Bougainville and the Bismarck Archipelago.

Americans who sweated and shivered with malaria and jungle itch as they crawled and fought across the tangled trails of thirteen-thousand-foot mountain ranges came to know the impenetrable jungles, blood-sucking flies, swollen rivers, great gorges and the towering white clouds of the awesome Owen Stanley Mountains. Those who were at Salamaua, Lae and Finschhafen, and the unsung heroes of Hollandia and Biak, saw New Guinea at its worst. Despite all this and much more—despite the intense heat, strange diseases such as the "laughing death," for which there is no known cure, and the lack of roads (few roads are safe for vehicles without four-wheel drive)—the Australian government still receives many letters from Americans interested in settling somewhere in this vast frontier where the Stone Age rubs shoulders with the twentieth century.

It is startling to a traveler to hear "Cock o' the North" being played to the skirl of bagpipes in a hot tropical town, but an old New Guinea hand knows that the pipers and drummers of the Pacific Islands Regiment Pipe Band are coming up the road. The traveler of today who is greeted by modern lap-lap clad Papuans and offered cool drinks and local-grown peanuts at Port Moresby's Jackson Airport and who watches these handsome people play cricket and soccer barefooted with as much skill and enthusiasm as Americans or Britons, finds it hard to believe that the interior of this island that does over a hundred million dollar import-export business is the last stronghold of the stone tool and the root-and-grub people.

Most known to outsiders are the rapidly increasing coastal Papuans and the air-minded Highlanders who are sufficiently advanced to have their own government councils and are developing coconut, coffee, peanut and cocoa plantations equal to European standards. Many sophisticated Papuans of Port Moresby and Rabaul have discarded their blue and red lap-laps for European dress of shirts and shorts. Some have small trucking or gardening businesses; others drive taxis or are carpenters, stevedores, medical practitioners, teachers or administrative assistants. These advanced people are still a very small percentage of the total population of the Territory, most of whom live behind or within a barrier of almost impenetrable mountains and are just beginning to emerge from a primitive society where some villagers still chop off a finger joint to express sorrow at a relative's death.

Papuans who became truck drivers, carriers, trackers and machete-men for the Allied Forces liked the free and easy spirit of the Americans. They also liked GI rations, and said so in beach-la-mar: "Belly belong me—fella 'e sing out." Despite the limitations of pidgin English they heard about "Stateside" life and about Rusefel (Roosevelt), the friendly King of America. They even learned something about the Boston Tea Party and the battles of Gettysburg and Bunker Hill.

U. S. wartime "magic from the sea" has been kept alive in the minds of some coastal people by cult leaders. In August 1960, several hundred villagers waited on the coast near Rabaul, New Britain, for a submarine which they had been told would take them on a voyage to the United States. After a day of peering seaward through a "bamboo belong look-look" (boy scout telescope) for the dream-boat that never arrived, Leonard the leader explained finally that the "ship-walk-along-bottom he got sore leg belong engine. He go back long way too much, thas' all," meaning that the submarine had developed engine trouble and turned back.

Early in 1961 an administration officer took custody of a collection of sorcerer's charms that included six eggs in a basket that the people of Watom Island asserted were landed from a U. S. submarine and in due time would hatch into American soldiers.

During the crucial period of the Kokoda campaign, when the Australian mainland was gravely threatened, the native people of the Territory of Papua and New Guinea rendered priceless service to the Allied cause. For many long months they labored over the little-known trails of the Owen Stanley Range with desperately needed supplies and on the return trip carried the wounded up and down the steep mountain sides on improvised stretchers. Their aid to

Nanabe Waki, a headman from the Western New Guinea Highlands, makes an important policy speech on election day.

Allied scouting parties and stranded airmen was invaluable. Without it, in some areas it would have been all but impossible for Allied troops to operate successfully. As a result they became widely known in Australia as "fuzzy-wuzzy angels."

The name of Golpak, a wise and courageous native of New Britain, became a byword among Australian and American troops. Golpak sheltered hundreds of GIs, smuggled them to safety and established a highly effective espionage system. Scores of other "Fuzzy-wuzzy Commandos," as they were affectionately called, carried wounded pilots through many miles of matted forest jungle and saved the lives of hundreds of Americans.

The war had very little effect on the remote mountain areas where a hard-working bride can still be purchased for several axes and possum pelts and some bird-of-paradise plumes. In some inland districts sorcery is still a common cause of death. When a native learns that a sorcerer has cast the evil eye on him—called "pointing the bone"—he frequently falls into an agony of terror which quickly undermines his health. Unable to eat or sleep, the terrified person quite often dies unless the voodoo man is placated.

In island courts when a Papuan is found guilty of murder and proves his act was justified by his deepest beliefs—traditional tribal custom—he is at most "sentenced to death," which usually means that he will spend a few years in jail learning new ways.

Tribal customs as well as art traditions are extremely varied. Ocher dyes, boars' tusks, shells and bird-of-paradise feathers are used for personal adornment and as status symbols. In preparing for ceremonial dances those who now live near trade centers and airfields find it much simpler to decorate themselves with a shilling's worth of store paint than to prepare natural pigments and ocher dyes laboriously from local materials.

The head-hunters of the upper Sepik always exerted the utmost care in preserving the heads of victims to retain what they believed to be the true beauty of the deceased. Not until the skull was properly "cured" was it given a place of honor on the family trophy pole. Grotesque wood carvings of human figures and faces still dominate Sepik River art and are eagerly sought by discriminating art collectors around the world.

Today's head-hunters live mostly in the swampy country along the riverbanks of the central part of the south coast of Dutch New Guinea, where they seek heads for religious and ceremonial purposes. The head-hunting season starts in June and is carried out in swift raids by canoemen who can paddle forty-eight hours on end when necessary to escape with their victims. A few enterprising, broad-minded missionaries have in some instances been able to convince villagers in this area to substitute "special" coconuts for heads in their ceremonies but the Dutch authorities are powerless to curb head raids that occur far outside their patrol areas. Often they don't know about a raid until weeks or even months later and sometimes they never know.

Conditions are rapidly changing in this vast region. New native movements are under way. Recent developments in the Congo, South Africa and Southeast Asia have not lessened the uneasy feeling among many of the Territory's twenty thousand Europeans (mostly Anglo-Saxons) about the future status and rights of the 1,840,000 native inhabitants.

Who are these emerging people who vary so greatly, from the hook-nosed Sepik River people and gloomy Kiwais of the west to the gay, music-loving Bamus, to intelligent businessmen, capable farmers and sophisticated town people of Rabaul, Moresby, Lae and Madang? Why are they so different? Where did they come from and how did they get here?

Long before there was any movement from the Malay Peninsula toward Micronesia and Polynesia, at a time when the pre-Homeric traders were still timidly coasting along the eastern end of the Mediterranean, an Oceanic Negroid people crossed into the South Seas by way of New Guinea and the Bismarck Archipelago.

This was no mass exodus. It took thousands of years for the roving band of short-statured, frizzy-haired people to cross the straits from Malaya to Oceania and to wander from island to island throughout Melanesia. Some preferred the thick-forested areas where they could hunt with bow and arrow, while others chose to settle in the plains and to hunt with spears and boomerangs. One of the first animals they brought with them was the dingo, known to us as the domesticated dog.

The native people who now inhabit the Territory of Papua and New Guinea and the neighboring islands are mostly of Papuan, Melanesian and Negrito stock, each different in customs, language and appearance. On the larger islands Melanesians and Papuans predominate, with an intermixture of Micronesian strains in the Admiralties and of Polynesians on several of the smaller eastern islands.

169

Many of the Caucasian-featured, often bearded, Papuans have a decided Hebraic cast. They prefer to live in thousands of small tribal groups that have little to do with one another, and their habits and social characteristics are extremely varied. It is impossible to travel more than thirty miles in almost any direction without encountering two or more different languages.

The tall, round-headed, frizzy-haired Melanesians who inhabit the coastal and river regions are darker-skinned and slightly taller than the typical Papuans, especially those of the northern and eastern coastal areas. The Negrito mountain dwellers are a small, three-to-five-foot pygmy people with woolly hair and broad noses.

The discovery of New Guinea and its adjoining islands came about as a direct result of the famous Papal Bull which divided the Pacific Ocean and much of the rest of the world between Portugal and Spain. Drawn from north to south across the Pacific at about 147 degrees east longitude, the Pope's line ran through the Australian continent and the northeast portion of New Guinea, both of which were undiscovered at the time. Had the Papal edict been recognized by all powers, most of Australia and almost all of New Guinea would have become Portuguese territory.

France, England and Holland refused to recognize the Vatican treaty. The French King Francis caustically remarked that he "would like to see the clause in Adam's will, which gave to Spain and Portugal the right to divide the world between them."

Nevertheless, Spain and Portugal continued to vie with each other for the fabulous Spice Islands' trade, to the exclusion of everyone else. Thus it was that the Portuguese first reached New Guinea by the long route around Africa while the Spaniards came across the Pacific from Mexico and Peru.

In 1527 Jorge de Menezes came upon the western shores of New Guinea while seeking a new route from the Malay Archipelago to the eastern Spice Islands. Surprised at finding an island inhabited by a Negroid rather than a Malay people, Menezes named it Ilhas dos Papuas, from the Malay *papuwa*, meaning "frizzy-haired."

When the first white inhabitants of Britain's Botany Bay penal colony turned to New Guinea and its nearby islands as likely havens of escape, a number of them succeeded in a small way by claiming to be special protégés of King George, "the great white chief," who would severely punish anyone molesting their persons.

In 1826 an American naval officer asserted that the harassed governors of the penal colony were unable to cope with the problem of escapees, and referring to the convicts who had descended like a plague on the various islands, added that British sailing masters had orders "not to molest these scape gallows, who as soon as out of reach of the halter, are considered fit subjects for increasing His Majesty's influence and even for giving laws to the South Sea Islanders."

When gold was first found in the hills behind Port Moresby, the news spread like wildfire throughout Australia. The gold rush that followed ended in failure for many, but succeeded in further stimulating colonial interest in the possibilities of the huge island—an interest that was prompted in turn by strategic considerations, the need for cheap labor on the northern plantations and the trading and other commercial opportunities.

With the development of European plantations and gold mining properties, the demand for docile native labor compelled the government to sanction a system of indentured labor. In lush years the human labor traffic provided some recruiters with as much as twenty-five thousand dollars. Early methods employed by the least scrupulous included the bribing of local chiefs and conspiring with native sorcerers. Some went well armed with magic tricks, a skill in ventriloquism, rubber snakes, flashlights and a wide number of sleight-of-hand accessories that never failed to impress the islanders and to persuade them of future possibilities if they signed up as indentured laborers.

Through the imposition of a head tax on all able-bodied men, which most were unable to pay, many of the best young men found it necessary to sign contracts by which they were strictly bound to white masters for a period of three years. At the end of their indenture most islanders had little to show for their years of labor aside from having paid their head tax regularly.

At the outbreak of World War I an Australian naval squadron took over the largest and richest of Germany's Pacific possessions, including all of German New Guinea, the northern Solomons, the Admiralties and the Bismarck Archipelago.

Confronted at once with the language barrier and lacking intimate knowledge of local native customs, the Australians issued a proclamation announcing the change in pidgin English (beach-la-mar) as follows:

> You look him new feller flag, he belonga English, he
> more better than other feller. Suppose you work alonga

171

Translating pidgin English into the local Mt. Hagen language in New Guinea.

new feller master; he look out you get plenty good feller *kai kai* (food).

You no fight other feller black man!

You no *kai kai* (eat) man!

You no steal Mary (wife) belongina other feller black man!

Me been talk with you now, now you give three cheers belongina new feller master. No more um Kaiser. God save um King.

During the long discussions over former German New Guinea, Australia held that she was entitled to outright annexation; President Woodrow Wilson felt that the territories should be administered by an international body that would assure the development of the native people toward self-governing status. Aghast at such a proposal for Australia's newly-acquired islands, Prime Minister Hughes exclaimed, "Self-government for New Guinea! Why Mr. Wilson—they eat people, up there!"

172

When President Wilson offered an amendment on racial equality, proposing that the "League of Nations guarantee to all alien nationals equal and just treatment in every respect, making no distinction on account of their race or nationality," Premier Hughes, father of the "White Australia" policy, violently protested against the inclusion of any amendment advocating racial equality, "no matter how mild or inoffensive."

The early administration of the eastern half of New Guinea was complicated by the physical, almost impenetrable, barriers of the country, by the widely variant religious beliefs, and by the vast differences between civilized and primitive logic and justice.

During this period of Australian rule the most serious native offense was murder. The natives often looked upon it as "pay back" (revenge), a part of ritual, and sometimes as an act of courtesy and kindness. Island murderers, when brought before white magistrates, offered strange reasons that were perfectly understandable and excusable according to the tribal point of view. There was the man who killed his uncle because "the old man was not much good;" and the two who, when asked by a sick man for aid in crossing a river, promptly killed him because he was too heavy to carry over and yet it would have been discourteous to refuse aid. According to primitive native logic they simply erased his problem of crossing the river and put him out of his misery at the same time.

The great Sir Hubert Murray, Australia's outstanding administrator of this area from 1907 to 1940, stated, during the early part of his administration, "We cannot leave the Papuan as we found him, a Stone-Age savage, often a head-hunter and a cannibal. We should most decidedly not turn him into a third-rate white man; we must try to turn him into a better brown man than he was before."

In the remote districts a blanket and a shiny steel axe are often the most prized possessions of a man who formerly took three months to shape and sandstone-sharpen an axe out of stone. On coming under direct supervision, such people give only a negative acquiescence, meaning that they bow to government authority out of fear of punishment. The more advanced people of the coastal areas, who have been under European influence for many years, have attained a considerable understanding of modern ways and confidence in their own ability to know what is best.

In 1942, when Japanese armed forces stormed ashore, southeastern New Guinea became known as the Australian Pearl Harbor.

Progressive teacher-training class in Papua keeps its curriculum closely related to village life.

Within two months the invaders were firmly intrenched in such key ports as Rabaul, Finschhafen, Lae and Salamaua. In July they began an incredible march up along the Kokoda Trail, lugging their heavy mortars and field pieces over the difficult Owen Stanley Mountains toward Port Moresby.

The invaders quickly penetrated to within thirty miles of the southern shores and were facing the Australian continent less than three hundred miles away when halted by veteran Anzac divisions rushed home from the Middle East. Greatly aided by native troop carriers, guides and stretcher-bearers, the Australians slowly pushed the Nipponese back to the northeast coast of New Guinea.

While American and Australian divisions were struggling slowly northwest along the coast from Buna and Gona into the Huon Gulf to attack Japanese bases at Lae and Salamaua, American aircraft subjected Rabaul and other bases to heavy bombardment. By 1944 the danger of an invasion of Australia had passed and the remaining

Japanese bases in New Guinea, the Bismarck Archipelago and the northern Solomons were neutralized.

The Commonwealth Government freed all native people from the yoke of indenture as a token of gratitude for their war service to the Allied cause. In addition they advanced a broad, new program providing facilities for better health and education. Land grabs were no longer possible, and one of the new regulations made it mandatory for Europeans who had children by native women to provide for their offspring.

Angry executives of the big copra, mining, rubber and shipping interests, long active in attacking government legislation, banded together in a campaign against the Commonwealth's progressive program. They strongly felt that government aid should be extended mainly to white settlers and corporations who had invested their money in exploiting New Guinea. Their spokesmen in Parliament and in the press protested violently against "wasting government funds on the welfare of indolent natives who have neither the desire nor the ability to develop their own lands."

In their final appeal against the government plan, the employers' groups held that the natives were "quickly and thoroughly civilized" by indentured labor and did not object to its features, that, on the contrary, they felt great affection and loyalty toward their employers. Mr. Ward, the Minister for External Affairs, replied that the natives could best show their liking for the indenture system and "their deep affection toward employers" by voluntarily signing on again if they wished. When informed that the old contracts were void and that they were free to sign new ones for one year if they so desired, ninety-five percent of the natives chose to return immediately to their home villages.

The "B-4's" (old-time New Guinea hands), government employees and missionaries are often a very divided people. A small group of fair-minded white settlers have as high a regard for native welfare as any of the capable government patrol officers. Contrarily, many "B-4's" are rugged, two-fisted men with contempt for government officials, missionaries, anthropologists and sophisticated Papuans. "Progress" to old New Guinea hands often means better transportation and higher prices for their copra, rubber, tea and other products, with a minimum of "sentimental stuff from the government" about native rights.

Today there is a new tone in the voice of the "big-fella-white-

175

master." He is learning to "talk soft along boy" and is frequently heard in Canberra seeking assurances that his rights and interests will be protected when self-rule is granted to the native people.

Rabaul, sitting as it does among a nest of volcanoes at the northernmost end of New Britain, has come a long way since the pre-United Nations' Trusteeship when the "Mastuh" of each Anglo-Saxon family hired five or more servants for ninety cents each per month. Several times destroyed by hot volcanic ash and warfare, Rabaul—with one of the finest harbors in the world—has been rebuilt this time into a thriving seaport town. Along its famous Mango Avenue (now lacking Mango trees because of street widening) there is a feeling of urgency and drive; there are new activities, new houses, modern business buildings and an increasing number of English-speaking native businessmen. This town where tea is served at 6:00 A.M. has a unique atmosphere. There are Europeans going to business in spotless tropic whites or playing golf, cricket, tennis or water-polo, or sitting reflectively in deep bamboo chairs at the exclusive New Guinea Club; there are busy Chinese storekeepers scurrying about, and easygoing native businessmen bringing a wide variety of products to the local market in their own trucks.

Modern commercial office blocks are mushrooming up in Port Moresby, the busy capital and principal city of the Territory. Sprawling along the hills above the harbor with its filmy casuarinas and crimson pomegranate trees, the refreshing greens of private homes surrounded by exotic gardens of bougainvillea, hibiscus, frangipani and coralita vines is like an oasis in this parched and windy coastal area of hard red soil and sparse kunei grass.

Before the arrival of American forces the only means of land transportation in Papua was by bridle path and a small twenty-five mile government road from Rouna Falls to Port Moresby. The United States spent several hundred million dollars on large-scale developments, from airfields, harbor facilities, and communication services to skyline roads, hospitals and drainage systems. Through massive engineering and field construction work, vast areas like Finschhafen, Milne Bay, Oro Bay and the Admiralty Islands have been developed almost beyond recognition. In addition to other much needed improvements, modern sanitation methods and malarial control have done much to pave the way for present population growth.

From its rich, beautiful plateau lands to its strange, pinnacled, limestone belt the Territory presents as great a contrast in terrain as can be found anywhere in the world.

From the humid, swampy regions bordering the lower courses of the large rivers to the snow-capped Central Highlands an extremely wide variety of plant life is found. Of the three thousand different species of plants and trees that have been classified, nine hundred are peculiar to the Territory alone.

Except for a few large river plains and coastal areas, the most striking features of the New Guinea mainland are its towering mountain masses. Extremely rugged and heavily forested, many are named after outstanding Europeans such as Mount Schopenhauer, Mount Gladstone, Mount Disraeli and the Bismarck Mountains, which form the principal range.

Isolated pockets of "uncontrolled people" remain who have never seen a white man and who have no conception of the sea. Each year thousands of square miles of new territory and tens of thousands of "new people" are being brought under administration influence by well-trained field officers. New patrol posts are being

Australian nurse and native trainees conduct a village clinic in Northern Papua.

established and far-ranging patrols are penetrating to the last strongholds of antiquity. Soon the Australian government will have complete control of this vast territory under a system of government that meets the moral and political standards of the modern world.

The great, rolling grasslands of the Eastern and Western Highlands are attracting an increasing number of white settlers. The beautiful mountain interiors of the Markham, Bulolo, Wadi and Purari offer rich agricultural areas in their malaria-free valleys and plateaus five thousand feet or more above sea level. Many former gold miners are now growing cabbages, corn and coffee in the wide fertile areas near Mount Hagen, one of the most pleasant places in the Highlands. A four-hundred-mile road is being built from Lae, on the north coast, up through beautiful gorges and misty mountain passes to Goroka, Mount Hagen and on through the heart of the Highlands.

Twenty to thirty planes may be seen at a time on the Eastern Highlands Goroka airstrip during the big event of the year, the Goroka Agriculture show. On this occasion more than ten thousand Highland natives in paint, fur, feathers and plastered mud are the biggest attraction as they compete in games and dance and chant in weird sing-sings to wild flute music and the thump of python-skin drums. Although Goroka, with its Rotary Club and civic leaders, is a fast-growing center for tourists and photographers, the show is still an authentic affair with gray mud-men from Asaro competing against men in string girdles and mobcaps from Mount Hagen and primitive wig men from Webang.

More than a hundred airfields dot these blue, mountain-rimmed valleys, and seven airlines are making possible the development of almost inaccessible regions long before roads are available— and in many cases where roads may never be available because of deep gorges and hundreds of rampaging rivers. Goods of all types, even bulldozers, go by DC-3's, and large numbers of cattle have been flown in to graze in the rich green meadows.

With whole towns and industries being maintained by air freighters, the Papuan farmers are as eager as Europeans for new airfields. Near Finschhafen, the Hubes, a group of primitive, coffee-growing people, have completed an airstrip in record time so that they can get their coffee promptly to market. Previously they had to carry it on their backs for two days to the nearest road.

In 1960 the United Nations' Trusteeship Council asked Australia to fix early target dates for political advancement in New Guinea. Australian Prime Minister Menzies, pointing out that political freedom without social and economic advancement is a mockery, stated emphatically that it was the administration's aim to grant the two million native people independence as quickly as they were able to stand on their social and economic feet.

The more than two hundred different languages that are spoken throughout the Babel-like Territory are one of the biggest obstacles to self-government. Only a small portion of the people can exchange views or even talk to one another. A somewhat Americanized version of pidgin English, called by Jack London the language without grammar or dictionary, has become the country's lingua franca. Its meager vocabulary requires amazing circumlocutions and its grammar is as unpredictable as its vocabulary. An "engine" to an unsophisticated Papuan can mean anything from a can opener to a bulldozer. A table fork is an "engine belong kau-kau." A knee is a "screw belong leg" and an ankle a "screw belong foot." A saw when it is not a "pull-him-he-come, push-him-he-go," is simply a "brother belong ax."

These enthusiastic people of New Guinea so strongly desire new roads that they sometimes leave the survey party far behind.

A simultaneous translation service similar to that used in the United Nations has now been installed at Port Moresby's Legislative Council quarters to provide translations of the two main languages, pidgin and Motu, spoken by native members of the Territory's highest political body. And, in an effort to develop the use of a common language, lessons in English are now being broadcast to Papuan children as a daily education feature.

On the credit side, Australia is improving health and food supplies and providing new and varied ways of making a living. All taxes are used for purposes directly beneficial to the island people and ninety-seven percent of the total land is still in native ownership and occupation. There are now free medical services and native schools in much of the Territory and in the crop areas the Department of Agriculture sends out experts, mostly on foot, to help Papuans get better crop yields from their land.

Farmers who set aside their bows and spears only a few years ago are learning to grow three crops of corn a year in the rich soil where tomatoes, potatoes, strawberries and even roses can be grown. Those who own their own trucks and tractors are steadily expanding their coffee acreage and more than half the Territory's entire copra production will soon be in native hands. Over two hundred and fifty co-operative societies operate retail stores; produce and market copra, rice, peanuts, coffee, cocoa, fish and garden produce; and operate tractors, large motor trucks and shipping fleets.

The pressure of Asia is being increasingly felt in the Southwest Pacific as Indonesia presses its claims for the Netherlands New Guinea, a territory larger than France. Many Australians, not forgetting for a moment the narrow margin by which they escaped possible destruction as a nation, feel that the greatest threat to their future security lies in the fact that someday the overcrowded people of Southeast Asia may inhabit New Guinea and the sparsely-settled islands of Melanesia.

H. J. Roethof, a Dutch expert on New Guinea, recently explained that the Dutch, in their half of New Guinea, are pressing ahead for independence, perhaps by 1970, because "Recent developments—particularly in Africa—convince us that it is no longer possible to develop colonial territories toward self-government in an orderly way."

Many Australians, also thinking of Africa, realize that despite the primitive conditions of a country an independence movement can develop speed very quickly and in unexpected ways.

"When people have to wait too long for independence, then they achieve it with ill will," Australia's Prime Minister Menzies has stated. "A friendly New Guinea is essential to Australia."

Late in 1960 the Australian Minister for Territories introduced a bill for the first stage of self-government in the Territory of Papua and New Guinea. The current rate of education and political advancement is being accelerated. Native councils scattered widely throughout this far-flung Territory, which is larger than New York State, Pennsylvania, Illinois and Maine, now give nearly three hundred thousand people the opportunity of gaining political experience through handling almost all of their own affairs.

A growing number of Papuans in authority, men like Simogun in the Sepik, Kandam in the Highlands, Stahl Salum of Madang and a number of others, have a wide and intimate knowledge of the problems of their people and a realistic approach to the solutions.

Typical Co-operative Society store near Port Moresby, Papua, keeps four clerks busy during peak hours.

Ismael Towalaka, of the English-speaking Tolai people of New Britain, is educating his eldest son to be a doctor "because this is the best way in which I can help in the development of our people." George Ambo of Papua, consecrated the South Pacific's first native bishop at thirty-seven, has complete confidence in the ability of his people to progress through their own efforts. Epinery Titimua, spokesman for the country's most progressive tribal group, demands early independence and envisions the Territory as a small, democratic nation advancing independently in the modern world.

Perhaps New Guinea's first president will be the university-trained son of a Sepik wood craftsman who carves heads for the curio trade or a former stretcher-bearer from the Kokoda Trail. His first prime minister could well be a successful coffee grower, a wealthy Tolai cocoa planter from the Gazelle Peninsula or one of the capable Highlanders who are now growing corn, cabbages and passionfruit.

Chapter Seven

THE INDEPENDENT STATE OF WESTERN SAMOA AND NEW ZEALAND'S POLYNESIAN DEPENDENCIES

Young, vigorous New Zealand, a nation smaller in size than the state of Nevada and with a population less than the city of Philadelphia, has jurisdiction over a widely scattered group of strategic islands in Central Polynesia and up until 1962 governed approximately one-half of all the Polynesian people in the Pacific.

For half a century New Zealand has led the rest of the world with its early social security system, unemployment insurance, universal free hospitals, complete free medical care, including doctors, surgeons and X-rays, free milk and dental care for children and reduced working hours for everyone. Still blazing a trail at home in advance of other democracies, New Zealand is also presently helping to establish Western Samoa as the first independent Polynesian nation created in modern times, the Independent State of Western Samoa.

Western Samoa

"Samoa is one of the finest countries under heaven—*L'Eldorado de la Polynesie!*" said the French geographer Lafond de Lurchy when he visited the Archipelago nearly one hundred and fifty years ago.

"They were so rich, and in want of so little, that they disdained our iron and stuffs. These islanders are undoubtedly the most happy inhabitants of the earth," reported La Pérouse, the first white man to set foot in the islands.

Samoa remains the finest group of islands in the South Seas and its romance is now of the challenging present and future, say the modern, well-educated Samoans. Fully aware of the important role they are about to play in the future of the Pacific, the competent island leaders have adjusted to the fast-changing world around them on their own terms in preparation for achieving their rightful place in the sun on January 1, 1962.

A courteous and hospitable welcome to visitors is part of a Samoan's strict social code. But bustling travelers who are in a hurry should know that Western Samoa, which even today is not easy to get to, is no archipelago of luxury hotels, pink catamarans, or beachcombers strolling the languorous beaches with shapely girls in lava-lavas; nor is it a lotus land of escape or a haven for weary businessmen. There are no bars that serve liquor, no drugstores, no brassy bands and no honky-tonks.

After one hundred years of European rule Samoa remains essentially Samoan and vastly different from the "better advertised islands" where the white man's enterprises return a high profit and hold the limelight. Western money-making ways have been little admired and local leaders are reluctant to open their islands to easy tourist dollars for fear of what it might do to the morals and morale of their people, who at present get most of the money they need by simple but unglamorous labor in their banana, coconut and cocoa groves.

Western Samoa in 1961 had the fastest-growing population in the world, more than half of whom were under twenty years of age. Unencumbered by television sets or hot rods, the young people excel in singing, dancing and many outdoor sports, especially cricket. They can dance the tango and rumba but are proud of their own island dances and can remind you that the hula originated in Samoa and was first performed as a serious dance, the fertility prayer of a proud people.

Though the young people could use some of the jobs and dollars that travelers bring, it seems certain that the new independent state will never allow the same unlimited influx of tourists and tourist conditions Tahiti has.

Once known as the "Irishmen of the Pacific," the prideful, energetic Samoans have many of the skills necessary to compete in the Western world, but prefer a simple yet productive way of life with ample leisure to one of maximum output and efficiency. Almost

This Samoan girl prefers her own traditional dress to the sarongs and lava-lavas found elsewhere in Polynesia.

alone of South Sea people they have preserved their traditional ways and native form of government little changed for centuries.

Samoan leaders who have been accused by rival Europeans in Apia of being too "puffed up with a sense of their own importance" know, without answering, that it is good to be proud of the right things; that every man needs aplomb and a decent amount of dignity. "A certain sea bird has a large feather in its tail," [the red-tailed tropicbird] said an early chief, "and whenever he loses it he loses his balance: so is dignity and tradition to the Samoan."

The importance given to relaxation, the relative unimportance of time, and the value placed on self-respect, racial individuality and courtesy to others remain unchanged. The lagoons, the thatched, beehive houses on coco-palm posts, the clean, picturesque villages with greensward and well-placed palms landscaped by people who love and understand simplicity are very little different from the way they were when the ruthless Dutchman Jacob Roggeveen discovered them two hundred and forty years ago. True, the numerous churches, schools, emporiums, taxis and lumbering buses are now there, but *fa'a Samoa* (the ways of our fathers) predominate.

Great respect is paid to old age. Unlike Westerners, who look back on youth with deep yearning, Samoans accept each phase of life gracefully and enjoy it to the fullest. Described by Robert Louis Stevenson as demigods, the handsome, silver-haired old men of Samoa are unmatched anywhere for their sagacity, quiet dignity and deep understanding.

A Samoan with a good house, a well-made canoe, a neat and well-formed wife, healthy children, a taro patch, coconut and breadfruit trees and a few pigs has always had the good sense to know that he is well off by any standards.

Samoa's fifteen islands (twenty-three hundred miles from Hawaii on the direct route to New Zealand) were divided long ago into two parts by the United States and Germany. Under this unnatural division the six eastern islands belong to the United States mainly because of Pago Pago, one of the best harbors in the Pacific.

Western Samoa's two main islands of Upolu and Savaii, plus a few islets, have fifteen times the area of U. S. Samoa and five times as many people. Besides size and population, one of the big differences between the Samoas is that it is much easier to forget about

186

Western ways in the quiet outer villages of Upolu, and even more so on Savaii.

Those who prefer peace and beauty to modern conveniences find it in Savaii, the largest and loveliest of the Samoas. This island of high mountains, dense forests, sparse settlements and *fa'a Samoa* —the old ways—remains one of the few unspoiled islands in Central Polynesia.

Upolu, which is slightly larger than Tahiti, has always been the most important and most populated island because of its harbors, its sheltered lagoons and the excellent agricultural areas in the valleys and along its forty-five miles of coastal hillsides. From the

Samoan craftsmen no longer use stone tools to carve the many-legged ava ceremonial bowls.

centrally-located capital of Apia on the shores of a curving bay, one hundred and seventy-two clean, spacious villages and sixty churches string out along the coast between coconut and banana groves.

Now that the destiny of these attractive green islands is again in the hands of a Polynesian people who ruled themselves for centuries, the high points of how and why they became pawns among major world powers should be known to understand the widely-held faith of the people in *fa'a Samoa*—a faith that warships, legislation and the administrators of three great nations couldn't destroy.

The Samoan Archipelago, three hundred miles long, was inhabited at an early date by Polynesian Vikings from the northwest and became a center for the development and distribution of Polynesian culture. It is believed that many of the outlying islands of the Central Pacific were first settled by far-ranging seafarers from Samoa.

The first white navigators to sail into these waters in ships moved by lofty yards of canvas were considered sailing gods or "Heaven-bursters" because their great white sails came over the horizon like clouds out of the sky. "*Papalangi*"—"The clouds are broken"— cried the Samoans when the bellying topsails of the first British ships were sighted. Later on they were less impressed with the "puny newcomers," some of whom became known as "pale barbarians."

White influence in Samoa dates from the beginning of missionary activities. In the early days, a number of white beachcombers and adventurers, quick to realize that they might gain wealth and fame by a pretended proficiency in the Bible, preached loud and long from almost any book at hand. Several devised an elaborate mumbo-jumbo ritual and administered "the holy sacraments" on a wholesale basis, for which they were well rewarded by the islanders.

Later, at the time when religious revival was sweeping through Scotland and the United States, the people of Samoa, delighted with the details of baptism and other functions of Christian ritual, experienced an overwhelming conversion to Christianity under the guidance of the London Missionary Society.

As the Reverend Murray of Pago Pago reported, "Melody, such as angels love to hear, arose from many hearts and tongues during those many long days and nights of prayer. There was only a break of half-an-hour near midnight. Bodily fatigue was disregarded in the intense desire to obtain the longed-for blessing." By June 1840 it was stated that the very last heathen in Pago Pago had accepted Christ.

Soon after the London evangelists were established, a printing press was set up and in three years the Reverend-printer J. B. Stair reported that publication had reached "79,000 copies of the principal portions of the New Testament which, with hymn books, catechisms, spelling books, a Life of Christ, sermons, etc., amounted to 7,721,000 pages."

In the middle of the nineteenth century, even before New Zealand had received a constitution from England, she was reaching out for a share of the islands in the South Pacific. A succession of her church leaders and statesmen, including, among others, Bishop Selwyn, Sir George Grey, Sir Julius Vogel and "King Dick" Seddon, worked diligently toward the annexation of a large island empire.

Commenting on New Zealand's Polynesian ambitions, Lord Kimberly, British Secretary of State for Colonies, felt that "The New Zealand government would do well to first get possession of the whole of New Zealand before undertaking to govern other territories. . . . They will have enough to do for years to come without embarking on quixotic schemes."

Despite a long series of official rebukes from Great Britain, New Zealand continued to maintain a keen interest in the Pacific isles. New Zealanders, like the Australians, were particularly averse to the thought of any non-British flags being raised in the island world, especially in Tonga, Samoa and the southwest Pacific area. The growing influence of American and German nationals at Apia and Pago Pago was especially resented as a menace to the Polynesian plans of the Dominion government.

In 1872, when Captain Meade of the U.S.S. *Narragansett* concluded a treaty with Chief Mauga of Tutuila for the cession of Pago Pago harbor to the United States, public opinion in New Zealand was bitterly aroused.

Almost from its first impact with white civilization Samoa was the object of international concern. High Chief Malietoa was harassed on all sides by plotting whites, American, British and German, each scheming and intriguing for annexation by their own country. A small but strongly armed white community set up a

European municipal area around Apia and maintained their own self-rule until 1900.

In other Pacific archipelagos where there was a single paramount chief or king, the transition to a unified government was made by gaining the adherence of the king to Christianity. But in Samoa such a course was not possible because, owing to family and district rivalries, the highest chief was not supreme over all districts.

A large class of unscrupulous whites encouraged native warfare in order to sell arms and ammunition to both sides. Rifles that were worth about six dollars each were sold for seventy-five dollars and ammunition was supplied at a thousand percent profit. It was in this manner that much of Samoa first came under foreign ownership. During the twelve years of intermittent warfare between Chief Malietoa and his rival nephew, thousands of acres of the best agricultural lands came into the hands of white opportunists in exchange for advice, guns and ammunition.

While the total land in Samoa was estimated at one million acres, acquisitive foreigners were soon claiming one million and seven hundred thousand acres, or nearly twice as much land as actually existed. Of this amount the British demanded the lion's share, about nine hundred and fifty thousand acres, seconded by American claims for approximately six hundred and fifty thousand acres. Canny New Zealand and American speculators bought up large tracts through questionable and often dishonest means and sold the less desirable sections back to the dispossessed Samoans at a huge profit. The Polynesian Land Company of California and McArthur and Company of Auckland acquired two-thirds of the total land on the largest island in Samoa.

Having first supplied the rival native factions with articles of warfare, the local whites soon were intervening directly in island affairs. While the Americans and British were almost always on the side of High Chief Malietoa, the Germans consistently supported the rival Tupua family led by Chief Tamasese. Beset and badgered on all sides by jealous consuls and foreign opportunists, Malietoa offered his "crown" to the United States, England and finally to New Zealand.

During this turbulent period, Robert Louis Stevenson became so outspoken in his sympathy for the Samoans and in his criticism of certain official white policies that the British High Commissioner for the Western Pacific seriously contemplated having Samoa's most distinguished resident deported as an agitator.

A few years after assurances were exchanged between Downing Street and the Wilhelmstrasse agreeing that both nations would respect the sovereign integrity of Samoa, Germany deposed and deported King Malietoa to the Cameroons in West Africa and installed the puppet Vice-King Tamasese in his place.

One of the first acts of the German-Tamasese government was to declare a fine of forty-seven thousand dollars against the people of Samoa with the provision that if they were unable to obtain the money in cash they could borrow it from German traders by mortgaging their communal lands as security.

To show their hatred of the German government, large groups of Samoans took to wearing the Union Jack as a lava-lava—much to the embarrassment of the British consul.

President Grover Cleveland openly voiced his strong disapproval of Germany's action in forcing her will upon the defenseless Samoan people. In his message to the American Congress the President pointed out that Germany's attitude made it plain that she was no longer content with a neutral position at Samoa. Accordingly, the President informed Congress, the commander of the Pacific Fleet had been ordered to proceed at once to Apia.

When Admiral Kimberly arrived at Apia aboard his flagship *Trenton,* the American sloop-of-war *Nipsic* and the corvette *Vandalia* were already at anchor opposite three German warships and the English cruiser *Calliope.* Feelings were tense between the rival captains and it was freely admitted that the slightest provocation would have precipitated a naval battle in the harbor.

Suddenly a terrific hurricane struck Apia without the slightest warning. During a wild night of chaos all six American and German warships were wrecked with the loss of one hundred and thirty lives in a disaster recorded by the British Admiralty as "unprecedented since the introduction of steam."

When pressed by the American and British governments, Chancellor Bismarck repudiated the strong-arm actions of German authorities at Apia and announced that the Kaiser had ordered the release of King Malietoa and his return to Samoa. It was also understood by all parties that henceforth Samoa was to be recognized as a neutral state with Malietoa as king.

As a result of the efforts of British missionaries the people of

Samoa developed a sincere respect for Great Britain while they continued to fear Germany as a strong, unsympathetic nation. Feelings toward the United States, whose interest was mostly strategic, fluctuated from friendly to uncertain.

At a time when Samoan affairs were approaching another crisis precipitated by the rivalry of foreign nationals, Great Britain, unknown to New Zealand or Australia, quietly renounced all of her Samoan rights in favor of Germany in return for concessions in West Africa and in the Solomons. Thus all of Western Samoa came under German rule, with the United States receiving Tutuila and the smaller eastern islands.

With the raising of the Imperial flag over Western Samoa the town and port of Apia became the official center for German development in this part of the Pacific. A large number of German settlers arrived. New copra plantations were laid out, improved methods of production were enforced, and the cultivation of cocoa, rubber, pineapples, coffee and vanilla was introduced.

In lamenting the penetration of "the democratic spirit of America—with its vulgar fashion of life," a high German official stated quite as a matter of fact that the success of the Imperial policy in Samoa depended upon the building up of German prestige "as a white man and master." During the fourteen years of Imperial rule two major outbreaks were suppressed with the aid of German warships. Following one action the governor announced, "This will teach Samoa a lesson and will cause all to bear in mind that there is only one head in Samoa and that is His Majesty the Kaiser."

On the credit side Germany laid the foundation of a modern health service, improved native hygiene, instituted the first effective campaign against yaws and provided free medical and surgical treatment for the island people. By 1913 trade had increased three times and the Group became known as the most prosperous Imperial dependency in the South Seas.

At the outbreak of World War I a New Zealand Expeditionary Force landed at Apia unopposed and took possession of Western Samoa.

New Zealand started her rule over Western Samoa with the best of intentions but failed to realize that a native system that had endured for centuries could not be changed overnight. All of her early administrators were former military career men with no understanding of Samoan ethnology and anthropology. Even had they not underestimated the importance of Samoan cultural problems, the former generals who became administrators lacked the tact and training to cope with the complex details.

Knowingly and sometimes unknowingly, the new *papalangi* cast aside hallowed customs and disregarded traditional taboos. In the flush of enthusiasm to change the Samoan quickly and give him some of the advantages of Western ways, his own rich culture was often disregarded and its deeper significance seldom understood.

Despite the white man's forceful qualities of leadership and of supposedly knowing what was best for Samoa, the native islanders were well aware that the papalangi bitterly quarreled among themselves over land, over politics, over nearly everything of material value, and sometimes even over spiritual affairs. Through bitter experience Samoans had long since ceased to regard the Anglo-Saxons and their rule as superior.

By temperament the Samoans are a gentle, hospitable people, extremely fond of music, dancing and all manner of entertainment. When civilized games were first introduced whole villages left their work and turned out to play for weeks at a time. "No occasion is too small for the poets and musicians," Robert Louis Stevenson has said, "a death, a visit, the day's news, the day's pleasantry, will be set to rhyme and harmony—song, as with all Pacific islanders, goes hand in hand with the dance, and both shade into the drama."

Possessing an excellent, highly-developed culture, the Samoans have always felt entirely self-sufficient. Their adequate leisure has allowed them to develop dignity and a way of life far in advance of their harder pressed Melanesian and Micronesian neighbors. "We have good houses, swift canoes, fine women and plenty of coconuts, taro, breadfruit and fish. What need have we for white man's things?" a famous chief has asked—and added, "A life filled with too much work is not worth living."

Considering their islands a worldly paradise and extremely proud of their own pleasant manner of living, they naturally scorn to labor as house servants or plantation drudges and decline to become enthused about improving their way of life along Western standards. When foreigners have proved too difficult they have simply boycotted their products and services.

While the Samoans are the most social of Polynesians, they are also the most independent. About one out of every four adult males is a chief of some sort, keenly sensitive to his personal dignity and to

Samoans love to sing and play. No occasion is too small for an impromptu dance.

that of his family. Of the two classes known as *ali'is* and *faipules*—chiefs and orators—the chiefs are paramount in all ceremonial affairs while the orators act as their spokesmen in political and other matters.

The national pride of the high-spirited Samoans was not easily reconciled to the fact that after World War I their country had been handed over to a foreign nation as though they were unable to govern themselves. Samoan statesmen asked—since they never had yielded their independence to any nation—on what basis the League of Nations could turn them over to New Zealand rule without first consulting the Samoans.

Early in 1927, the growing opposition of the Samoan people to the New Zealand government policies began to unite in a single articulate body for "more recognition of our sense of what is due to us as a people." Taking as their motto *Samoa mo Samoa* (Samoa for the Samoans) they formed a cultural and political movement known

194

as the Mau. Led by native orator groups, who were aided by friendly local whites and part-natives, the Mau movement became the national party of the Samoan people and soon grew to include over ninety percent of the total population.

When the New Zealand Labor Government came into power one of its first acts was to legalize the Mau as a legitimate Samoan political party. Labor ministers met the Mau leaders at Apia in a frank and open discussion of their grievances and shortly after that they were granted a much greater share in their local government. Since that time the progressive steps toward self-rule have been steadily advanced.

The majority of the Samoan people feel that the political division of their islands, now split between the United States and Independent West Samoa, should be terminated in the interest of Samoan national unity. In protesting to the United Nations Trusteeship Council against "the unnatural division of the islands of the Samoan Group, enforced by the Three Powers in the past without the consent of the Samoans," the majority leaders have emphasized that a people who are fundamentally one in history, culture, language and ways of life should not be arbitrarily divided under two flags by the two powers most often heard defending "the democratic rights of smaller nations."

High Chief Tuitele of American Samoa said in 1961 that his Samoa would "never unite with Independent West Samoa." Chief Tuitele and a few conservative leaders of tiny Eastern Samoa's seventy-six square miles fear mostly that they will be outranked if the two Samoas are united. The average Samoan, not particularly concerned with the status rivalry of the chiefs, strongly resents having to pay for a special permit to visit the other Samoa.

Most visitors to Western Samoa arrive at Faleolo Airport (twenty miles out of Apia) where they are greeted with a gracious "*Talofa lava*" ("Hello to you"), roughly the equivalent of Hawaii's *Aloha*. The ninety-mile flight between American and Western Samoa can be made any day in the week but the best way to first see the steep, rugged hills and purple valleys of Upolu is to sail over from Pago Pago on the schooner *Mauna Tele* or the *Sulimoni*. These small but shipshape copra and banana schooners maintain a regular service between Pago Pago and Apia and take a few passengers at moderate fares.

Graceful coco-palms enhance the fine sandy beaches and coast lines of Upolu. Pandanus and banyan trees, hibiscus, gardenia, convolvuli, orchids and frangipani are all there too. But countless rickety outhouses on stilts (privies-by-the-sea), add nothing to the beauty. These weathered, forlorn little sentry boxes jut out at the end of short jetties along some of the loveliest bays in Samoa until it has become difficult to find a marine view without a stilted privy or two. It is rumored that steps will soon be taken to improve the coastal seascapes by solving the sanitary problem in a less conspicuous manner.

Though Apia still has less than one hundred good hotel rooms available, things are vastly different from the days of the once-a-month steamer. There are now over fifteen thousand people in this tropical center of sprawling wooden-frame buildings and wide verandahs painted white. A dozen hotel rooms with private showers are available and Aggie Grey's insect-proof cottages now have hot water and private baths.

A few of the most colorful personalities in the Pacific may be met almost any day along Apia's Beach Road or perhaps in the lounge of Aggie Grey's unpretentious but famous Aggie Grey Hotel where complimentary tea is served to guests twice daily.

West of Apia, the town of Mulinu'u has the Pacific's most complete geophysical observatory; Foxtrot Beach has the best swimming; Mulifanua has one of the world's largest copra plantations; and across the island quiet little Lefaga has the most charming village and the loveliest blue lagoon in Upolu. To seasoned travelers who have overlooked the inconveniences and discovered the rich colors, remote villages and deep peace of these not-easily-reached green islands, Samoa is the heart of the South Seas.

In contrast to the idiom of the motor-scooter and motorcycle enthusiasts and the modern cricket-playing Samoans of Upolu, the traveler hears again and again the words *"fa'a Samoa"* spoken in the soft island dialect. And they say it proudly. It is heard among school children, at public gatherings or in a circle of *matais*—ranking men of the community—sitting cross-legged on Council House mats.

Overlooking Apia, at Vailima, is the house where Robert Louis Stevenson lived. And directly above, at the top of Mount Vaea— under his "wide and starry sky"—is Stevenson's tomb, inscribed with the words from his immortal *Requiem*.

Stevenson fought hard for Samoan rights. He spoke publicly,

wrote letters, interceded with influential people on their behalf; visited the proud chiefs when they were thrown in jail; took care of them and their families when they were ill. When free, they came direct to "our truest friend" whom they called *Tusitala* (Teller of Tales). The well-worn trail to Stevenson's home was a difficult one and the chiefs decided to build him a good road all the way to Apia as a token of their gratitude. The four-mile road proved a difficult task, with aristocratic chiefs and commoners laboring long hours in the scorching sun for many days and weeks. Two venerable chiefs who were old and sick insisted on working with the others until the road was finally completed and became known as *Ala Loto Alofa*— The Road of the Loving Heart.

When Stevenson died there was great sorrow in Apia and in the many small villages of Samoa. Loving hands cut a difficult pathway up the thick, forested mountain at the rear of Vailima and six of the strongest Samoans carried their "staunch friend" up the long precipitous slope to the flowering summit of Mount Vaea. "When Mataafa our leader was imprisoned, who was our support but Tusitala?" said the oldest chief when they had reached the top. "He cared for us when we were sick and made us well. We were hungry and he fed us. The day was no longer than his kindness—*Tofa* [Farewell] Tusitala: sleep well."

Stevenson died in 1894, but today his memory still warms the hearts of the Samoan people. If you speak of Tusitala to a Samoan in Apia more often than not he will glance up toward Mount Vaea, the highest peak in Upolu, where "Tusitala overlooks the sea."

Most of the slightly more than one hundred thousand people of Western Samoa live in small, immaculate villages in the best-designed thatch houses in the South Pacific. There are no doors, windows or partitions in the round, open-sided Samoan houses; simple coconut-frond shutters can be raised or lowered at any side to let the sun in or to shut out the rain. Meals are served on the clean, pandanus-matted floor from large fresh banana leaves. Samoans and guests sit always cross-legged. Those who are too old or stiff-legged to do so cover their feet with a mat, as it is considered bad manners to sit with your feet pointing toward anyone.

It has been said of the ample, stalwart Samoans, many of whom weigh over two hundred and fifty pounds, that "their psychology revolves around their stomachs." This of course could also be said of Hawaiians, Tahitians and others who live on bountiful islands, and might also be said of many Americans and Europeans, some of whom belong to gourmet and diners' clubs. The truth is the Samoans love fine food as well as anyone else and their way of life frequently provides an event calling for a feast with all the trimmings.

In the small rural villages part of the routine of everyday life is taken up with agricultural work on Friday; preparation for the Sabbath on Saturday; church, hymn singing, feasting and more singing on Sunday; recuperating on Monday; meetings, oratory, games or fishing on Tuesday, Wednesday and Thursday.

Belted lava-lavas, shirts and sandals are popular everyday attire for the men, except on Sunday when they attend as many as three long church services in double-breasted white coats, white starched lava-lavas, white shirts and black ties—perhaps with a black umbrella to ward off the noon sun.

The solid, earthy Samoan women, whether dressed in their Sunday missionary-influenced, usually-white attire with pandanus hats or in flowery everyday lava-lavas, have a proud, graceful bearing. As one might expect from the open-sided houses there is little false modesty in Upolu or Savaii. Dances are frequently held and the girls all know that it is pleasant to walk beneath the palms with a *tane* (man).

Independence for the people of Western Samoa has brought new problems in its wake. The islanders now have a much greater share than ever before of the natural wealth of their islands. New tropical industries have been put into operation and the production of copra, cocoa and bananas has advanced. But the present agricultural lands, even if fully developed, will not be adequate to support the rapidly increasing population. This, with the lack of business opportunities in Apia and the preference given to age and rank in village affairs, is increasing the drift of young Samoans to Wellington and other port cities where their future is far from assured.

Considering the modern and liberal views of the Prime Minister of Western Samoa, the Honorable Fiame Mataafa, the matai system with its special privileges for chiefs will very likely be modified to provide more opportunities for young citizens and to conform with the democratic principles of the new Samoan nation.

In the midst of complexity and twentieth century speed-up most Samoans continue to retain the best of the old ways and to take only what they want of Western civilization, which is very little. Serene,

198

tolerant and politically mature, they remain the purest of Polynesians.

The modern Fono, or Legislative House, a masterpiece of contemporary Samoan architecture, has recently been wired for the best auditory effects. Sewing machines and small modern radios hum in palm-thatch houses, but the people still live close to the fruitful earth. They dry copra and cocoa beans, cultivate bananas, sow their taro patches and look forward to the next shark or turtle hunt.

Cook Islands, Niue and the Tokelaus

The tropical island dependencies that remain under New Zealand administration are the Cook Islands, Niue, and the isolated Tokelau Group. (The Dominion also shares in the control of the rich phosphate island of Nauru, in the Gilberts.)

Samoan chief's house and meeting hall. Traditional Samoan architecture is the most distinctive in Polynesia.

Like Pitcairn, Rarotonga is an island without harbors and everything has to come ashore the hard way.

The late, renowned Dr. S. M. Lambert, who probably did more to better health conditions among South Sea Islanders than any other single individual, has said more than once that "It would probably be better for the Polynesians if New Zealand were to govern them all."

New Zealand's far-flung Cook Islands, extending from the low northern atoll of Tongareva, east to Puka Puka, south to Palmerston and southeast to mountainous Mangaia, form a long central-Pacific arc of islands located between Tahiti, Samoa and Tonga.

The high, southern islands comprise a beautiful, verdant group, of which Aitutaki, Mangaia and Rarotonga are the most important.

Of greater area and fertility than the low coralline atolls of the north, they contain eighty-five percent of the total population.

Rarotonga, the administrative headquarters for the Cook Islands, is the most attractive island in this part of the Pacific, with a climate unsurpassed in any tropical area. A central mountain chain extends the length of the island with craggy mountain peaks and purple valleys. Plantations are numerous along its low coastal areas and in the well-watered valleys where nearly all tropical and subtropical fruits and vegetables are easily grown.

Sometimes called the Tahiti of the Cook Islands, Rarotonga is preferred by some travelers to any island in French Polynesia, which is saying a lot. With its spectacular skyline of green, volcanic peaks, its patches of tomato plants, rows of oranges and lemons, incredibly blue lagoons and roads lined with flamboyant trees, Rarotonga is an ideal retreat for those who would have a quiet vacation near a fine sea beach on an island where mangos, oranges and bananas still grow wild.

The people of the Cook Islands, the Niueans and the Tokelau Islanders are among the finest of Polynesians. Intelligent, kind and courteous, they are a well-built people of light skins and fine features. "*Kiaora ana!*"—"May you live!" is the traditional Rarotongan greeting to a newcomer. It is said with garlands of flowers—called *ei*— and often followed by a feast which includes fish and prawns in a sauce of coconut cream and fresh lime juice, breadfruit baked or fried in coconut oil, taro tops cooked with pork or chicken, and fresh banana poi.

Tourists are granted temporary permits for short visits if they meet a few simple requirements, but as elsewhere in Polynesia, the day of the happy-go-lucky beachcomber is definitely gone. Niue now has a dog tax and even bicycles have licenses in Rarotonga. Outsiders are allowed permanent entry permits only at the discretion of the Resident Commissioner at Avarua, the port of entry. His permission is difficult to acquire and is based largely on the applicant's political background, health, financial standing and ability to show visible means of support.

One hundred and forty miles north of Rarotonga, the rich, fruit-producing island of Aitutaki contains a large, magnificent lagoon entirely surrounded by small islets. Formerly an American air base, it is second to Rarotonga in size and commercial importance. Mangaia, the southernmost of the Cooks, is a fertile, highly productive island about thirty miles in circumference.

The Northern Cook Islands, Palmerston, Suvarov, Tongareva, Rakahanga, Manihiki, Puka Puka and Nassau, extend from three hundred to seven hundred and forty miles north and northeast of Rarotonga. They are mostly of coral and sand and inhabited by Polynesians darker than others from long exposure to the sun in fishing, diving and carrying on their numerous atoll and lagoon activities. The main exports of the Group are copra and pearl shell.

Isolated Niue, the largest Polynesian island under New Zealand rule, lies three hundred and fifty miles southeast of Samoa. Its land area of one hundred square miles is almost equal to the entire Cook Group. One of the most intense hurricanes experienced in the Pacific, with winds up to one hundred and twenty miles an hour, swept the island in 1959, devastating entire villages. Another damaging hurricane struck in 1960. More than five hundred new "hurricane proof" houses being built with government help will class the Niueans among the best-housed islanders in the Pacific.

The eighteen hundred people of the Tokelaus who live on three clusters of islands about three hundred and fifty miles northeast of the most easterly Samoan Islands have no crime, no jails, no newspapers and no motor vehicles—not even a bicycle. A priest and a Catholic nun are the only Anglo-Saxon residents, and travelers are not allowed to visit the Group. Rarely seen by outsiders, the Tokelaus are less touched by Western ways than any other Polynesian community.

The early Polynesian discovers and explorers of the Cook Islands —the wise and fearless Kupe, Hui-te-Rangiora, long-wandering Ru and others—were among the best of the world's primitive navigators.

Rarotonga was the last stopping place of the wandering Maoris, during the period of their long migrations to New Zealand. Between November and March, when the northeast trades were strongest, whole communities sailed forth in great double canoes bearing such names as *Te-Manu-ka-rere* (flight of the birds), *Tokomaru* (the southwest wind) and *Te-Arawa* (the shark). With each canoe loaded with as many as two hundred men, women and children, kumara seeds, gourds of fresh water, taro and the Maori dog, they sailed out through the reef of Rarotonga in November, and the course steered kept the bow of the canoe just to the right of where the sun sets in

202

the day and the moon and Venus at night. By following this ancient advice today one sails from Rarotonga to the northwest, the compass direction of New Zealand.

In 1773 Captain James Cook made his first discovery in the islands that were destined to carry his name, and a few years later Lieutenant Bligh discovered Aitutaki two weeks before mutiny broke out on his vessel, H.M.S. *Bounty*.

The early history of the Cook Islands is closely interwoven with the activities of the Reverend John Williams and other evangelists of the London Missionary Society who sowed the seeds of salvation far and wide throughout the Group.

Influenza and other epidemics invariably followed contact between the natives and the early whites. When a terrible plague swept through the islands shortly after the evangelists arrived they explained to the islanders that it had been sent by Jehovah as a final punishment for the long years in which they had lived in wickedness.

Williams relates that "It is a very remarkable fact that in no island of importance has Christianity been introduced without a war." On Mangaia the zeal of the Christian natives was aroused to such a feverish pitch that in Williams' own words the devout islanders exterminated many of "their heathen enemies by hewing them in pieces while they were begging for mercy."

Williams, a former London ironmonger, put his Cook Island missions on a paying basis by strongly exhorting the natives to a keen rivalry in which they strived to outdo each other with contributions of coconut oil, pigs and other salable products.

Of the natives of Aitutaki, Williams wrote, "They have subscribed 270 hogs, which I shall dispose of for the Society at the earliest opportunity. As hogs are very inconvenient animals—breaking down fences, etc. it was determined not to subscribe hogs again; and as the island produces neither arrowroot nor coconuts, I made a rope machine for them and taught them to make rope which they are to contribute this year for the purposes of the Society."

No place in the world observed a stricter Sabbath than the Cook Islands that fell under Williams' edicts. No work, sport or relaxation of any description was permitted. The entire day and evening was given over to scripture reading, prayers, sermons and to the interpreting of Gospel messages and catechizing. No fire was allowed— not even a cooking oven. As Williams relates in a description of Mangaians, "Saturday was their principal rat catching day—as they were desirous of having animal food to eat with their cold vegetables on the Sabbath."

Under the firm reign of a Brother Buzacott, Rarotonga became a center of Calvinist righteousness, and bronzed native puritans in long-tailed frock coats became a common sight in the mission square.

Among his many accomplishments Brother Buzacott published a native spelling book and a hymnal containing two hundred and seventy-nine hymns—two hundred and four of which were of his own composition. At first the Rarotongans used the spelling books, with their monotonous A,B,C intonations, as a new charm against danger. And occasionally, when the Reverend was not around, the Rarotongan youths could see no harm in dancing a sensuous *tarekareka* to the rhythm of the Buzacott hymns.

Under the constant prodding of the evangelists the islanders constructed a huge church at Avarua, Rarotonga, which was hailed by missionary journals as the "best specimen of Gothic architecture in the South Seas." That this opinion of the church was not entirely unanimous was attested by the Earl of Pembroke who described it as "that vile, black and white abomination paralyzing one of the most beautiful bits of scenery in the world."

The Cook Islands were held up as inspiring jewels in the Protestant missionary crown. For nearly sixty years Rarotonga retained a stringent record of piety and set an example of Puritanism unexcelled by any other island in the South Seas. This period, widely known as "The Period of the Blue Laws," extended well into this century. During their long reign, the London Missionary Society gradually perfected a system of laws which applied to temporal as well as spiritual matters. By quietly usurping the power of the native chiefs they came into virtual control of every phase of island government.

Just when it looked as though the French Catholics were about to invade the Calvinist paradise in an attempt to bring it within jurisdiction of the French Administration in the Society Islands, British warships visited the Group and formally declared them to be under the protection of Great Britain. Shortly after, a British consul was appointed to Rarotonga—paid for by New Zealand.

The tight grip of the missionaries was gradually taken over by a New Zealand administration. The grim blue laws and lack of easy money to be made from the natural resources discouraged any large number of white adventurers from settling in the Group and interfering in Polynesian affairs. Though considerably changed, the strict Calvinist code is still not entirely gone and as late as 1958 arrests were still being made for minor infractions of the modified local blue laws.

Cook Islanders have had a say in their own government for over half a century, but despite a long succession of Island Councils and finally a Legislative Council, the real power remains in the hands of the nonelective Resident Commissioner. All acts of the Legislative Council are subject to his veto. A big step forward was taken in 1958 through the creation of a much-enlarged elective Legislative Assembly with increased powers and responsibilities.

Notable improvements have been made in sanitation and health. Under the Cook Islands Act all islanders are given free medical and surgical care. Modern mosquito inspectors, copra inspectors and other skilled and capable islanders have come a long way from the 1930's when they still thought that a stethoscope would cure almost any ailment. Many have become excellent doctors, nurses and public health officers. Health standards are high but a persistent complaint of Rarotonga health authorities is that it is "too close to Papeete for good health."

When interisland vessels with Polynesian crews arrive from Tahiti some of the Rarotonga girls find the bottles of French perfume hard to resist. While the churches (mainly London Missionary Society) remain the strongest influence in island life, the Cook Islands' *hura,* which is more graceful than the hula, is still danced at occasional beach parties to British hymns or American jazz. Goatskin drums, hollowed-log drums, empty kerosene can "drums," ukuleles and guitars provide the music.

All of the land in the Cook Islands is owned by Polynesians and may not be sold, mortgaged or diverted to others except through long-term leases; hence the fruit industry, the economic backbone of the main islands, is made up of hundreds of small growers. Sometimes a year's work of a grower is gone overnight when a hurricane tears through, doing great damage to the fruit crops and "skinning the land." The poor condition of much of the land is due to gradual soil depletion through lack of conservation in previous years.

Conflict between the old ways and the new is revealed sometimes in the reluctance of older islanders to destroy a coconut tree that has passed its peak of production and replace it with a new one because they consider the aged tree an old and valued friend.

Experimental farms are helping to improve agricultural methods, and islanders who are dependent on the New Zealand market as an outlet for their tomatoes and citrus products have adopted modern equipment and co-operative methods in marketing and purchasing.

New Zealand's Polynesian Dependencies all have rising populations, over half of whom are under twenty years of age. Education is free and compulsory and the principles of co-operative movements, especially agricultural, is a part of the school course. A large number of disillusioned young islanders point out that although they are given free education by a government that means well, the economic development of their home islands has fallen behind and they now lack the opportunity to live up to the modern ways to which they have been educated. Thousands have sailed away to live permanently in New Zealand.

Contrarily, several hundred New Zealanders have come to live in the islands, mostly in and about Rarotonga where living conditions are as pleasant as anywhere in the Pacific. Every village has its scent of yellow, pink or red frangipani and *tiare maori* (Rarotonga gardenia). Each Polynesian home has its patch of taro and kumara, and most have some jasmine or hibiscus. But even when the local flame trees and Christmas lilies are coming into bloom some of the former New Zealanders still miss their sharp, frosty days, beefsteak-and-kidney pies, skylarks, daffodils and mountains topped with snow. Their feeling is best expressed by the remark one of them made when remembering, in November, "It is spring and rose-time at home in Auckland." Then he turned and said, "Ah yes, but Rarotonga is a fine place too."

By a more efficient use of the available land, increased mechanization and better transportation, these islands that are famed for their high-quality Valencia and Rarotonga Seedless oranges are capable of supporting more than twice their present population.

In addition to the growing citrus and copra exports, diversified crops such as pineapples, mangos, avocados, peanuts, coffee, and tomatoes, which can be grown in coconut groves, are expected to provide new jobs and raise standards of living during the next ten years. A clothing factory is doing well and a modern cool depot facilitates the export of citrus products. Tomatoes and other produce can be air-freighted to New Zealand markets.

A new generation of educated young islanders feel that they are entirely capable of handling all of their own affairs, including the offices of department heads (still mostly held by New Zealanders). Increasingly able to stand on their own feet economically and politically, the sons of noble Polynesian families, some of whom can trace their ancestors through ninety generations, are certain to acquire the key positions and play the leading role in the future of their home islands.

Chapter Eight

AMERICAN POLYNESIA

Eastern Samoa

Now that it is cheaper and easier to get to American Samoa than to any other archipelago south of Honolulu, American interest in these seven small islands and atolls is on the increase. It will soon be "on the jump," say island officials pointing out that jet planes can make the twenty-six hundred mile flight from Hawaii to Pago Pago's fast expanding Tafuna Airport in only four and a half hours.

The dreams of tourists sometimes fade quickly among the harsh realities of modern Pacific port towns. Pago Pago (pronounced rhythmically Pango Pango), the capital of American Eastern Samoa, is one of the exceptions. Green, mountainous Tutuila, with the cleanest capital town and one of the best harbors in Oceania, still has and will always have the natural beauty that an unspoiled South Sea Island ought to have.

The handsome, golden-skinned Polynesian people who live in the more than fifty villages of American Samoa take much pride in the flower-lovely background and landscaping that surround their unique, round *fales* (dwellings). Unlike Hawaii's Waikiki Beach version of a bamboo-and-thatch village, those on Tutuila are the real thing.

East from Pago Pago there is Leloaloa, Laulii, Fagaitua and lovely Alofau surrounded by coco-palms and breadfruit trees. There are the Japanese fishing boats near Anua, dancing spectacles at Laulii, turtle and shark songs at Vailoga and the artisans of Aua where wooden *ava* (ceremonial) bowls are hand-crafted out of filele, a local hardwood. The out-of-the-way villages on the north side of the island, reached by the short, steep road to the coastal village of Fagasa, are the best. Beyond the grandeur and deep greens of

208

Fagasa Bay are small beaches and happy communities of peace and quiet.

Some of the finest deep sea fishing is off the Rose Islands—the ancient reserve of native kings. Sharks are lassoed with hand-made sennet ropes off Manua, a group of three small islands whose hard-working inhabitants produce most of the copra and remain less sophisticated than the Tutuilans of Pago Pago. A number of them, men of stature such as Chief Tufele of Tau, look like bronze Greek gods.

With all of their unspoiled beauty, these are not dreamy islands of total escape from the pressures of reality, and never were. Like almost any other part of the Pacific they are not without problems. The capital of American Samoa, though only eighty miles and twelve hours by motor vessel from Apia, has become a much different place from the capital of Independent Western Samoa, and there is an even greater difference between the neat, punctual attitude of official Pago Pago and the *laissez-faire* of Papeete, Tahiti.

The impact of American ways is seen and felt almost everywhere in Pago Pago today. "Excuse me, sir," says your young Samoan

Pago Pago, on the island of Tutuila, the capital of American Samoa, has one of the loveliest harbors in the Pacific.

friend as he hurries off on his motorcycle to a baseball game. With all of its charm, there is an artificial cut to the town that is perhaps inevitable in an outpost that has been dominated for over half a century by the United States Navy.

When a ship is in port the town's three honky-tonks come alive and on occasion provide a customer for the *pooe pooe,* the local jail. If it happens to be Saturday night the more conservative Goat Island Club comes alive, too.

Behind the facade of picturesque villages drastic changes are taking place. Today there is overpopulation, a faltering economy and a keen rivalry for land and prestige in these "paradise islands" of the travel posters and magazine advertisements.

Those who come thinking, as many do, that all is bountiful and that everyone helps himself to the abundant products of land and sea soon find that they are mistaken. The coconut palm, mango, bread-fruit trees and thousands of pink-blooming *futu* (Barringtonian) trees are all there. Taro, bananas, sugar cane, yams, pineapples and papayas are there too and so are the cassavas, but since the population has doubled in the past twenty years under American rule the economy is no longer the same. The health, happiness and prosperity of a family is often dependent on such a small area of land that the ownership of every single coconut and breadfruit tree on an island is known and important.

Where a large amount of land is available for a people, as in Tahiti, attitudes and standards can be vastly different from a situation where every square yard of soil has to be carefully cultivated, as in American Samoa. Most of the coconut trees on Tutuila are over-age and more than a few plantations are in poor soil on slopes so steep that they would be considered of no agricultural value at all in the United States.

The area of land in American Samoa suitable for growing crops is barely enough to maintain the present twenty thousand people, and since the Navy pulled out no attempt has ever been made to turn Tutuila into a modern naval base. Yet more than eight hundred acres of the best shoreside land on the island has become almost entirely a government villa taken up by rambling adminis-tration buildings, bungalows, green gardens that stretch to the shores of the bay, recreation grounds and a golf course—all part of an administration system that costs American taxpayers a mil-lion and a half dollars yearly.

The lack of agricultural land and the limited food supply leaves hardly anything for export. This means almost total dependence on government and town employment for money for church donations, to pay taxes and to buy kerosene, matches, soap, lava-lavas, tobacco and town clothes. Everyone knows that the economy of American Samoa is artificially propped up, but for the average Samoan it's not propped up enough. Despite benefits the United States has in added security through control of the harbor of Pago Pago, Samoans feel that it has been niggardly in economic aid. In December, 1960, the leading high chiefs asked United States Senators Oren Long and Ernest Gruening to petition Washington in their behalf for a twenty-five million dollar grant-in-aid loan.

To know something of the impact of the West on Eastern Samoa, and the sort of problems we are faced with in ruling a race of people with patterns of culture centuries old, a brief look at the background will help.

With the early growth of United States commerce and trade in the South Pacific, it was repeatedly pointed out by mariners, traders and the consular representatives that Samoa was in the direct path of such trade routes and that something should be done to make certain that it would always be open to American commerce. The early official policy of the United States was to avoid taking any part in Polynesian affairs. But, through the activities of its nationals, the United States government eventually became involved in native matters on Tutuila.

Commander Meade was sent to Pago Pago in 1872 with orders to obtain rights for a coal depot and a treaty with the local chiefs "to frustrate foreign influence which is at present very active in seeking to secure the harbor." On reaching Samoa in the U.S.S. *Narragansett*, Captain Meade drew up a treaty with High Chief Mauga extending to the United States government "the exclusive privilege of establishing a naval station in Pago Pago Harbor."

President Grant looked upon the treaty with favor and gave his approval to a petition for direct annexation which arrived from the chiefs shortly after. Because of Grant's unpopularity in the Senate, the treaty failed to be ratified and the petition for annexation was turned down.

The following year, President Grant sent a Colonel Steinberger out to Pago Pago to obtain "full and accurate information in regard to the islands." When he returned to Washington, Steinberger recommended that a United States protectorate be established over the Samoan Islands as well as over the Gilbert and Ellice Groups.

Upon his return to Samoa with friendly greetings and presents from President Grant for the native chiefs, Steinberger received a great welcome and shortly afterwards was made Prime Minister of "the Kingdom of Samoa." Upon his advice a constitution was drawn up, a bill of rights was declared and a set of laws were put into effect based upon the highest principles of Christianity. Steinberger's judicious advice to the chiefs on how to handle their foreign affairs with a minimum of friction and in a manner calculated to keep the jealous foreign consuls in their place was much resented by the latter and in time precipitated his downfall.

For business as well as personal reasons S. S. Foster, the American consul, hated Steinberger and did everything in his power to undermine him in the eyes of the white community. Previously, with the full knowledge of the State Department, Steinberger had traveled to Germany to further the cause of the Samoan Government. While at Hamburg he entered into business negotiations with Godeffroy and Co., none of which were of political import since all were disavowed by him on becoming premier.

On learning of Steinberger's visit to Germany Foster exploited the fact to the utmost. With the aid of the British Consul, Steinberger was illegally arrested, given a mock trial by Captain Stevens of H.M.S. *Barracouta* and deported to Fiji. Because of its international nature, the highhanded affair caused immediate reaction in Sydney, London and Washington. For their part, Foster and the British Consul, S. F. Williams, were removed from their consulate posts and Captain Stevens was dismissed from the British Navy.

The Samoans remained loyal to the memory of Colonel Steinberger for, as Mr. Griffin, the American Consul who replaced Foster, stated, "He was self-denying, earnest and enthusiastic in his efforts to ameliorate the condition of the people and to raise their government and country to the dignity and independence of a well-ordered and independent nation, and was long remembered by the natives as the wisest and safest ruler and best friend that their country has ever had."

During the turbulent eighteen seventies three native appeals to America for annexation of Samoa were refused. "Our policy of nonintervention," Seward wrote when he was Secretary of State,

High chief's daughter. Tutuila, Eastern Samoa.

"straight, absolute, and peculiar as it may seem to other nations, has thus become a traditional one which could not be abandoned without the most urgent occasion, amounting to a manifest necessity."

During the third quarter of the nineteenth century, as commercial and political rivalry increased at Apia, the United States was forced to take a more active interest in Samoan affairs and was confronted with more than one crisis "amounting to a manifest necessity."

Malietoa Laupepa, who had been recognized as king by the United States, Britain and Germany died in 1898 and Mata'afa, the former pretender to the throne, was selected by a group of leading chiefs to be the new monarch. A small opposing faction, backed by British and Americans, insisted that Malietoa Tanu should acquire the throne.

Upon the outbreak of civil warfare and the establishment of a provisional government by Mata'afa, additional American and British warships were rushed to Samoa. Four days after his arrival in the U.S.S. *Philadelphia,* the American commander, Admiral Kantz, declared the Samoan provisional government deposed. Marines were landed to attack the Mata'afa forces and American and British warships bombarded the town of Apia, destroying considerable native property.

Despite American and British opposition and the fact that the U.S.S. *Philadelphia* was supplying the Malietoa forces with guns and ammunition, Mata'afa, supported by the majority of the Samoan people, was able to defeat his opponents again and again. In the following weeks American warships repeatedly bombarded the native islanders under Mata'afa while detachments of marines from the U.S.S. *Philadelphia* engaged them in open warfare.

Local Germans, recalling the indignant attitude of the American press over strong-arm action by German vessels ten years previous, were shocked to see American and British naval officers resorting to the same tactics. At Berlin, in a private conversation during a meeting of the Reichstag, Admiral von Tirpitz remarked to Prince von Bülow, "It is clear that the action of the British and Americans points to the determination to go to war with us in order to destroy us before our fleet has been hatched out of its shell. Otherwise one would have to assume that both John Bull and Jonathan had gone mad."

214

After the failure of tripartite rule and before Germany and England had come to any final agreement about dividing the people of Samoa under two separate flags, Ambassador Hay, in an impatient dispatch to the American Ambassador at London, cabled, "If there is any doubt of the American attitude as to the partition of Samoa, you may say to Lord Salisbury that we are favorable to it, provided that satisfactory terms can be made, and that we shall be content with that portion of the islands east of the one hundred and seventy-first meridian."

In 1900, following the signing of a treaty of partition with Germany, President McKinley placed the islands of Eastern Samoa under the direct control of the Department of the Navy on February 10. Thus the United States and Germany divided an archipelago between them over which neither had any legitimate claim.

The artificial division of the Samoans, who are one in history, language and ways of life, into two parts did not pass without a number of severe criticisms by prominent statesmen. Democratic Senator Pettigrew protested strongly against simply taking over the islands and people of Samoa as though they were helpless pawns. . . . "we blot out, then," he charged, "a sovereign nation, a people with whom we have treaty relations, and divide the spoils."

In 1900, when a naval party established military rule over Tutuila, the local high chiefs were persuaded by the American commander to cede their islands to the United States and did so on April 10.

The native chiefs of Manua, not so easily convinced of the advantages of military rule as their Tutuila kinsmen, were slow in responding to Naval "tact and persuasion" and refused repeatedly to cede their islands to the new papalangi.

Considering Samoa as the world's navel, these islanders never forgot that in their own high state of culture they had ample leisure to develop their national arts and crafts to perfection and that, long before the papalangi arrived to enforce a new way of life with cannons and warships, their native methods had made the land prosperous, had given them more time for stories, songs and legends— and much more of grace and beauty.

In a bitter dispute over ceremonial customs the Manuans resorted to an open rebellion in which their highest ranking native judge was thrown into prison by the Naval Commandant. It was not until 1904 that they were sufficiently reassured as to the honesty of the

215

Navy in regard to their land rights and other affairs to sign a deed of cession.

With the people of Tutuila encouraged to feel that they had been saved by the United States from the harsh German Administration at Apia, Christian missionaries and the governing authorities were successful at first in setting up new standards of morals and property rights, and with them new prejudices and rivalries.

Little was heard from American Samoa during the years leading up to World War I, but in the disposition of former German territories Samoa was included once again in international discussions. While President Woodrow Wilson was expounding his high ideals to the ministers of foreign nations (who had already privately divided the Pacific spoils among themselves in their secret treaties), Breckenridge Long, bright young man of the American Commission at Paris, was forwarning his colleagues of the importance of acquiring Western Samoa and other islands for the United States.

In 1926, after a quarter-century of naval rule, Senator Lenroot introduced a bill in the United States Senate providing for the establishment of a civilian government over American Samoa. "There never has been any legislation for the government of these islands," Senator Lenroot stated before the Senate, "and our rule has been an absolute dictatorship. Since 1900 the government has been administered by a naval officer who has exercised supreme executive, legislative and judicial power. From his decision there is no appeal. He holds the power of life and death in his hands. Such dictatorship as now exists . . . is utterly at variance with all our history of which no American can be proud."

In 1929 Congress finally annexed the islands of Eastern Samoa as a Territory of the United States but side-stepped the main issue by conveniently forgetting to make any provision for the establishment of a civil government. Instead, a commission was appointed to proceed to Pago Pago and investigate the matter.

The Congressmen's report recommended that the people of Eastern Samoa be granted full American citizenship, that the Samoan chiefs be given full legislative powers and that a bill of rights be granted to the Samoans similar to the first ten amendments of the United States Constitution. When the proposals were presented to the Senate by President Hoover they were quickly passed and sent to the House of Representatives. In the House the bill met the powerful opposition of naval officials and after repeated delays was defeated.

Naval governors reminded critics that the cost of medical services, education and other advantages which the Navy provided free would exceed by many times the native income if natives had to pay for these services. They were able to point out that the native population had more than doubled under naval rule. Also, they said, the Navy prevented American traders and planters from exploiting the islanders.

People in Hawaii and California continued their efforts to convince officials at Washington that military rule over a freeborn people was unconstitutional. Naval rule, they claimed, established false standards and created a regimented type of naval servants and Samoan "yes chiefs" who no longer represented the people of Samoa.

It was asserted that Tutuila was run like a battleship, with native initiative and liberties limited as though they were Indians on a reservation. It was also shown that Navy policy gave slight attention to Samoan political and cultural advancement and in forty-six years had failed to raise the educational standards of Eastern Samoa above the sixth grade level.

During the early United Nations days American Samoa was frequently included in discussions considering the placing of key islands under a trustee form of government. While favoring trusteeship rule for the island territories of other nations, naval "policy makers" strongly insisted on retaining outright or majority control of their own island areas. For forty-seven years the Navy was able to defeat every attempt in the Lower House of Congress to grant the Samoans organic acts, constitutional rights, domestic self-rule and American citizenship.

In 1947, after seeing their hopes repeatedly dashed and having grown weary of the role of flag-saluting satellites, four hundred native chiefs of American Samoa drew up a bill calling for self-rule and sent it to key members of the U.S. Congress.

In the House of Representatives, Republican Congressman Norris Poulson of California openly called upon the Secretary of the Navy "to put an end to the undemocratic and un-American forms of government which exist in Guam and American Samoa." Congressman Poulson stated that the inhabitants of American Samoa "are governed under a form of military autocracy which is a disgrace to our democracy" and "await the day when the United States will restore to them the human dignity and pride in living enjoyed by other free Americans."

Even at this late date (1947) Navy four-stripers and admirals were effective enough to have civilian government for Samoa delayed until June 29, 1951, when the President of the United States directed that the administration of American Samoa be transferred from the Navy Department to the Department of the Interior.

Flag Day, the anniversary of the raising of the first American flag over Eastern Samoa, now also commemorates the raising of the first Samoan flag and the establishment of constitutional government, both of which took place April 17, 1960. It is Pago Pago's biggest day of the year, a gala event of singing, dancing and athletic events. It is said that when Samoan visitors from Apia (Western Samoa) hear the Tutuilans play the "Star Spangled Banner" on Flag Day they forget all about "God Save the King." Some want to remain in Pago Pago with their eastern relatives and forget all about Apia.

In addition to Tutuila, the islands of American Samoa, with a total area slightly larger than the District of Columbia, include tiny, uninhabited Rose Atoll in the extreme east; one-square-mile Swain's Island; and Tau, Olosega and Ofu of the Manua Group. Extending over an area of about sixteen miles the Manuas are located between sixty and seventy miles east of Tutuila. All are fertile, with heavily forested mountain peaks rising fifteen hundred to three thousand and fifty feet above the sea.

The island of Tutuila, centrally situated in the South Seas, is about eighteen miles long by two to six miles wide, with a total land area of about forty miles. A range of densely wooded mountains spread out over its entire length, with peaks fifteen hundred to twenty-one hundred feet high and deep fertile valleys reaching out and down to the coast. Out from Pago Pago principal villages scatter along the east and west coasts beside the forty miles of coastal roads. The great natural beauty of Tutuila and the splendid Samoan houses and landscaping have done more than anything else to keep the Pago Pago area with its odd assortment of tin-roofed houses and ex-GI buildings from becoming another typical government-style outpost like Guam.

Encircled by a chain of mountains, Pago Pago Bay is about three miles long, shaped somewhat like a foot. The town of Pago Pago is situated on a narrow strip of land between the hills and the shore. Old Rainmaker Mountain, towering two thousand feet high to dominate the fiordlike side of the bay and the town, takes all the moisture from the clouds and trade winds and sometimes sends it down on Pago Pago in solid sheets.

There is a decided difference between the islanders of the Manua Group and the people of Tutuila. The Manuans, because of their relative isolation, continue to cling to many of the old customs that have been discarded in the Pago Pago Bay area in favor of American ways. Most of the approximately three thousand Manuans are engaged in subsistence agriculture and the production of copra for export. Whatever may happen to Tutuila with its new jet airport, Manua will always remain a stronghold of Polynesian culture.

To a newly arrived tourist one of the most bountiful crops of Eastern Samoa sometimes appears to be its happy groups of chil-

On Flag Day (April 17) in American Samoa the whole island comes alive.

Happy, friendly children are one of the principal "crops" in American Samoa.

dren. Some chiefs are fathers of ten or more youngsters. Several have more than a dozen. "We are not concerned with world politics," a Samoan chief will tell the visitor. "What really matters to a Samoan is his family and the welfare of his island people."

A few *palagis* (American residents) will tell you that what really matters to a Samoan chief is dignity, pride and prestige; to a young modern Samoan, baseball, a government job and some day a palagi-style house and second-hand car; to proud aristocrats of the old order, more respect from young people for the *matai* (village chief) system.

The fabric of small village life is very different from what it may appear to be at the *malae* (town green) on "Boat Day" in Pago Pago. A large amount of unpressed free time is considered as necessary to a rural Samoan as eating or drinking. The thirty to forty families of the average village take much pride in their leisure activities and group singing, as befits a people who live in hand-jointed houses made without nails, roofed with sugar cane or pandanus thatch and lashed together with hand-braided sennet.

Marriage for the first few years among these soft and gentle Polynesians is often an indefinite arrangement depending on the continuing satisfaction of both parties. If a wife is unhappy with her husband she simply goes home to her own family. Then, unless the husband makes amends and regains her interest, they both are free to seek new mates.

Many mainland ways engulfed Samoa when thousands of American GIs were there. Yet, despite a whole new pattern of sophistication, young girls still dance the siva-siva, perform ceremonial functions and gather flowers, as they always have, to weave into garlands on feast days; the reefs gleam with the torches of fishermen on dark nights; children chase land crabs as always—but more than a few teen-age girls, who wear lava-lavas for ceremonial affairs, are saving up their money to buy a "Honolulu-style dress."

The great value of land hasn't affected the wild taro and yams that still grow in the steep forests with arrowroot and *ifi* (Tahitian chestnuts). Villagers haven't forgotten how to make lamps out of coconuts, or how to trap eels and lobsters on the coral reefs and cook with hot stones. Although green beans, cabbages and other temperate-area vegetables can be grown, islanders are not especially interested in them, much preferring their own highly nutritious vegetables and the national dish of coconut, prepared in taro leaves and cooked in stone ovens.

In comparison with the modern town trend toward boiling food quickly in metal pots, the superiority of the old ways is readily apparent in the delicious flavors of yams, taro, breadfruit and roast suckling pig that have been wrapped in leaves and baked between layers of hot rocks. Coconut-fed roast pork with crab, a bit of octopus and banana poi is a luscious meal in any language.

Islanders learning to cope with the methods of the modern world have not hesitated on occasion to add to the administration's problems. More than once when highbred, imported pigs were distributed by the government experimental farm to promising young students they were killed and eaten a few days later by order of the village matai, who believed that the choicest pork is always best for a village feast. When, in an effort to eliminate ravages of coconut beetles, chiefs were required to gather weekly quotas or be fined, they set up beetle farms to assure a good supply for the beetle inspectors. When rats were a problem the government offered a bounty for the tail of each rat killed. As the number of tails that were being cashed in greatly increased, the rat-tail inspector investigated and found that several enterprising farmers had started breeding pens to maintain a wholesale "cash crop" of rat tails.

The environs of Pago Pago are not without a few slum areas that are partly made up of sad-looking "American-style" dwellings built out of discarded lumber and scraps of corrugated metal roofing. Neglect, the tropic climate and casual patching has made these dilapidated shacks a considerable eyesore. Other fairly well built palagi-style (American) houses are increasing in the Pago Pago Bay area and out along the good roads. But, except for the fact that the metal roof of a board and frame house lasts longer, most of the native-owned imitations of American cottages are inferior in every way to the better-designed, oval-shaped Samoan *fale*.

Young Samoans who do not care to leave their homeland and who formerly would have become Navy employees and possibly members of the elite *Fitafitas* (local marines), now look toward government jobs as laborers, clerks, carpenters and mechanics. Some, learning "non-native ways," find that combining the old with the new is beset with more than a few dilemmas. Formerly a man's social standing was marked not by what he had but what he gave to others. Young moderns with new ideas, seeing the acquisitive and status-seeking ways of Westerners, are upsetting some of the social traditions and challenging some of the prerogatives of the older, conservative chiefs.

Prospects are not bright for the educated young Samoan whose ambitions lead him far beyond the possibilities of his home islands. As elsewhere in the South Seas, the pressure of overpopulation and lack of acceptable local employment has created a drift of young islanders to Hawaii and Pacific Coast cities where thousands of uprooted Samoans have formed sizable groups.

Many palagis feel that the matai system and its communal ownership of property must go if Samoans are to achieve the highest possible output from their land. A democratic system that encourages individual initiative and land rights may come to American Samoa a lot sooner than some of the high chiefs think. Whatever happens, much that is of permanent value from the old Samoan ways will always remain.

With the completion of the seven-million-dollar Tafuna jet airport, opportunities for increasing cash incomes center on the fast-developing tourist industry and its many by-products which include local arts and crafts and the manufacture of island curios. A large-scale swordfish and tuna fishing and canning industry centered at Anua is increasing its efficiency and production for export. Cacao is being developed as a cash crop and a large number of islanders are now working toward the best possible use of their valleys and coastal strips with high-yielding crops.

Backed by the weight of their own tradition, Samoans have developed an efficient system of local self-government and feel that their astute leaders are increasingly able to take over a large number of government positions now held by mainland Americans.

In 1961 it was difficult for Samoans to understand a political system that removed their native-born, republican Governor Peter Tali Coleman, known as one of the best administrators in the Pacific, simply because a democratic political victory thousands of miles away in Washington decreed that a Democrat should be appointed. When a Chicago lawyer, Miss Marie Berger, was slated as the new governor many Samoans objected. "The governor is our highest office and we see him as a father, not a mother," said Sinira Fuimaono, expressing the sentiments of many. To emphasize her point, Mrs. Fuimaono asked, "Why don't Americans elect a woman as President of the United States?" Samoan protests resulted in the appointment of a male, H. Rex Lee, as governor.

As intelligent, capable human beings with decided opinions of their own, Samoans want a say and the right to vote for their own governor and other heads of government. In December, 1960, the chiefs once again asked the United States to grant U.S. citizenship to their people, install a Samoan representative in Washington, D.C., and make Eastern Samoa an incorporated territory of the United States.

Having long since come of age politically, Samoans who love freedom, independence and their own flag (red, white and blue with an eagle in flight), have a well-developed loyalty to the United States and prefer to remain under the Stars and Stripes providing they can do so as American citizens.

American Outposts in Polynesia

The most valuable "pearls" in the South Seas today, so far as official Washington is concerned, are probably the "million dollar"

Midway albatross feeding its young. These greatest of sea birds have a wing spread of 7½ feet.

Sooty tern with nesting egg.

American airplane atolls in Central Polynesia that are without native islanders, traders, missionaries, taro, breadfruit, or banana groves. Even the smallest and remotest of these land specks provide excellent air facilities without any of the complicated problems of a native population.

Millions of red-tailed tropicbirds, sooty terns, frigates, wandering tattlers, bosun birds and the great albatrosses—"kings of the seaways"—live on these dots in the wilderness of the Pacific with hermit crabs, rats and the occasional sea turtles that come to lay their eggs in the coralline sand. On a few islands there are not enough edible scraps to support even a healthy rat population. The most impressive fact about them is the vast open spaces of long-rolling seas that surround them, yet several of the most barren have become important transocean stopovers for air liners spanning the Pacific.

On a droning and booming jet-age outpost of American Polynesia, where planes roar in every day, sometimes every hour, under the flags of many nations, the landing strip is the center of everything. There are always the control tower, the navigational aids, radar screens, small weather station, fuel tanks, radio masts, hotel, fire department, maintenance shop and hangars. The "natives" are mostly Americans from the mainland and Hawaii and imported Guamanians, Filipinos, Fijians and Gilbert Islanders.

Twice already, these tropic pinpoints that scatter over so wide an area have proven to be inextricably linked with our destiny and it is only a few years ago that Wake and Midway became household

A frigate bird (left), "king of the sea-ways" of Central Polynesia; red-tailed tropic bird (right) and young daughter on Midway.

words known and heard frequently around the world. Not so well known are the lesser island possessions of the United States that were acquired by early discovery, daring and adventure.

Yankee exploring south of Honolulu began when traders from Stonington, Salem and other New England ports cruised widely in the South Seas seeking profitable cargoes of bêche-de-mer, sandalwood, turtle shell, edible bird nests and other exotic products in demand at San Francisco, Canton and New York.

Whalers and sealers from Nantucket and New Bedford followed the China traders, and there were a handful of others, including a merchantman, a frigate, a trading brig and a sloop-of-war. The resolute men who sailed them, men such as Captain Ingraham in the brigantine *Hope;* Captain Fanning of the *Betsy*—the first to take an American ship around the world from the port of New York— and Captain Porter in the *Essex*, were the earliest navigators to carry the Stars and Stripes to the remote islands of Polynesia.

Between 1791 and the year 1840, when smoke from the tryworks of over six hundred American whalers was smudging the blue Pacific skies, American shipmasters discovered more than twenty-five islands in the South Seas. American adventurers and guano prospectors, extending the Oregon and Santa Fe trails across the Pacific Ocean, laid claim to more than fifty islands and atolls near the equator. Owing largely to the efforts of those early shipmasters and enterprising guano seekers, much of the Central Pacific came to be known as American Polynesia and was so labeled on the maps of a number of German and British cartographers.

Lacking in size and safe harbors and without sandalwood, bêche-de-mer, copra or native girls in lava-lavas to attract traders and trading vessels, these low, wind-and-sea-swept specks of land remained scarcely visited until guano became of commercial importance.

By 1850, in an effort to break the Peruvian guano monopoly, American sailing ships were scouring the little known Pacific waters for uninhabited islands. During this period the Stars and Stripes was raised over fifty-seven guano islands including Christmas Island and the fifty-two islets of Palmyra, one of the most beautiful atolls under the American flag.

America's lesser-known possessions in Polynesia include a number of small steppingstone islands that lie scattered between Samoa and Hawaii beginning more than six hundred and fifty miles north of

Pago Pago. Besides Canton and Enderbury, which are shared with Great Britain, they include Howland and Baker, isolated Jarvis, Palmyra and Kingman Reef, the smallest deep sea island in the world. Others that lie more to the north, and west from Hawaii, are Wake, Kure, Midway and isolated Johnston—one of Hawaii's permanent fortress islands.

Eighty years after the famed clipper ship era, the historic 1935 flight of Pan American's *China Clipper* from San Francisco to Manila via Honolulu, Midway, Wake and Guam heralded the dawn of a new life for the isolated land-specks of American Polynesia.

In the first of a series of fast-moving events that occurred after the successful inauguration of transpacific air service, an air scout was dispatched to examine every island, rock and sand spit between Hawaii and Samoa that might be useful to air travel. From Honolulu he proceeded to Kingman Reef and Palmyra, both of which were already included in the Territory of Hawaii; then to solitary, uninhabited Jarvis Island, fourteen hundred miles due south of Honolulu; and from there one thousand miles west to Baker and Howland.

Impressed by the survey reports on Jarvis, Baker and Howland, the Bureau of Air Commerce consulted the State Department as to their sovereignty and was informed that all three belonged to the United States, although Great Britain would doubtless attempt to claim them. Acting at once to re-establish valid American claims, the Department of Commerce settled twelve volunteer Hawaiians on the three islands. The whole affair was accomplished with the utmost secrecy. Lead plaques were erected on each island asserting American rights followed by a bold "No Trespassing Allowed."

Eight months later when news of the colonizing venture finally leaked out it created an immediate stir around the world. France was "disturbed"; Great Britain refused, at first, to admit America's title; and Japan was inclined to interpret such secret colonial subterfuge as a strategic maneuver.

The importance of Canton and Enderbury to transpacific aviation was readily realized by President Franklin Roosevelt, who in 1938 placed them under the Department of the Interior, thus serving notice that the two islands were considered as American territory. Three days later Britain formally announced that she was reserving her rights in both islands.

After more than a year of proposals and counter-proposals between an American committee of three and the British ambassador it was finally agreed that the United States and Great Britain would administer Canton and Enderbury Islands jointly for fifty years, "without prejudice to their respective claims."

Solitary Jarvis Island, approximately fourteen hundred miles due south of Honolulu, rests almost directly on the line where the 160th meridian crosses the equator, a point considered on most government maps as the exact center of the Pacific. Lonely island outposts such as Jarvis, Howland, Baker, Palmyra and others are invaluable in time of war as landing places in case of emergency and as advance observation bases. In this respect they are often called "the eyes of the fleet."

Midway

Tiny, one-and-a-half-square-mile Midway, America's first outpost on the air route to the Philippines and the Orient, lies eleven hundred and fifty miles northwest of Honolulu. It is a nearly circular atoll, about five miles in diameter, enclosing two small islands and a large sheltered lagoon.

At the beginning of the twentieth century, Midway was made an important relay cable station on the main line between the United States, Hawaii and the Orient. It again came into national prominence in 1935 as a much-needed steppingstone on the air route to China. In that year Pan American Airways erected a modern airport and a small settlement with all conveniences, including a hotel, refrigeration, a power plant and a radio station. By the end of 1935, when Captain Musick landed the *China Clipper* at Midway on the first transpacific flight to the Philippines, the resident population had increased to over a hundred. After the importation of thousands of tons of soil and a wide variety of trees, shrubs and plant life they soon transformed the tiny atoll from an almost barren sand area to a modern tropical paradise with purebred livestock, poultry, well-kept gardens, a tennis court and a golf course.

After years of blasting and dredging by the U.S. Engineers, a wide, deep entrance was cleared through the coral reef and the lagoon to permit large naval vessels to moor safely within. Many millions of dollars have been spent and are still being spent on submarine and air base facilities at Midway and the main anchorage can now hold a small fleet of warships.

228

Midway's important strategic position in relation to Hawaii and Asia has made it one of America's key defense outposts.

In 1960 Midway had thirty percent (645,000) of the world population of Laysan albatrosses, sometimes dubbed gooney birds because of their intricate mating dance accompanied by a musical score of hoots, squawks and clattering. These wide-winged, greatest of sea-birds require large, flat areas for take-offs and are therefore very fond of the United States Navy's major air facilities on Midway.

In the battle between the Navy and the friendly albatrosses that is still going on the Navy has lost every tactical move. The burning of old tires and the firing of bazookas and mortars in the nesting areas have had no effect. When their nesting eggs were taken the birds wailed dismally for a while and then promptly laid some more. Finally the Navy packed large numbers of them into transport planes and flew them to Japan and to the Puget Sound, four thousand miles away. After recovering from plane sickness these lonely birds, that drink sea water and can circle the world, flew unerringly back to the naval facilities on Midway.

In the latest move the Navy has constructed an airport for albatrosses on nearby Kure Atoll (last island in the sixteen hundred mile long Hawaiian Archipelago) with special fifty-foot-wide gooney runways. High ranking officials hope that now these great birds will no longer defy the United States Navy.

Wake

Wake, an international port-of-call without a harbor or a dock, is Oceania's most remote gas and service station for planes flying the Pacific north of the equator. Today winging west over twenty-one hundred miles to this unique aerial center takes only a few hours from Honolulu.

Like a strange, isolated airdrome on another planet, the most important part of Wake is confined within two square miles of flattish coral, sand and gravel. Despite this, the island is now a booming miniature aviation city on a pinpoint of macadam and concrete. In 1961 the strip was enlarged for the latest fan-engined turbojets to come in and the same year over ten thousand planes were landing day and night around the clock.

During 1935 to 1938, the real pioneering years in transpacific aviation, Wake's convenient location and completely sheltered four-mile-long lagoon made the early flights to the Orient possible. It soon became one of the two most important air links between the United States and the Far East.

Almost immediately after the Pearl Harbor attack two Japanese squadrons swooped down on the tiny atoll and in a matter of minutes destroyed almost all of the valuable installations and eight of the island's twelve small fighter planes. During the epic fourteen-day defense by a handful of marines and civilians, powerful Japanese naval and air forces were held at bay and a number of their warships and bombers destroyed before the small garrison was forced to surrender. The island was retaken by American forces in 1945 and it was on Wake that President Harry Truman met General Douglas MacArthur and relieved him of his Far East Command.

More than a thousand well-paid permanent residents of Wake are employed to service the huge planes that arrive at an average of thirty a day. In the course of any single night in the crowded, noisy terminal residents meet Chinese, Australians, Dutch, English, Korean and other transocean travelers during their brief stopover on this small international world.

The more than one hundred young people of Wake go to school to the continual roar of engines warming up or settling down. They also eat, sleep, play tennis and go to the "Windy Palace," an outdoor movie, to the same around-the-clock sound of planes roaring in from around the globe.

Beyond the rusting guns, bomb fragments, old pillboxes and dugouts there is fine swimming and fishing and lots of clean, fresh air, a few loyal old-time "natives" will point out. There is also good health, they say, and tropic beauty on nights when Polaris and the Southern Cross reflect in the still waters of the lagoon. When the full moon rises over the horseshoe-shaped island, over its red beacons and tall missile and satellite trackers, fork-tailed terns wheel overhead and it is usually bright enough to read by moonlight.

At some future date Wake and other key American outposts may be bypassed by long-range jets but they never again will be unimportant. Their value for satellite tracking, radar posts and meteorological stations will keep them "alive." To a pilot with engine or other plane trouble or low on fuel there is no more welcome sight on earth than one of these mid-Pacific atolls. That fact will never change.

Taking little notice of the planes that roar down on these white sea-bones of coral land, the man-o'-war birds, bosuns and tropics with foot-long red tails continue to hover and glide without effort in the sea-wind, and albatrosses with rudderlike tails rise splendidly in great, wide circles against the trades as they have for centuries.

Chapter Nine

THE FUTURE OF THE SOUTH SEAS

The emergence of the fan-engined turbojet liners, streamlined airports, jet strips and supersonics that now pierce the blue Pacific skies marked the end of an epoch in the South Seas. Isolation for key islands is now a thing of the past. Lotus eaters, "white shadows" and the days of "cheap native labor" are gone.

Today it is only a thousand miles from brooding, mysterious Stone-Age valleys of New Guinea to Kwajalein Island's weird, fire-bolt equipment for knocking missiles or even satellites out of the sky.

Micronesians who still value ancient beliefs have found themselves thrust overnight into the center of the Atomic and Missile Age. With new awareness, and new values, standards and ways of life, a new worldliness is ahead for the Pacific's key islands of romance.

Despite all this the Pacific is still big and raw, and some areas remain aloof and mysterious. Out of the future will still come strange, true stories of adventure and mystery. Volcanic islands appear and disappear and there will always be typhoons and tsunamis like the one that recently swept inland a mile, bent parking meters level with the ground and took sixty lives in downtown Hilo. More recently a new radar-equipped government ship completely disappeared off the Solomon Islands without leaving a trace.

The two halves of Samoa and the two halves of New Guinea point up contrasts, civilized and primitive, that exist within single mountainous archipelagos. The part of Samoa (American) that wants tourism was planning for its first jet planes while the other and far larger part (Western Samoa) had no present plans for welcoming jets and was not at all certain that it wanted "easy tourist dollars" or the problems that go with them.

In large areas of Western New Guinea the jet age is still unheard of and human power remains cheaper than bullock or horse power because humans eat less. A few hundred miles away in the eastern half of this same vast island, as well as in other parts of Melanesia, excited, air-minded people, only just emerging from primitive ways, are hastily building their own isolated airports with the crudest of makeshift tools.

The current air schedule at one of the latest native-built airports in the New Hebrides reads:

TANNA PLANE
E out long 8 clock e faldown long Loasia after e go long Erromanga e faldown back agen. After e go long Vila. After e cumback long 5 clock, long place eer. [Plane leaves at 8 for Loasia, Erromanga, Vila and returns at 5 to Tanna.]

Tannese people who have invested their slow-earned money to buy a share in the new airline watch the schedule and the passenger list closely and urge their friends to take a flight to Vila—cost: five pounds, or about eleven U.S. dollars.

Now that jet liners, winging across the Pacific at thirty-five thousand feet, have brought once-remote Tahiti within eight hours of Los Angeles things are happening fast in the "little Paris of the South Seas." The highest prices ever heard of in Polynesia are being offered for land by popaas as new beachheads are secured around the island for the expanding tourist trade.

The airlines to Tahiti expect five jet flights daily into Papeete within a few years, and if present plans of energetic American promoters are carried out, Tahiti and its neighbor islands will rival Waikiki and Miami beach-fronts in little more than a decade.

Construction of hotels and tourist sidelines is booming with exclusive lagoon-beach type cabanas and ersatz native houses, called *fares*, that rent for one hundred dollars a week, taking the lead. Even tiny Bora Bora in the *Iles Sous le Vent* has its own twenty-seven dollar per person per day de luxe hotel.

For the present and immediate future the French have said no to ambitious plans for sleek, tall Miami and Waikiki-beach type concrete hotels. And some Americans don't like it a bit.

"Can you believe it!" shouted one angry hotel man from Honolulu, pounding the table at Vaihiria, the sidewalk cafe on the Quai Bir Hackeim. "They build an eleven million dollar jet airport and then hope to keep the place on a one-cylinder, coco-palm standard."

An American speculator from the Pacific Coast who has never before had his plans turned down demanded, "What's wrong with high-rise hotels? You invite civilization and American dollars with one hand and with the other hope to hold everything to a French snail's pace and keep the place a sleepy paradise. Does that make sense?"

The French think it does and have advised outside investors that it is to their own interest to contribute to the preservation of the charm and beauty of the island. In an eleventh-hour, almost desperate effort to preserve "Tahiti's traditional style," architects are closely watched and warned that their designs must be guided by the island's Gallic-Tahitian character.

Island leaders, seeing non-Tahitians by one subterfuge or another gain control of choice parcels of their best land and quickly convert them into high-yield investments, accuse the French administration of allowing the new tourist industry to slip almost entirely into the hands of Americans.

The popular weekly *Tribune Tahitienne*, whose opinions are supported by most educated Tahitians, recently lamented seeing the island overrun "with American speculators of every sort" and pointed out that instead of going "to the tourist factories of Honolulu for advice the administration should have sent to Switzerland, Normandy or the South of France" for quiet commercial ideas more suitable to the soft beauty of Tahiti. "Thanks to our tourist office, eighty percent of our hotels are owned by Americans," reported the *Tribune Tahitienne*. "The most beautiful homes are also owned by Americans who rent them out. And where do you find a Tahitian in all this?"

Twitting the administration for lacking the get-up-and-go to develop basic industries and create opportunities for capable young Polynesians, Tahiti's Protestant monthly *Vea Porotetani* regretted seeing educated Tahitians limited to menial servitude in the tourist industry and asked, "Under such a system what sort of a future awaits the new generation of Tahitian youth?"

Educated Polynesians, who look on glamour and "quaint native ways" to solace tourists as an affront to their character and intelligence, say, "We are not a supine people ready to smile or dance

234

the tumare at a nod and a few francs from the Office du Tourisme." The popular "Tahiti for the Tahitians" program elected their candidate to the territory's highest office and their demands on the government to divert funds toward development of natural resources resulted in the establishment of a five-year plan for social and economic advancement in 1961-1965.

Tomorrow's jet travelers will have a hard time finding a pure-blooded Polynesian. Distinctive new Oceanic people are emerging. On some islands one-half of the children born in recent years are part Oriental, American or European young people of outstanding character and attractiveness. In the French Group there will be increasingly more Chinese, American and French strains, which often means more shapely physique and an exotic beauty for the vahines, although the essential Polynesian characteristics remain.

Copra schooners will eventually disappear and be replaced by interisland motor vessels, but for the next few years those who want to see Polynesia unsweetened and unlacquered can still book passage on authentic trading schooners out of Papeete.

Modern travelers who encourage the dances and ways that missionaries once frowned on are doing much to reverse the Mother Hubbard trend. The Dorcas Societies of New England who sent thousands of flannel nightgowns and ankle-tied pantalets of early Boston vintage to the South Seas would be astounded to see the latest Parisian-designed pareus in Papeete.

Evangelists have learned much since their early mistakes. The Gothic Apostle of the Lord in glazed hat and black alpaca coat is long gone from the island scene. And so are many of the ideals that islanders were told about but seldom saw in practice.

In recent Christianization of native religious rites in New Guinea, a tattooed dove, symbol of the Holy Ghost, has been substituted for the traditional crocodile in tattooing rites of the young people of Korogo on the Sepik River.

Some missionaries travel about with portable organs, and the latest trend is to combine church activities with competitive sports. Today, missionaries frequently are qualified doctors who go evangelizing with the Bible in one hand and a hypodermic needle with penicillin in the other. Some are nurses and linguists; others have degrees in anthropology, ethnology or tropical agriculture. The best are flexible, broad-minded individuals who look with understanding on what is left of native culture and the old ways.

Less than eighty years ago it was believed that the South Sea people who had welcomed the white man as a friend were doomed by him to extinction. Now, to cite but one example, Western Samoa—with the fastest growing population in the world—is expected to double itself by 1981.

So far as the intelligent, capable Polynesians are concerned, the Westerner in the South Seas has as much to learn as to teach. Loti, Gauguin, Stevenson and other discerning men of genius have pointed out that natural Polynesian life, free from pressures and competitive strife, is the real civilization. Several authorities like the late world-renowned Dr. S. M. Lambert have felt that the Polynesian is potentially the superior of the white man. In Hawaii, New Zealand and other modern centers they have proved capable of the highest standards and have become outstanding doctors, lawyers, anthropologists, members of parliament and cabinet ministers.

After two centuries of contact with Westerners the Polynesians remain people of immense kindliness. Ten years or ten decades of the jet age will never destroy their grandeur.

Some remote Polynesian people, remembering perhaps that their language has no word for tomorrow, prefer to be left alone. The out-islander, listening to his tiny, trade-store radio in a lonely, sometimes wind-swept, thatch hut, looks out over the blue lagoon and knows that he is immeasurably better off than his neighbors a few jet-hours away who are beset with the space-age rivalries, fears and pressures of modern living.

When the moon comes up in the night sky over Avarua, Apia or Nukualofa—the quiet capitals—it's sometimes hard to believe that, as Americans tell the islanders, "there is no stopping progress." Yet, in the long struggle to hold to time-honored ways against the onslaught of the West, only islands destitute in material things prized by whites have escaped "civilized benefits."

In several parts of the South Pacific the twilight of the papalangi —white men, or "sailing gods," as they were once called—is at hand. Large native-owned co-operatives, awakened to new needs, now operate their own sailing vessels, trade stores and agricultural projects. The beachcomber, small trader, and small trade-schooner-owner-captain have all but vanished from the South Sea scene. The small landholder controlling hundreds of black, brown or Oriental laborers is also going. White colonial pukka sahib settings with private "gin and tonic" clubs closed to Indians, Chinese and others, remaining in a few key port towns (notably Moresby and Suva), will go, too.

Even the great trading firms that have acquired vast holdings and enormous profits, such as the giant British Unilever combine, and Burns Philp Ltd., are streamlining their organizations and operations to meet the new challenge.

Dried meat from the nuts of fifty million coconut trees in the South Seas will continue to decide the way of life of more islanders than any other product. The coconut economy of dollar-limited islands affected by copra substitutes and dependent on world market prices will remain unstable, partly offset in some archipelagos by copra stabilization funds.

Hawaii's influence continues to expand as the education and cultural center of the Pacific island world. Suva will grow as a tailoring and mercantile center and in some sections a miniature India. Chinese seamstresses, who have apprenticed under famous Parisian couturiers, may make Papeete the tropical fashion center of the South Seas where, as in Hong Kong, any fashion or mode of dress can be had or copied.

Fishing is the islands' best potential, and seagoing vessels are carrying out extensive research looking toward further large-scale fishing enterprises based primarily on tuna. Atomic-powered ships that will greatly reduce the sea time to key island ports will boost exports of perishable cargoes, and international free ports may develop to help the islanders compete in the complex economy of tomorrow.

In Western Samoa where voting has always been limited to the *matais* (chiefs) a United Nations plebiscite in 1961 provided the first opportunity in the history of those islands for the common (untitled) men and women to vote. Stevenson's "sweetest people God ever made" are also having to face some bitter facts of life. Though some are not particularly interested in material development, the needs of their increasing population make it mandatory.

As the great Polynesian leader Sir Maui Pomare declared, "The tide of progress is moving on and we must go with it. Education is our paddle." Unfortunately the solution is not that simple. Only a very small percentage of native islanders have found stability and a satisfactory way of life within the modern setting. They alone are ready and able to play a vital role in the future of the South Seas.

Smaller Pacific islands are already overflowing with more people than their coconut trees, lagoons and taro patches can support. Islands such as Tonga, the Ellices and Gilberts, some Micronesian atolls and others are faced with the dual problem of rapid population increase and paucity of natural resources.

On main islands where there is no lack of educated young islanders there is a dearth of opportunities for them to use to the fullest their new-found skills. Rivalry for ways to make a living, town jobs and social prestige is increasing, and island after island, volcanic as well as low atoll, is moving toward economic crisis due to overpopulation and underdevelopment.

Most of the high islands could support at least twice their present population. Even Fiji with its four hundred thousand people could support three times that number. But the planning, know-how and drive needed to meet complex problems is seldom noticeable in island legislative council meetings. As long-time Fiji resident Mrs. Lema Low put it, "Expert footballers and cricketers are of

Suva, the capital of the Fiji Islands, is the true crossroads of the Pacific.

little use to the country. What Fiji needs is more young leaders of stability and character to replace the Council Chiefs who lack initiative to act, who talk too much and do too little."

Meanwhile the formalities and ritual of colonial rule in the pukka tradition still goes on in modern Suva and all real power remains in the hands of three British colonials.

The astute leaders of Fiji's two hundred thousand East Indians consider the rising international prestige of their homeland, the swift progress of native independence in island areas and the growing influence of the Afro-Asian bloc people as the best news of this century.

As the impetus toward self-government is increasingly felt all over the South Pacific, the status quo, pro-administration leaders, often called "yes chiefs," are losing out to younger, more nationalistic-minded men. Some fast-rising leaders, thinking beyond their council meetings and island boundaries, are beginning to take an all-Pacific view. Those who are able to take a world view realize that the key problem of the Pacific in the next decade is not the Indonesians against the Dutch, nor the United States against China or Russia but the survival of the human race.

In April 1957, a French scientist claimed that a new, mysterious disease was attacking the Marquesans, caused by the eating of radioactive fish impregnated from bombs exploded by the United States in the Marshall Islands. At Atuona, Hiva Oa and on Nuku Hiva the great, great grandsons of Marquesan cannibals were at first dismayed, then saddened to learn of still another danger from civilization and the "big shoots that kill everything."

Hearing of new missiles and of astronauts going around the world in one hundred and eight minutes, many native people who contributed heavily to preserving the freedom of the Pacific, who have had their lives profoundly affected, their islands boned and scraped raw and their people moved to atolls they didn't want to go to, watch the horizon with uneasy eyes and wonder when Westerners will tire of "bigger and better bangs" and live in peace.

In December 1960 a Russian ship launched the first meteorological rocket in the tropical atmosphere belt. With the British improving their nuclear base at Christmas Island; with the United States increasing its Polaris-equipped submarines, building up its Micronesian bases (including a seventy-five million dollar intricate radar and missile-killer base in the Marshalls); and with the

239

Soviets lobing multi-stage test rockets into the Palmyra Island area, the awesome possibilities are of increasing concern to everyone living in the Pacific area, brown, black or white.

Some advanced islanders, like some Americans, are beginning to know something about Antarctica, and about modern problems of outer space and earth satellites. To these descendants of the most daring seafarers the world has ever known, people who for centuries knew intimately the movements of heavenly bodies, air and sea currents and the intricate lore of sea and sky phenomena, the news of space flights by astronauts came as no great shock except that, hearing of humans out on the vast sea of electricity beyond the reefs that surround the earth they, like other races, wonder if the future in the age of space will mean a new tropic dawn and islands in the sky.

Those who think deeply about it would probably concur with Norman Cousins, who has said, "Why not orbit poets into space?" Polynesia, Melanesia and Micronesia could furnish more than a few natural poets who can meet all of the physical requirements, are familiar with the galaxies of bright, blue stars and who can think co-operatively and creatively.

The long record of the papalangi in the South Seas is by no means a fine one and the "South Pacific Six"—Britain, France, the United States, Australia, New Zealand and the Netherlands, are being called on to avoid repeating many of the tragic mistakes of the past. In recent years all nations involved in the South Pacific have made promising statements regarding their dependent island people. If those promises are to be more than a United Nations dream it remains to be seen to what extent they are put into practice.

Australians looking apprehensively toward Indonesia, their nearest neighbor, see President Sukarno, backed by eighty-five million people and several hundred million dollars worth of Soviet weapons, planes and sea power, claiming Western New Guinea as part of Indonesia. In this last Pacific link of the once-great Dutch colonial empire only a few thousand Hollanders remain. Dutch Eurasians continue to sail for Amsterdam and the Zuider Zee, and native self-government, if it comes, must come within the next ten years. Many question the wisdom of this. Others who question the time element feel that it is too soon and that unless more time is given to the development of native administrators and an export economy the

United Nations will have another Congo-type problem on its agenda.

Old European hands in Melanesia who were always inclined to be highly critical of educated and sophisticated natives are beginning to realize that when and if independence comes to Netherlands New Guinea, Papua and Australian New Guinea cannot remain too far behind.

In Samoa, Micronesia and elsewhere south and west of Hawaii, the United States stands committed to a trust and a responsibility that cannot be overlooked. Though, historically speaking, the United States certainly was no great white savior, today in the South Seas over two million islanders look with hope toward Uncle Sam—variously known as "Papa," "Sam," "George" and "the USN." From Papeete to Port Moresby and from Apia to Rabaul native people long accustomed to "God Save the King" and the jubilant notes of the "Marseillaise" are now familiar with the "Star Spangled Banner" and like it well. Some prefer it even to "Yankee Doodle."

The granting of statehood to Hawaii greatly enhanced American prestige throughout the Pacific island world. It also renewed the

Where the twain will meet: East-West Center, a unique experiment in understanding, education and the exchange of ideas among the people of the Pacific.

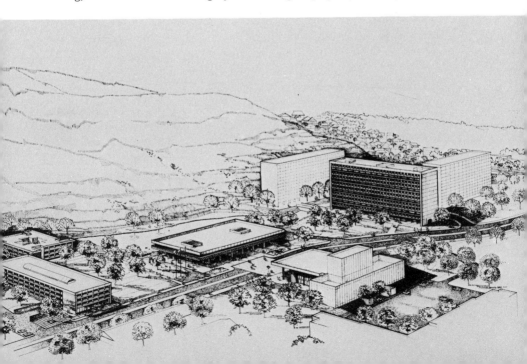

hopes of a loyal people who have lived sixty years under the Stars and Stripes without the basic rights of citizenship. Many who look to "Sam" as a champion of the human rights of dependent people wonder when the Samoans will be granted American citizenship.

Early atrocities and brutalities of Westerners are almost beyond belief and the excuse that native ways were almost as bad doesn't soften the facts. But it cannot be denied that in the past decade the nations involved in the South Pacific have worked toward unifying the island people and solving some of their major problems. Health services are greatly expanded. Populations are increasing. Yaws, elephantiasis, gonorrhea, tuberculosis and other once prevalent diseases are greatly reduced. Education facilities have been vastly improved and the standard of living raised. The Central Medical School and the yearly South Pacific Conference are examples of the pooled efforts toward the advancement and well-being of the South Sea Islanders.

High above Honolulu in a green mountain valley, Hawaii's new thirty million dollar East-West Center may do more to further understanding between Americans and other peoples of the Pacific than anything put forward in the past half century.

Here where Hawaii's unique aloha spirit and multi-racial atmosphere prevails, some Fijians, Asians, Americans and other scholarship students are living and studying together in an atmosphere of American democracy. When the Center's full complement of two thousand racially mixed people take up the curriculum of their choice some will be potential leaders from Melanesia, Micronesia and Polynesia who may be directing the destiny of their island homelands much sooner than most Westerners think.

In 1905 Theodore Roosevelt declared, "This Century will be the Century of the Pacific." How well events have borne him out so far the world knows. Those who are thinking about the dimensions of tomorrow realize even more sharply how America's future is bound up with the Pacific area and the islands that inhabit its vastness. As the jet age reaches out to new islands, the generation ahead will have a new perspective and the opportunity to fulfill some of the all-but-forgotten promises of our civilization.

This sophisticated vahine of Papeete is part Tahitian, French and English.

APPENDIX

Summary of Latest Basic Facts

Island or Group	*Discovery*
Australs	Cook, 1769–77; Gayangos, 1775
Carolines (and Palaus)	Villalobos, 1543; Hunter, 1791
Cook Islands (and Niue)	Cook, 1774
Easter Island	Roggeveen, 1722
Fijis	Tasman, 1643; Cook, 1774
Gambiers	Wilson, 1797
Gilbert and Ellice Colony	Grijalva, 1537; Byron, 1765
Guam	Magellan, 1521
Marianas	Magellan, 1521
Marquesas	Mendana, 1595; Ingraham, 1791
Marshalls	de Saavedra, 1529; Marshall and Gilbert, 1788
New Caledonia (Territory of)	Cook, 1774
New Guinea (Eastern)	d'Abreu, 1512; de Saavedra, 1527–8
New Guinea (Western)	d'Abreu, 1511; de Menezes, 1526–7
New Hebrides	de Quiros, 1606; Bougainville, 1768
Papua	de Menezes, 1526
Pitcairn Island	Carteret, 1767
Samoa, Eastern	Roggeveen, 1722; Bougainville, 1768
Samoa, Western	Roggeveen, 1722; Bougainville, 1768
Societies	Wallis, 1767; Cook, 1769
Solomons	Mendana, 1568; Carteret, 1767
Tahiti	Wallis, 1767
Tonga	Tasman, 1643; Wallis, 1767
Tuamotus	de Quiros, 1606; Schouten, 1616

Status (1962)	Area (Sq. miles)	Population (1960*)
Colony of France	110	4,039
U.S. Trust Territory	461	51,795
New Zealand Dependency	121,238 (acres)	22,435
Dependency of Chile	28	260
British Crown Colony	7,083	197,957 Indians 167,474 Fijians 35,390 Others
Colony of France	6	622
British Crown Colony	369	45,893
Territory of U.S.	206	66,910
U.S. Trust Territory	380	9,134
Colony of France	492	4,284
U.S. Trust Territory	380	14,907
Colony of France	8,548	70,987
Australian Trust Territory	93,000	1,410,083
Dutch Colony	160,000	742,600
British-French Condominium	5,700	61,210
Territory of Australia	90,540	480,000
British Possession	2	148
Unincorporated Terr. of U.S.	76	20,050
Independent State	1,133	110,000
Colony of France	646	60,804
British Protectorate	12,000	123,956
Colony of France	402	36,300
Constitutional Monarchy under British protection	269	61,899
Colony of France	337	8,643

* In several groups there has never been a complete census and figures are necessarily estimated. But whenever possible figures given are from the latest reports.

SOURCES AND ADDITIONAL READING

For general references I have found the latest official year books with trusteeship reports to the United Nations, and the Pacific Islands Year Book (Sydney, Australia) most useful. For cultural facts the Honolulu Bishop Museum publications and journals of the Polynesian Society (Wellington, New Zealand) are invaluable, as are the authoritative works of Felix Keesing, John Coulter, Douglas Oliver, Bengt Danielsson and other Pacific area anthropologists and ethnologists.

No one book can answer all the questions about the South Seas and seldom do any two see it the same way. Some find tawdriness, others find loveliness. Several modern writers see humor—interpret as comedy what Robert Louis Stevenson, Paul Gauguin, Robert Keable, Pierre Loti, Jack London and other men of large talents saw and would still see as tragedy.

In personal narrative and fiction James Michener, the late Robert Dean Frisbie and James Norman Hall have written as perceptively about island life as anyone. Teuira Henry, Peter Buck (Te Rangi Hiroa), "Johnny" Frisbie and others with direct Polynesian backgrounds have each in his own way contributed much.

INDEX

BIOGRAPHICAL NOTE

Captain Charles A. Borden's knowledge of the Pacific matches and complements his love of island landfalls. After twenty years as a writer, engineer and master mariner in the South Seas he knows in a curiously intimate way what is happening today in the main island groups and port centers.

A lifetime student of Pacific affairs and life member of the Polynesian Society (an organization devoted to the history, anthropology and cultural life of the people of Oceania), he has had access to authoritative sources and combines extensive research with the latest up-to-the-minute facts.

Because of his deep interest in the people of the South Seas Borden is acutely aware of their problems and writes of them with clarity and perception. Much of his information comes firsthand from a large circle of island friends and from men who are never interviewed by correspondents hurrying through these islands off the beaten paths: the harbor masters, skippers of interisland trading schooners, keepers of hotels on whose verandahs gather all the big fish of the South Pacific—the plantation overseers, port superintendents—men who don't talk to strangers; Dutchmen, Frenchmen, Englishmen and Yankees in a dozen tropical ports south, east and west of Hawaii.

MARIANA ISLANDS

MICRONESIA

WAKE ISLAND

ISLANDS

PALAU ISLANDS

GILBERT ISLAND

NEW GUIN

A

ES

FIJI ISLA

AUST

ALTY ISLAND

ONIA

ISLANDS

NEW ZEALAND